GUINNESS WORLD RECORDS

GUINNESS
WORLD RECORDS®

GAMER'S EDITION

2019

British Library Cataloguing-in-Publication Data: a catalogue record for this book is available from the British Library.

UK: 978-1-912286-47-8
US: 978-1-912286-44-7
US: 978-1-912286-45-4

Check the official website at guinnessworldrecords.com/gamers for more record-breaking gamers.

ACCREDITATION:
Guinness World Records Limited has a very thorough accreditation system for records verification. However, while every effort is made to ensure accuracy, Guinness World Records Limited cannot be held responsible for any errors contained in this work. Feedback from our readers on any point of accuracy is always welcomed.

Guinness World Records Limited does not claim to own any right, title or interest in the trademarks of others reproduced in this book.

© 2018 Guinness World Records Limited, a Jim Pattison Group company

GAMER'S EDITION 2019

Gaming Editor
Mike Plant

Layout Editor
Chris Bryans

Consultant Editor
Stephen Daultrey

Editor-in-Chief
Craig Glenday

Senior Managing Editor
Stephen Fall

Senior Editor
Adam Millward

Editor
Ben Hollingum

Head of Publishing & Book Production
Jane Boatfield

VP Publishing
Jenny Heller

Senior Information & Research Manager
Carim Valerio

Head of Pictures & Design
Michael Whitty

Picture Editor
Fran Morales

Picture Researcher
Wilf Matos

Talent Researcher
Jenny Langridge

Proofreading/fact-checking
Stace Harman,
Matthew White

Designer
Alvin Weetman at
magazine-designers.co.uk

Artworker
Terry Stokes

Cover Designer
Billy Waqar

Original Illustrations
Maltings Partnership

Production Director
Patricia Magill

Production Coordinator
Thomas McCurdy

Production Consultants
Roger Hawkins,
Tobias Wrona

Reprographics
Res Kahraman at Born Group

Original Photography
James Ellerker,
Paul Michael Hughes,
Ben MacMahon,
Kevin Scott Ramos

Indexer
Marie Lorimer

Printing & Binding
MOHN Media Mohndruck
GmbH, Gütersloh, Germany

GUINNESS WORLD RECORDS

CORPORATE OFFICE
Global President: Alistair Richards

Professional Services
Chief Financial Officer: Alison Ozanne
Financial Director: Andrew Wood
Accounts Receivable Manager: Lisa Gibbs
Management Accountants: Jess Blake, Jaimie-Lee Emrith, Moronike Akinyele
Assistant Accountants: Yusuf Gafar, Jonathan Hale
Accounts Payable Clerk: Nhan Nguyen
Accounts Receivable Clerk: Jusna Begum
Senior Finance Analyst: Elizabeth Bishop
General Counsel: Raymond Marshall
Senior Legal Counsel: Catherine Loughran
Legal Counsel: Kaori Minami
Legal Counsel, China: Paul Nightingale
Trainee Solicitor: Michelle Phua
Global HR Director: Farrella Ryan-Coker
HR Officer: Monika Tilani
Office Manager: Jackie Angus
Learning & Development Manager: Alexandra Popistan
IT Director: Rob Howe
IT Manager: James Edwards
Developer: Cenk Selim
Desktop Administrator: Alpha Serrant-Defoe
Analyst / Tester: Céline Bacon
Head of Category Management: Jacqueline Sherlock / Victoria Tweedy
Senior Category Manager: Adam Brown
Category Manager: Sheila Mella
Category Executives: Danielle Kirby, Luke Wakeham, Shane Murphy

Global Brand Strategy
SVP Global Brand Strategy: Samantha Fay
Brand Manager: Juliet Dawson
VP Creative: Paul O'Neill

Global Content & Product
SVP Content & Product: Katie Forde
Director of Global TV Content & Sales: Rob Molloy
Senior TV Content Executive & Production Co-ordinator: Jonathan Whitton
Head of Digital: Veronica Irons
Senior Content Manager: David Stubbings
Social Media Manager: Dan Thorne
Front-End Developer: Alex Waldu
Director of Video Production: Karen Gilchrist
Digital Video Producer: Matt Musson
Junior Video Producer: Cécile Thai
Audience Development Manager: Sam Birch-Machin
Head of Global Production Delivery: Alan Pixsley
Marketing Director: Helen Churchill
Senior Product Marketing Manager (Brand & Consumer): Lucy Acfield

B2B Product Marketing Manager (Live Events): Louise Toms
B2B Product Marketing Manager (PR & Advertising): Emily Osborn
Product Marketing Executive: Rachel Swatman
Designer: Rebecca Buchanan Smith
Junior Designer: Edward Dillon

EMEA & APAC
SVP EMEA APAC: Nadine Causey
Head of Publishing Sales: Joel Smith
Sales & Distribution Manager: Caroline Lake
Publishing Rights & Export Sales Manager: Helene Navarre
Publishing Sales Executive: Natalie Audley
Commercial Accounts Services Director: Sam Prosser
Senior Account Manager: Jessica Rae
Business Development Manager: Alan Southgate
Commercial Account Managers: Sadie Smith, Fay Edwards, William Hume-Humphreys, Irina Nohailic
Commercial Account Executive: Andrew Fanning
Country Representative – Business Development Manager, India: Nikhil Shukla
Commercial Executive, India: Rishi Nath
Marketing Director: Chriscilla Philogene
Head of PR: Doug Male
Senior Publicist: Amber-Georgina Gill
Senior PR Manager: Lauren Cochrane
Publicist: Georgia Young
PR Assistant: Jessica Dawes
Head of Marketing: Grace Whooley
Senior Commercial Marketing Managers: Daniel Heath / Mawa Rodriguez, Saloni Khanna
Marketing Manager: Kye Blackett
Content Marketing Executive: Imelda Ekpo
Head of Records Management APAC: Ben Backhouse
Head of Records Management Europe: Shantha Chinniah
Senior Records Manager: Mark McKinley
Records Managers: Christopher Lynch, Matilda Hagne, Daniel Kidane
Records Executives: Lewis Blakeman, Tara El Kashef
Senior Production Manager: Fiona Gruchy-Craven
Production Manager: Danny Hickson
Country Manager, MENA: Talal Omar
Head of Records Management, MENA: Samer Khallouf
Records Manager, MENA: Hoda Khachab

Senior Marketing Manager, MENA: Leila Issa
Digital Content Executive: Aya Ali
Senior Commercial Accounts Manager: Khalid Yassine
Commercial Account Managers, MENA: Kamel Yassin, Gavin Dickson
VP Japan: Erika Ogawa
Office Manager: Emiko Yamamoto
Director of RMT Japan: Kaoru Ishikawa
Records Managers: Yoko Furuya, Lala Teranishi
Records Executive: Koma Satoh
Senior PR Manager: Kazami Kamioka
PR Assistant: Mina Haworth
Designer: Momoko Satou
Content Manager (Digital): Masakazu Senda
Senior Project Manager: Reiko Kozutsumi
Commercial Director: Vihag Kulshrestha
Senior Account Managers: Takuro Maruyama, Masamichi Yazaki
Account Managers: Yumiko Nakagawa, Yumi Oda
Commercial Marketing Manager: Aya McMillan
Official Adjudicators: Ahmed Gamal Gabr, Anna Orford, Brian Sobel, Glenn Pollard, Jack Brockbank, Kevin Southam, Lena Kuhlmann, Lorenzo Veltri, Lucia Sinigagliesi, Mariko Koike, Paulina Sapinska, Pete Fairbairn, Pravin Patel, Richard Stenning, Şeyda Subaşı-Gemici, Sofia Greenacre, Victor Fenes, Joanne Brent, Brittany Dunn, Solvej Malouf, Swapnil Dangarikar, Justin Patterson, Mai McMillan, Rei Iwashita, Fumika Fujibuchi

AMERICAS
SVP Americas: Peter Harper
VP Commercial Account Services: Keith Green
Head of Commercial Account Services: Nicole Pando
Senior Account Manager: Alex Angert
Account Manager: Mackenzie Berry
Account Executive: David Canela
Junior Account Executive: Michelle Santucci
VP, Publishing Sales: Walter Weintz
Publishing Sales Manager: Valerie Esposito
Head of RMT, North America: Hannah Ortman
Senior Records Manager, North America: Michael Furnari
Records Managers, North America: Kaitlin Vesper, Spencer Cammarano
Records Executive, North America: Christine Fernandez

Junior Records Executive, North America: Callie Smith
Marketing Director: Sonja Valenta
Senior Marketing Manager: Kerry Tai
Junior Designer: Valentino Ivezaj
Head of PR, Americas: Kristen Ott
Assistant PR Manager, North America: Elizabeth Montoya
Digital Coordinator: Kristen Stephenson
PR Coordinator, North America: Rachel Gluck
Office Assistant: Vincent Acevedo
Head of Brand Development, West Coast: Kimberly Partrick
Director of Latin America: Carlos Martinez
Senior Records Manager, Latin America: Raquel Assis
Senior Account Manager, Latin America: Ralph Hannah
Records Manager, Latin America: Sarah Casson
Account Managers, Latin America: Giovanni Bruna, Carolina Guanabara
PR Manager, Latin America: Alice Marie Pagán-Sánchez
Marketing Manager, Latin America: Laura Angel
Official Adjudicators, North America: Michael Empric, Philip Robertson, Christina Flounders Conlon, Andy Glass, Claire Stephens, Mike Marcotte, Casey DeSantis, Kellie Parise
Official Adjudicators, Latin America: Natalia Ramirez Talero, Carlos Tapia Rojas

GREATER CHINA
Global SVP Records & General Manager, Greater China: Marco Frigatti
VP Commercial, Global & Greater China: Blythe Fitzwiliam
Senior Account Managers: Catherine Gao, Jacky Yuan, Chloe Liu
Account Managers: Jing Ran, Elaine Wang, Jin Yu
Head of RMT: Charles Wharton
Records Manager: Alicia Zhao
Records Executive: Winnie Zhang
Head of Production: Reggy Lu
Production Manager: Fay Jiang
Head of PR: Wendy Wang
PR Manager: Yvonne Zhang
Digital Executive: Echo Zhan
Marketing Director: Karen Pan
Marketing Managers: Maggie Wang, Vanessa Tao, Tracy Cui
Content Director: Angela Wu
HR & Office Manager: Tina Shi
Office Assistant: Crystal Xu
Official Adjudicators: John Garland, Maggie Luo, Dong Cheng, Peter Yang, Louis Jelinek, Wen Xiong, Iris Hou

Guinness World Records Limited uses both metric and imperial units. The unit used when the record was originally measured is given first, followed by a converted figure in parentheses. The sole exceptions are for some scientific data where metric units only are universally accepted, and for some sports data. Where a specific date is given, the exchange rate is calculated according to the currency values that were in operation at the time. Where only a year date is given, the exchange rate is calculated from 31 Dec of that year. "One billion" is taken to mean one thousand million.

Appropriate advice should always be taken when attempting to break or set records. Participants undertake records entirely at their own risk. Guinness World Records Limited has complete discretion over whether or not to include any particular record attempts in any of its publications. Being a Guinness World Records record holder does not guarantee you a place in any Guinness World Records publication.

INTRO

Hello readers – Stampy Cat here!

The people at Guinness World Records have asked me to introduce this year's *Gamer's Edition*. As I am literally obsessed with videogames, I was so excited when I heard that they wanted me to be involved with this book! If I'm not playing them, I'm making videos with them or watching them being played online. Seeing as this book is all about celebrating the most incredible achievements across all of gaming, I'm so glad that I was chosen to introduce it.

The thing I love most about videogames is how they are always changing. There are new TV shows, films and books every year, but you always enjoy them in the same way. Videogames are always re-inventing themselves, as technology improves and the developers have cool new ideas.

If you told an eight-year-old version of me, who was playing his Game Boy after school, that in 20 years people would be playing games online against opponents from all over the world, while wearing a virtual reality headset – I probably wouldn't have believed you!

The types of records that are possible expand each year. It's not all about getting a high score or beating a game quickly. There are so many ways to be creative with what you do. So there are near-endless opportunities to break unique records or do something no one has done before.

I thought it'd be a good idea to try to set a new record myself. As two of my greatest loves in life are *Minecraft* and cake, I decided to combine them and set the record for the **fastest time to make and display 10 cakes**. More on that later (see pp.100–01). I also found out that I hold the record for the **most viewed *Terraria* video** (9,336,915 views as of 24 Apr 2018)! It's a brilliant feeling knowing that you have achieved something no one else has. That's what this book is all about.

Seeing all of the amazing achievements, from the **largest collection of *Final Fantasy* memorabilia** (pp.54–55) to the **highest-earning eSports player** (pp.168–69), is really motivating. We all share a love of gaming. This is a chance to celebrate the people that make gaming officially awesome!

CONTENTS

BE A RECORD-BREAKER

Whether you're an expert gamer, an eSports superstar, a pioneering developer or a collector of gaming memorabilia, Guinness World Records wants to hear from you!

1 MAKE AN APPLICATION

The first stop for any would-be record-breaker should always be our website – **www.guinnessworldrecords.com**. Go to the "Records" section to see how the process works and how to register an account. Email us with which record you'd like to attempt.

READ THE RULES 2

It takes about six weeks to process an application. If you want to beat an existing record, you'll be sent guidelines. If it's a new record we like the sound of, we'll compile rules for it. Many ideas are turned down at the application stage, but we will explain why. Use this book and the website to see the kinds of records we like, then try again!

3 PRACTICE MAKES PERFECT

GWR record attempts are just like a sports competition – you need to train hard to make sure you're in peak condition to take them on. The more hours you practise, the greater your chances of success will be.

MAKE YOUR ATTEMPT 4

Once you're certain that your gaming skills are in prime condition, you're ready to take on the record. Make sure you have everything in place to meet the guidelines – you'll need a good-quality video recorder, witnesses and anything else we've specified you require for a valid claim.

5 SEND YOUR EVIDENCE

Preparation can ensure that your potential new record isn't missed or rejected because of technical issues. When filming videos, do a trial run to make sure that the lighting is right and that there are no obstructions. After you've filmed your attempt, package up the evidence and send it to GWR. Easy!

FRAME YOUR CERTIFICATE 6

You did it! Successful record-breakers will be sent an official certificate to show off to their friends. If you're very lucky, you may even be one of the fortunate few to make it on to these pages next year. And if you've missed out, there's no need to despair – you can always try again.

EDITOR'S LETTER

It's my absolute pleasure to welcome you to the *Guinness World Records Gamer's Edition 2019*. As regular readers might have already spotted, there's something different about this book: me.

Yes, that's right, I'm new here – although I like to think I'm a little more on top of things than a fledgling *Fallout* Vault-dweller about to venture out into the Wasteland for the first time!

My background is in reviewing games, for both videogame websites and magazines. But one of the best things about editing this book is that it has allowed me to step away from critiquing games. Instead, I've been able to focus solely on finding things to praise and enjoy about my – and your – favourite pastime.

More than that, though, this book has given me the opportunity to work with and award certificates to people who simply love games. And I'm not just talking about games developers – I mean YouTubers, speed-runners, cosplayers, eSports pros and everyone else with a passion for gaming. People exactly like you.

Find out what happened when "Stampy Cat" visited our London HQ (pp.100–01)

You won't believe how much Xbox Raymond Cox played for his record! (pp.70–71)

MORE THAN YOUR AVERAGE GAMER

One of the most interesting people I've met in the job so far is "Mega Ran" (below left), a chiptune artist who takes the soundtracks from famous games and constructs entire new songs around them. In fact, he's remixed so many of the songs in Capcom's *Mega Man* games that we were able to award him a unique record (see pp.52–53).

Then, of course, there's the wonderful Joe Garrett – "Stampy Cat" himself (above). He's the perfect example of what can be accomplished when you have a passion for what you do and are willing to put in

How many songs can one person base on *Mega Man*? A lot, as it happens... (pp.52–53)

Not a scene from *Tron*, but the most subscribed VR-dedicated YouTuber (pp.86–87)

the hard work to make it happen. Those who have watched his videos will know that his *Minecraft* avatar has a particular fondness for cake – I think we indulged his sweet tooth rather well! See pp.100–01.

But, as I said, our pages aren't reserved for YouTubers or musicians. Anybody with a particular talent for gaming can find themselves immortalized here.

One of my favourite records in the whole book belongs to Raymond Cox, aka "Stallion83" (pictured in his games cave, far left). His ludicrous record is having the **highest Xbox Live Gamerscore** of all time. He told me that there have been times when he's played games for 16 hours in a day! His reward? A certificate from us and recognition from Microsoft, which presented him with some very cool goodies (see pp.70–71).

GENRE-BUSTING RECORDS

I'm also proud of the breadth of games – and records – that you'll find in this book. We've covered just about every genre of game you'd care to name. But I'd be lying if I didn't admit that part of the fun of being Editor is being able to dig further into the games I've enjoyed playing myself.

That's why you'll find a page dedicated to *The Legend of Zelda* (pp.48–49); why there's a rather special *Cuphead* record on our shoot-'em-ups page (pp.76–77); and why you'll find *Monster Hunter: World*'s 10 largest monsters ranked on pp.116–17.

Find out why Lorenzo Ramondetti decided to brave *Resident Evil* for his marathon (pp.38–39)

See why "SilentcOre", aka Dan White, brought a donkey to a gunfight (pp.18–19)

2018 AND BEYOND...

Whatever your favourite videogames are, I hope you enjoy reading about them in the book. But don't just *read* about record holders – become one yourself! On p.5, you'll find our guide that explains how to apply for records. If you're short of inspiration, then turn to pp.104–05 to find four *Minecraft* records created specifically for our readers to beat.

For those who want all the latest *Gamers* news, you can follow us on Twitter @GWRGamers. And be sure to look out for our new *GWR Gamer*'s podcast, full of gaming news, reviews and record holders!

Mike Plant

Mike Plant
Editor,
GWR Gamer's Edition

Meet the man who proposed to his wife at a *Final Fantasy* concert (pp.54–55)

YEAR IN GAMING: PART 1

The gaming world doesn't stand still for a second, with amazing announcements, noteworthy news and frivolous fancies turning up on a daily basis. Here are some favourites since our last book…

MAY 2017

Activision Blizzard to bring more structure to eSports
The eSports industry might be thriving, but Activision Blizzard's Major League Gaming division believes there's plenty more that can be done to bring it further into the mainstream. It announced plans to make events more palatable to younger audiences by creating localized tournaments and teams.

Free DLC: live spiders
Even grizzled customs officials in Mexico were surprised by the discovery of 73 phials secreted in bootleg Super Nintendo cartridges. They contained exotic and very valuable spiders. Bound for the US state of Maryland, they weren't the sort of bugs gamers usually expect to contend with.

JUNE 2017

Nintendo and Universal Studios reveal Super Nintendo World
On 7 Jun, Nintendo gave us a sneak peek of what we can expect when Super Nintendo World opens in 2020 at Universal Studios in Osaka, Japan. Visitors will be able to race in a *Mario Kart*-themed ride and explore the castles of both Princess Peach and Bowser.

AI achieves *Ms. PAC-Man* perfection
As reported on 14 Jun, an artificial intelligence-based system, developed by Microsoft's Maluuba "deep-learning" start-up, played the perfect game of *Ms. PAC-Man* on Atari 2600, scoring the maximum possible points tally of 999,990. It's a score that no human has ever come close to achieving.

AUGUST 2017

No chocobos were harmed in the making of this pizza
After a deal was struck between Domino's and Square Enix to make *Final Fantasy*-branded pizzas in Australia, fans of the famous JRPG were able to order toppings containing choice cuts of chocobos and moogles. Thankfully, there was a veggie option in the guise of the "Curious Cactuar" deep pan.

JULY 2017

Pokémon GO FEST fans leave empty-handed
The 20,000 tickets for the event that marked a year of *Pokémon GO* sold out rapidly. But the crowds that descended on Grant Park, Chicago, USA, on 22 Jul were left frustrated. Server issues denied gamers the chance to snare some very rare Pokémon.

Riot blames *League of Legends* price hikes on Brexit
Adding to the many adverse effects laid at the door of the UK's decision to leave the European Union, Riot Games announced that, as of 25 Jul, the exchange rate of Riot Points in games such as *LoL* would drop sharply, reflecting the plunge in the value of sterling against other currencies.

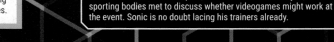

Will gamers get a medal opportunity at the 2024 Olympics?
Could eSports play a part in the Games of the XXXIII Olympiad, to be held in the French capital, Paris? It's a definite maybe, after sporting bodies met to discuss whether videogames might work at the event. Sonic is no doubt lacing his trainers already.

FK
WN'S BATTLEGROUNDS gamer "Mysterion157"
racter in a bath while he got a bite to eat.
okes of luck conspired to create possibly
t AFK (away-from-keyboard) winner, as all
each other and themselves up.

Going round the (U) bend – is Mario a plumber or not?
A Japanese Nintendo profile page revealed that Mario – the world's most famous plumber – isn't a plumber at all! The page stated that Mario "seems to have worked as a plumber a long time ago". But Nintendo backtracked on that in Mar 2018, confirming that he *is* still a plumber, although "his activities don't stop there".

OCTOBER 2017

A new era for the Nintendo World Championships?
After a surprise one-off reprise in 2015 to celebrate its 25th anniversary, the Nintendo World Championships returned in a more permanent capacity on 7 Oct 2017. The overall winner was "Thomas G", who defeated the 2015 champion "John Numbers".

Studio closes and takes Star Wars game down with it
Viscera Games was closed down by EA on 17 Oct and the studio's hotly anticipated Star Wars action game – codenamed *Ragtag* – was "pivoted" (read "completely re-done") to be a *Destiny*-like "game-as-a-service" title.

Nintendo® World Championships 2017

OVEMBER 2017

open to all
events had descended on Las Vegas, London and
's MineCon Earth was a little different. It was a live-
v that fans could watch no matter where in the world
to be. Billed as a "MineCon for everyone", the event
with news on all the latest developments, including
s Bergensten on the underwater Update Aquatic project
et *Minecraft* players delve under the sea.

HINECON EARTH

The cults, cells and kooks of *Animal Crossing: Pocket Camp*
Nintendo's life sim for mobile phones lets players create a friendly campsite where visitors go out of their way to help each other. But some players have exploited the game's features to suit their own peculiar purposes by creating strange cults devoted to, of all things, lampshades, or by using fences to create makeshift prisons (above).

YEAR IN GAMING: PART 2

… And here are the gaming headlines that caught our eye during the rest of the year – including a particularly controversial story about some of gaming's oldest records.

DECEMBER 2017

Even Mario can't believe it…
Finishing any *Super Mario* platformer without jumping seems unlikely. But "Gamechamp3000" (USA) did just that, becoming the **first to complete *Super Mario Odyssey* without jumping** on 10 Dec 2017. "Gamechamp3000" exploited a quirk in the game that means wall and pole jumps, and jumps done while possessing enemies, don't count as Mario jumping!

Mega Man returns – with a modern new look
Fans of Capcom's *Mega Man* series had a pleasant surprise on 4 Dec. To mark the franchise's 30th anniversary, the publisher announced that the long-awaited *Mega Man 11* would arrive in late 2018. This would be the first new adventure in the main series since *Mega Man 10* in 2010. The hero's new, high-definition, 2.5D looks divided opinion, but fans are coming round.

JANUARY 2018

Popularity of Game Jam spreads
On 26–28 Jan, the 10th annual Global Game Jam was staged in Cairo, Egypt. This year's theme was "Transmission", with participants creating a total of 8,606 games that reflected the concept. The 2,114 registered jammers in Cairo was the **most participants in a game jam in a single location**. While the 42,811 jammers in 108 countries around the world was the **most participants in a game jam across multiple venues**.

Saying goodbye to the voice of Bulma
Hiromi Tsuru, the actress who provided the voice of the plucky heroine Bulma (aka Buruma) in the *Dragon Ball* franchise for 30 years across anime, film and videogames, died (at the age of just 57) and was laid to rest in a private ceremony in Nov 2017. Fans took the chance to pay their respects to the actress in a Tokyo-based memorial service in Jan 2018.

THE RECORDS THAT NEVER WERE…

In 1982, Todd Rogers (USA, left) set the fastest time in *Dragster* (Activision, 1980). Fast-forward to 2017 and no one had come close to breaking his 5.51-sec mark. He was given a GWR certificate in Apr for the **longest-standing game record**, but the absence of challengers raised suspicion. In Jan 2018, our partners at Twin Galaxies (TG) confirmed that his time was not technically possible and he was stripped of the record – though Rogers still insisted it was a legitimate time.

On 12 Apr 2018, TG repeated the act by stripping Billy Mitchell (USA, right) of all his records. These included two active Guinness World Records: the **highest score on *PAC-Man*** and the **first perfect score on *PAC-Man***. TG member Jeremy Young was able to prove that Mitchell's submitted scores were obtained while using MAME (arcade emulation software), something that's forbidden according to TG's rules.

FEBRUARY 2018

Teenage Mutant Ninja Turtles get a pizza the action
On 13 Feb, nearly 30 years since their first videogame, the Teenage Mutant Ninja Turtles took to YouTube to announce their debut in the Warner Bros. superhero fighter *Injustice 2*. The "Heroes in a Half Shell" joined other DLC characters from *Mortal Kombat* and *Hellboy* as they brought the fight to DC's villains.

A Blizzard of *Warcraft III: Reign of Chaos* rumours
Warcraft III (2002) turned 16 years old in 2018, so why would Blizzard revisit it with a new patch now? Patch 1.29 might have added some cool new features – not least widescreen support and multiplayer lobbies that hold 24 players (up from 12) – but could this all be a smokescreen ahead of a remaster of the classic strategy game? Let's hope so!

MARCH 2018

Nintendo closes the door on WiiWare
Gamers wanting to plug the old-school gaps in their WiiWare collection had to meet a 26 Mar deadline. That was the last date on which Wii owners could buy Wii Points, required to make WiiWare purchases. Among the pick of the titles was *Contra ReBirth*, Konami's 2009 run-and-gun shoot-'em-up (above).

Welcome to *Overwatch*
The 27th *Overwatch* hero was announced as Brigitte Lindholm. The daughter of weaponsmith Torbjörn Lindholm (and goddaughter of Reinhardt) was first seen in 2017's animation *Honor and Glory*. Blizzard's Jeff Kaplan said: "We just want you to fall in love with her the way we have."

APRIL 2018

If you go down to the woods today...
Square Enix continued the gaming community's tradition for April Fools' Day pranks by promoting the *Final Fantasy XIV GO* (Gathering Outdoors) app. A short YouTube video showed eager gamers attaching their phones to "Harvesting Sticks" (that looked suspiciously like selfie sticks), then smashing their new tools against rocks and trees to harvest resources that could be used in *Final Fantasy XIV*. In one scene, a gamer is even seen using the Harvesting Stick to cast his phone into a lake to catch fish!

A street fight on your tabletop
A Kickstarter campaign for *Street Fighter: The Miniatures Game* that began on 4 Apr had almost tripled its goal of £280,440 ($394,252) after just 12 days. A total of £674,242 ($959,623) was pledged as fans of the series hurried to back it. The strategy game will put our favourite World Warriors at the mercy of the dice roll, as Ryu, Ken and co. team up to take on the evil Akuma and M. Bison. Turn to pp.68–69 to see our picks of other videogames reimagined for the tabletop...

AWARDS ROUND-UP

It looked odds-on that *The Legend of Zelda: Breath of the Wild* would take all the "best game" gongs at the major award shows after winning the first five. Find out which show foiled its clean sweep…

35TH GOLDEN JOYSTICK AWARDS
17 Nov 2017, London, UK

AWARD	WINNER
ULTIMATE GAME OF THE YEAR	The Legend of Zelda: Breath of the Wild
Best story	Horizon Zero Dawn
Best visual design	Cuphead
Best audio	The Legend of Zelda: Breath of the Wild
Best gaming performance	Ashly Burch (as Aloy in Horizon Zero Dawn)
Best indie game	Friday the 13th: The Game
Best multiplayer game	PLAYERUNKNOWN'S BATTLEGROUNDS
Studio of the year	Nintendo Entertainment Planning & Development
Best VR game	Resident Evil VII: Biohazard
eSports game of the year	Overwatch
Best streamer/broadcaster	"Markiplier"
Handheld/mobile game of the year	Pokémon Sun and Moon
Life achievement	Sid Meier

The Legend of Zelda: Breath of the Wild conquered all but one awards ceremony.

Cuphead won multiple awards for its animation and sound.

GAME DEVELOPERS CHOICE AWARDS
21 Mar 2018, San Francisco, USA

AWARD	WINNER
GAME OF THE YEAR	The Legend of Zelda: Breath of the Wild
Best audio	The Legend of Zelda: Breath of the Wild
Best debut	StudioMDHR (Cuphead)
Best design	The Legend of Zelda: Breath of the Wild
Innovation award	Gorogoa
Best narrative	What Remains of Edith Finch
Best technology	Horizon Zero Dawn
Best visual art	Cuphead
Best VR/AR game	SUPERHOT VR

THE GAME AWARDS 2017
7 Dec 2017, Los Angeles, USA

AWARD	WINNER
GAME OF THE YEAR	The Legend of Zelda: Breath of the Wild
Best game direction	The Legend of Zelda: Breath of the Wild
Best narrative	What Remains of Edith Finch
Best action game	Wolfenstein II: The New Colossus
Best art direction	Cuphead
Best role-playing game	Persona 5
Best fighting game	Injustice 2
Best family game	Super Mario Odyssey
Best action/adventure game	The Legend of Zelda: Breath of the Wild
Best score/music	NieR: Automata
Best audio design	Hellblade: Senua's Sacrifice
Best performance	Melina Juergens (as Senua in Hellblade: Senua's Sacrifice)
Best ongoing game	Overwatch
Best handheld game	Metroid: Samus Returns
Best VR/AR game	Resident Evil VII: Biohazard
Best strategy game	Mario + Rabbids Kingdom Battle
Best sports/racing game	Forza Motorsport 7
Best multiplayer game	PLAYERUNKNOWN'S BATTLEGROUNDS
Best independent game	Cuphead
Best debut indie game	Cuphead
Best eSports game	Overwatch

SXSW GAMING AWARDS
17 Mar 2018, Austin, USA

AWARD	WINNER
GAME OF THE YEAR	**The Legend of Zelda: Breath of the Wild**
Excellence in visual achievement	Horizon Zero Dawn
Excellence in technical achievement	NieR: Automata
Excellence in SFX	Super Mario Odyssey
Excellence in narrative	What Remains of Edith Finch
Excellence in multiplayer	PLAYERUNKNOWN'S BATTLEGROUNDS
Excellence in musical score	NieR: Automata
Excellence in gameplay	The Legend of Zelda: Breath of the Wild
Excellence in design	The Legend of Zelda: Breath of the Wild
Excellence in convergence	Star Wars: Battlefront II
Excellence in animation	Cuphead
Excellence in art	Cuphead
Most promising new intellectual property	Horizon Zero Dawn
Most fulfilling community funded game	Night in the Woods
Matthew Crump cultural innovation award	Doki Doki Literature Club!
Trending game of the year	PLAYERUNKNOWN'S BATTLEGROUNDS
eSports game of the year	PLAYERUNKNOWN'S BATTLEGROUNDS
VR game of the year	Resident Evil VII: Biohazard

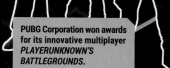

PUBG Corporation won awards for its innovative multiplayer *PLAYERUNKNOWN'S BATTLEGROUNDS*.

DICE 21ST ANNUAL AWARDS
22 Feb 2018, Las Vegas, USA

AWARD	WINNER
GAME OF THE YEAR	**The Legend of Zelda: Breath of the Wild**
Action game of the year	PLAYERUNKNOWN'S BATTLEGROUNDS
Adventure game of the year	The Legend of Zelda: Breath of the Wild
DICE Sprite Award	Snipperclips: Cut It Out, Together!
Fighting game of the year	Injustice 2
Handheld game of the year	Metroid: Samus Returns
Immersive reality game of the year	Lone Echo/Echo Arena
Mobile game of the year	Fire Emblem Heroes
Outstanding achievement in animation	Cuphead
Outstanding achievement in character	Hellblade: Senua's Sacrifice
Outstanding achievement in game design	The Legend of Zelda: Breath of the Wild
Outstanding achievement in online gameplay	PLAYERUNKNOWN'S BATTLEGROUNDS
Outstanding achievement in original music composition	Cuphead
Outstanding achievement in sound design	Super Mario Odyssey
Outstanding achievement in story	Horizon Zero Dawn
Outstanding technical achievement	Horizon Zero Dawn
Racing game of the year	Mario Kart 8 Deluxe
Role-playing game of the year	NieR: Automata
Sports game of the year	FIFA 18
Strategy/simulation game of the year	Mario + Rabbids Kingdom Battle

BRITISH ACADEMY GAMES AWARDS (BAFTA)
12 Apr 2018, London, UK

AWARD	WINNER
BEST GAME	**What Remains of Edith Finch**
Artistic achievement	Hellblade: Senua's Sacrifice
Audio achievement	Hellblade: Senua's Sacrifice
British game	Hellblade: Senua's Sacrifice
Debut game	Gorogoa
Evolving game	Overwatch
Family	Super Mario Odyssey
Game beyond entertainment	Hellblade: Senua's Sacrifice
Game design	Super Mario Odyssey
Game innovation	The Legend of Zelda: Breath of the Wild
Mobile game	Golf Clash
Multiplayer	Divinity: Original Sin II
Music	Cuphead
Narrative	Night in the Woods
Original property	Horizon Zero Dawn
BAFTA Fellowship	Tim Schafer

Night in the Woods' off-beat narrative style made it a winner at the BAFTAs.

HARDWARE

Videogame technology moves ever onwards, but not always in the direction you might think. Sony and Microsoft are pushing the envelope when it comes to console power. But, as you'll see in our round-up of recent hardware developments, sometimes there's more power in being portable.

Clash of the titans

Microsoft's Xbox One X (left) and Sony's PS4 Pro (above) are currently slugging it out in a bid to be the number-one ultra-high-definition (UHD) console. Launched in Sep 2016, Sony's console had a whole year on Microsoft's machine, which finally arrived in Nov 2017. But the Xbox One X's added power meant that its games' visuals could, theoretically, look superior.

Which is faring better? Well, both manufacturers have been coy about their console's sales. In a statement in Dec 2017, Microsoft announced that the launch of the Xbox One X helped Xbox hardware revenue rise 14%. In Jun 2017, Sony commented that "one out of every five PS4s sold was a PS4 Pro". It looks like the jury's out until both announce official sales figures…

A new dimension for VR?

Early reports from those few tech journalists who got to try out the new HTC Vive Pro VR headset have been very positive. The Pro's improved screen resolution displays 1400 x 1600 pixels per eye, compared with 1080 x 1200 p on the current Vive, making for a sharper image. It also includes built-in headphones and a more adjustable head strap. The bad news? It's set to cost $799 (£563) and its release date keeps being pushed back. Jun 2018 is the current date (unless that gets moved, too).

A Link to your own arcade

On 23 Jan 2018, we got our first look at The Steam Engine Arcade. No, you didn't miss the release of a new console. Instead, this was how "Inferno156" used a Steam Link (Valve's device that streams games from PC to TV) to create a mini arcade cabinet, complete with joysticks – the **first Steam Link arcade cabinet**. "It came out even better than I'd hoped," he said.

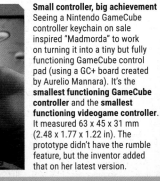

Small controller, big achievement

Seeing a Nintendo GameCube controller keychain on sale inspired "Madmorda" to work on turning it into a tiny but fully functioning GameCube control pad (using a GC+ board created by Aurelio Mannara). It's the **smallest functioning GameCube controller** and the **smallest functioning videogame controller**. It measured 63 x 45 x 31 mm (2.48 x 1.77 x 1.22 in). The prototype didn't have the rumble feature, but the inventor added that on her latest version.

Stars of Nintendo drive impressive Switch sales

The poor sales of the Wii U were suddenly a distant memory for Nintendo when the Switch became the fastest-selling console in the US. In 10 months from 3 Mar 2017 to 3 Jan 2018, it sold 4.8 million. Those figures were driven by the hit titles *Super Mario Odyssey* and *The Legend of Zelda: Breath of the Wild*.

Sega's mini Mega Drive

No doubt taking note of the success of Nintendo's NES Classic Mini and Super NES Classic Mini (right), Sega took to the stage at 2018's Sega Fes event in Apr 2018 to announce the Mega Drive Mini. The company hopes to release the tiny version of the Mega Drive (known as Genesis in the US) in time for the 30th anniversary of the original console's launch, which was on 29 Oct 1988 in Japan.

There was no news on which games will be included at the time we went to press. But Sega's classics such as *Sonic the Hedgehog*, *Golden Axe*, *Streets of Rage*, *Dynamite Headdy*, *Comix Zone* and *Gunstar Heroes* are all likely candidates.

A gaming legend returns…

In a second and extremely successful demonstration of the strength of its back catalogue, Nintendo followed up 2016's NES Classic Mini with the Super NES Classic Mini in Sep 2017 (European version pictured above; US version pictured right). The company announced it had sold over 4 million units by the end of Jan 2018. Rumours abound that a Game Boy Classic Mini is next in line…

Making a switch to Nintendo Labo

On 20 Apr 2018, Nintendo released Labo for Switch – the **first augmented reality videogame to require construction**. Gamers have a choice of two sets, the "Variety Kit" (that includes a fishing rod kit, left) and the "Robot Kit" (below).

Labo kits consist of cardboard that has to be folded into shape before it can be used. Other examples of these controllers – which Nintendo dubs "Toy-Cons" – include a piano game, a remote-controlled car and a motorbike. Each Toy-Con uses the Switch console, or its Joy-Cons, in a novel way to create new gaming experiences aimed especially at younger players.

ALL-TIME BEST-SELLING CONSOLES

Sony's PS4 has been selling like the proverbial hotcakes, but it has a way to go to be the all-time best-selling console. In fact, no console released in the last 18 years has toppled the current champion. At least Sony can "console" itself with the fact that the title holder is one of its own.

1 PLAYSTATION 2
157.68 MILLION
Release: 4 Mar 2000 (JPN)

2 NINTENDO DS
154.90 MILLION
Release: 21 Nov 2004 (USA)

3 GAME BOY
118.69 MILLION
Release: 21 Apr 1989 (JPN)

4
PS ONE
104.25 MILLION
Release: 3 Dec 1994 (JPN)

5
WII
101.64 MILLION
Release: 19 Nov 2006 (USA)

6
PLAYSTATION 3
86.90 MILLION
Release: 11 Nov 2006 (JPN)

7
XBOX 360
85.80 MILLION
Release: 22 Nov 2005 (USA)

8
GAME BOY ADVANCE
81.51 MILLION
Release: 21 Mar 2001 (JPN)

9
PLAYSTATION PORTABLE
80.82 MILLION
Release: 12 Dec 2004 (JPN)

10
PLAYSTATION 4
75.59 MILLION
Release: 15 Nov 2013 (USA)

Figures correct as of 10 Mar 2018, as verified by VGChartz.

OPEN WORLD

From the highest mountain peak to the darkest depths of the ocean, open-world games let you delve into every nook and cranny of their environments. Here, we'll guide you through these vast games as we delve into the past, explore the present and put one foot into the future...

"I GALLOPED ACROSS THE MAP SO MANY TIMES THAT I MEMORIZED THE RHYTHM OF SPRINTING TO PROLONG MY DONKEY'S STAMINA!

DAN "SILENTCORE" WHITE ON HIS THUMB-NUMBING FEAT

MOST *RED DEAD REDEMPTION* NPCS HOGTIED IN THREE MINUTES

Dan White (UK), better known among gamers as YouTuber "Silentc0re", has not one but two records to his name for feats in Rockstar's best-selling western.

First, he proved his dexterity with a lasso by hogtieing 16 non-player characters (townspeople by any other name) in just 3 min. "I found the best place to hogtie NPCs was in Casa Madrugada, a shady backwater in Mexico," he told us. "The authorities there would pass a blind eye as I tied up piles of townsfolk."

For his second challenge, he galloped out on to the open plains on the back of the game's most unglamorous mount – a donkey. He achieved the **fastest time to ride from Dixon Crossing to Gaptooth Ridge**, completing the journey in just 11 min 7 sec. "When it comes to riding a donkey in *Red Dead Redemption*, you should be prepared to be late to all of your appointments," he said.

Both records were achieved on 21 Sep 2017 at Guinness World Records' London HQ.

HISTORICAL

Danger in these worlds can come from the fiercest saber-tooth tiger, the most-wanted outlaw of the Wild West or the mummified remains of the pharaohs of ancient Egypt, so be on your guard. Only the most fearless gamer will survive long enough to make history...

MOST ASSASSINATIONS IN ASSASSIN'S CREED: SYNDICATE

Players are free to roam the fog-filled streets of *Assassin's Creed: Syndicate*'s Victorian-era London at their leisure, picking up as many optional side-missions as they please on their travels. As of 12 Feb 2018, "ANA PAULA FBI" had successfully completed 12,243 assassination side-quests on Xbox One, as verified by TrueAchievements. The tally was just over 2,000 more hits than the second-most-lethal assassin, "ChereneC17".

YOUR NEW FAVOURITE GAME

SKULL & BONES
Platforms: PS4, Xbox One, PC
Gamers who enjoyed the pirate life in *Assassin's Creed IV: Black Flag* (Ubisoft, 2013) will soon find the high seas calling them again as Ubisoft's *Skull & Bones* makes ready to drop anchor. Only the best captains will be able to avoid Davy Jones' Locker.

MOST OUTPOSTS CAPTURED IN *FAR CRY PRIMAL* ON XBOX ONE

Using stealth, planning, spear, club and the help of his ferocious bestial companions, Xbox One gamer "Taylor Shrout" had cleared out 105 camps in the spin-off to Ubisoft's popular open-world franchise as of 13 Feb 2018, according to TrueAchievements.

For the intrepid gamer "wheelhorse50", exploration was more interesting than conquest, with plenty of scope for travel in *Far Cry Primal*'s huge open world. The Xbox One expert had covered a heel-shredding 4,597,967 ft/1,401,460 m (870.8 mi/1,401.4 km), which is the **farthest distance travelled in *Far Cry Primal***. Let's just hope that his caveman character works out how to make some decent footwear soon.

LEAST-AWARDED ASSASSIN'S CREED ORIGINS ACHIEVEMENT

Few gamers have found their way to every location, tomb and secret chamber concealed within *Origins*' vast ancient Egyptian wilderness. The "Old Habits" achievement – awarded to gamers who find and complete all locations – had been picked up by only 17.25% of Xbox One players as of 13 Feb 2018, according to TrueAchievements.

On the PS4, "Old Habits" is the second-rarest trophy (aside from *Origins*' Platinum). It has been narrowly edged out in the rarity stakes by a trophy simply called "BOOM!". It is a reward that can be obtained only when skilled (or lucky) players cumulatively kill 30 enemies by successfully shooting a fire arrow at oil pots, after which the oil spreads and burns.

Q&A: DR GARRY J SHAW

A doctorate in Egyptology makes Garry J Shaw the perfect person to tell us if *Assassin's Creed Origins* sticks to the facts or takes liberties with history...

Q Were there really traps inside the pharaohs' tombs?

A There weren't, but the Egyptians did make it as difficult as possible for thieves to reach the royal burial chamber. Sometimes, the Egyptians placed doorways high up near the ceiling of a chamber or they hid the entrance to the next chamber behind large blocks of stone. Any thieves would need to dig through this stone to reach the burial chamber. Unfortunately, their tombs were still robbed.

Q *Origins*' main character, Bayek, is a Medjay. Who were they?

A A people from Nubia, an area in the far south of modern Egypt and northern Sudan. They were famous as warriors. Later, Medjay worked as guardians of the Valley of the Kings, the burial place of such famous pharaohs as Tutankhamun. They kept an eye out for tomb robbers.

Q What would you say is the least accurate part of *Assassin's Creed Origins*?

A Hmm. I can say for certain that the ancient Egyptians didn't spend their time climbing up pyramids and then sliding down the sides – these were sacred locations!

MOST FOLLOWED GAME PUBLISHER ON TWITTER

Rockstar Games' total of 9,160,346 Twitter followers as of 12 Feb 2018 was bettered only by PlayStation (15,362,173) and Xbox (12,587,196) – though both, of course, are makers of consoles as well as games. Of Rockstar's tweets, its Oct 2016 announcement of *Red Dead Redemption II* (above) performed best, with 142,599 retweets (many more than the 16,922 retweets of the news of its delay).

Most failed case in *L.A. Noire*
It's back to the training academy for the gamers who failed to crack open the case of "The Fallen Idol" in Rockstar's 2011 open-world detective game. As confirmed by Rockstar (statistics released on 31 Oct 2017), the case – involving a fading actress and an upcoming starlet who accuse their movie producer of attempted murder – was too much for 8,219,654 would-be detectives to solve.

High flier
Leonardo da Vinci's flying machine was spectacularly brought to life as a means to take out a target in Ubisoft's *Assassin's Creed II* (2009).

Most expensive collector's edition for an action-adventure game
Of the six different editions of *Assassin's Creed Origins*, the *Dawn of the Creed Legendary Edition* was the priciest, costing $799.99 (£631) – no wonder Ubisoft limited it to 999 copies. For that, you got the game, a resin statue of Bayek and his eagle, a Certificate of Authenticity, a resin replica of Bayek's eagle-skull amulet, a steelbook case, lithographs signed by the studio's artists and even more goodies.

Fastest 100% completion of *Red Dead Redemption*
It was many decades before the western frontier was tamed in real life, but "Renzo Bos" (NLD) galloped through Rockstar's western in just 41 hr 10 min 50 sec. He left rivals in his dust at the TwistDock Endurance Gaming Challenge in Rotterdam, Netherlands, in Jul 2010.

Most "Platinumed" PlayStation game
Players need skill and determination to grab every trophy in a PlayStation game and secure that ever-elusive Platinum. The most-collected Platinum ever is that of *Assassin's Creed II* on PS3. According to PSNProfiles, 156,569 gamers had taken it as of 13 Feb 2018.

Most followed action-adventure game series on Twitter
Ubisoft's *Assassin's Creed* Twitter channel had 4,237,650 followers as of 13 Feb 2018. That's the most for an adventure series and makes it the ninth most followed gaming account.

Most arena champions defeated in *Assassin's Creed Origins*
The gladiatorial ring holds no fear for Xbox gamer "LESCHBOMBER". As of 13 Feb 2018, the deadly fighter had defeated 228 arena champions, as verified by TrueAchievements.

ALTERNATIVE PRESENT

If fantasy realms and deep space aren't your thing, then there are always open worlds to explore in the here and now. Developers aren't content to recreate humdrum aspects of real life, though, instead filling their games with hitmen, superheroes, special forces and more...

FASTEST STEAM EARLY ACCESS GAME TO SELL ONE MILLION COPIES

In a feat totally unheard of for an Early Access game, *PLAYERUNKNOWN'S BATTLEGROUNDS*, released on 23 Mar 2017, needed just 16 days to reach sales measured in seven figures, according to SuperData. Emphasizing its impact, the same game set the **fastest time for a Steam Early Access game to gross $100 million** – just 79 days. That's how to announce your arrival!

YOUR NEW FAVOURITE GAME

SPIDER-MAN
Platform: PS4
He's back in Marvel films and now he's coming to your PS4. Get ready for a web-slinging adventure that lets gamers play as Spidey and Peter Parker. Here's hoping it's the wall-crawler game that can finally outdo *Spider-Man 2* (Activision, 2004).

MOST *HITMAN* MISSIONS COMPLETED WITH FIVE STARS

Assassins who successfully eliminate targets in the open-world thriller *Hitman* are graded out of five, based on factors including time taken and the total of non-target casualties. As of 12 Feb 2018, Xbox player "UnknownGamer477" had become the ultimate hitman, with 2,550 of his missions getting the five-star treatment, according to TrueAchievements.

142,925

The steady aim of "AshenHero" had helped the American gamer set the mark for **most enemies killed in *Tom Clancy's Ghost Recon: Wildlands***. His formidable total of 142,925 downed foes, as verified by TrueAchievements on 12 Feb 2018, put him far ahead in the sharp-shooting stakes for Ubisoft's 2017 tactical open-world game. He was way beyond second-placed gamer "ChancierSet6", who had 74,090 kills.

Least-killed Elusive Target on *Hitman*
Only 23% of players have been able to assassinate wily Xander Haverfoek – aka "The Fixer" – in the 2016 open-world shooter. The character's resilience was confirmed by Square Enix on 17 Mar 2017. Eliminating an Elusive Target can bring Agent 47 rewards such as new outfits.

Most viewed Twitch broadcaster (individual)
Twitcher "ShadbaseMurderTV" had a formidable view count of 332,187,004 as of 12 Feb 2018. It was the highest for an individual and the fourth most viewed Twitch channel overall. Although predominately an artist, the masked broadcaster also streams himself playing games such as *PUBG* as well as *A Hat in Time* (Gears for Breakfast, 2017).

Most successful FOB defences in *Metal Gear Solid V*
"中国人 Invincible Dragon" had defended his Forward Operating Base (FOB) 1,502 times in Konami's 2015 open-world shooter, as of 12 Feb 2018 and according to Steam Leaderboards.

Most solo kills in a game of *H1Z1*
As verified by Twin Galaxies on 27 Feb 2017, "Ninja" (USA), aka Richard Tyler Blevins, achieved a record of 38 solo, all-weapons kills while playing Daybreak Game's 2018 survival shooter. The gamer had to face-off against 150 other players within the game's sprawling environment to hit the high score.

FACT!

In Jul 2016, *Hitman* (2016) featured a target based on a real person. In the game's second episode, "World of Tomorrow", US actor Gary Busey made a surprise cameo.

MOST DIGITAL SALES OF A PC VIDEOGAME

Some games seem to come out of nowhere, and *PLAYERUNKNOWN'S BATTLEGROUNDS* (*PUBG*) is one of them. PUBG Corporation's survival shooter was setting records while it was still under development, shifting 26,868,058 copies in 2017, according to the digital-sales tracker SuperData. It has set plenty of other new benchmarks along the way. For example, it was the **first game** with 3 million concurrent players on Steam. That figure hit a peak on 13 Jan 2018. At a point on that day, a remarkable 3,236,027 gamers were busy playing *PUBG* at the same time. The same total made it the **most actively played game on Steam**, gave it the **most concurrent players for a Steam Early Access game**, and was the **most concurrent players on Steam for a non-Valve game** – a significant feat.

48 TITLES

Late US author Tom Clancy had an eye for technical detail that clearly struck a chord with generations of gamers. As of 7 Mar 2017, some 48 titles bore Clancy's name, the **most games headlined by a real person**. That total is made up of 18 titles in the *Tom Clancy's Rainbow Six* series and 15 in *Tom Clancy's Ghost Recon*, as well as endorsed games in the *Splinter Cell*, *The Division*, *H.A.W.X.* and *EndWar* series.

Most first-place finishes in *Fortnite Battle Royale* (solo)
As the last player standing on 1,853 occasions, PS4 gamer "AlexRamiGaming" (UK) has more than earned his place on these pages. That is especially true when you consider he's won way over a quarter of the 4,449 Battle Royales he's started in Epic's survivalist sandbox.

Elsewhere, "NinjasHyper" (USA) registered the **most kills in *Fortnite Battle Royale***, taking out 30,851 players over the course of 4,407 games.

The title of **most matches of *Fortnite Battle Royale* played** was set by "FusIoNoNeR", who had competed in 9,010 encounters, as verified (as are all the above) by fortnitetracker.com as of 12 Feb 2018.

FUTURISTIC

Will the future bring peace to all? Not if various open-world titles set in far-flung alternative societies are correct in their depictions. Some imagine worlds are ruled by robots, others by dinosaurs, and at least one by robot dinosaurs – and none of the above are ever pleased to see us...

FASTEST COMPLETION OF *HORIZON ZERO DAWN: THE FROZEN WILDS*

German PS4 gamer "Schattentod" obviously sets high standards for himself. On 18 Nov 2017, he took just 1 hr 24 min 30 sec to complete *The Frozen Wilds*' story campaign, but he still wasn't happy. "Schattentod"

commented on his feat, saying that it was a "pretty good run, [but] could still be a lot better", citing a death in one of the game's challenging cauldrons as one of the areas in which his time could be improved. As it was, his run

still slashed over 4 min off a mark set by "EverydaYAussiEHD" (AUS), who had, just four days previously, completed *Horizon Zero Dawn*'s DLC campaign in 1 hr 28 min 54 sec, as verified by Speedrun on 14 Nov 2017.

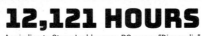

12,121 HOURS

According to SteamLadder.com, PC gamer "Discorrdia" (CAN) had invested the greatest aggregate time on Studio Wildcard's *Ark: Survival Evolved* (2017). As of 28 Mar 2018, the Canadian had spent 12,121 hr on the dinosaur-themed game of dodging mighty beasts. That equates to just over 505 days!

Fastest completion of *inFAMOUS: Second Son* (100% evil karma)

To complete the super-powered open-world game with evil karma, players must execute enemies that are trying to surrender and disrupt peaceful protests. "SpiderHako" (DEU) embraced his dark side as he finished in 6 hr 35 min 24 sec on 6 Jul 2017, a time that was verified by Speedrun.

Choosing a much more peaceful path was "Gamecuber" (ZWE), who achieved the **fastest 100% good karma completion of** *inFAMOUS: Second Son* on 22 Sep 2016. Proving once and for all that nice guys really do finish last, he took 7 hr 20 min 29 sec. For his good karma run, he had to complete the game while saving the lives of hostages and subduing bad guys as he went.

Most followed dedicated videogame character on Twitter

As of 26 Feb 2018, the "personal" Twitter account for mouthy-but-loveable robot Claptrap (@ECHOcasts), of 2K's *Borderlands* series, had 124,000 followers. That exceeds the total for any fictional game character dedicated to issuing "personal" tweets.

Most successful co-op operations in *WATCH_DOGS 2*

Xbox One player "Neohidro" (LVA) had hacked his way through 1,948 co-op operations in Ubisoft's 2016 action-adventure as of 26 Feb 2018, as verified by TrueAchievements. *WATCH_DOGS 2*'s randomly generated missions task players with stealing vehicles, downloading restricted data, rescuing prisoners and completing other similar objectives.

Fastest completion of *Fallout 4*

The questionably named "tomatoanus" (USA) holds the any% speed-run record for Bethesda's 2015 post-apocalyptic RPG with a time of 40 min 38 sec, set on 7 Mar 2018, as verified by Speedrun. "Wew, good run besides [The] Institute," he said of his attempt. As it stands, he's only 15 sec faster than the second-quickest Vault-dweller, "BubblesDelFuego" (USA), in what's a hotly contested record.

Largest LEGO® brick *Horizon Zero Dawn* custom scale model
After creating LEGO masterpieces inspired by *Halo* and *Titanfall*, Marius Herrmann put together *Horizon Zero Dawn*'s fearsome Thunderjaw. His model (above) measures 42 x 30 x 65 cm (16.5 x 11.8 x 25.6 in). He presented it to Guerrilla Games, who have it on display in their offices in Amsterdam, Netherlands.

FACT!
Fallout 4's robot butler Codsworth can address players by one of 1,259 pre-recorded names in the game's English version – the **most names spoken by a robot in a videogame.**

YOUR NEW FAVOURITE GAME

ANTHEM
Platforms: PS4, Xbox One, PC
The next big release from BioWare is an open-world action game set on a monster-dominated planet. The last line of defence for humans, who have taken refuge in a walled city, are Freelancers – warriors protected by Iron Man-style suits called Javelins.

EXPANDED FRANCHISE

As of 8 Feb 2018, Bethesda's online store let *Fallout* fans prepare for life in the Vault with 53 items of clothing, the **most items based on a Bethesda franchise**. The "Ladies Heather Vault-Tec ANGL Hoodie" (left) was the most popular.

777,439

Most popular female games broadcaster on Twitch
Self-proclaimed "full-time dragon slayer, part-time sniper" "OMGitsfirefoxx", aka Sonja Reid (CAN), boasted 777,439 followers as of 15 Mar 2018. This put her ahead of fellow female games broadcaster "KittyPlays", who had 771,593 followers as of the same date.

SPACE EXPLORATION

OPEN WORLD

Whether you believe it's the final frontier or a place where no one can hear you scream, there can be no denying the intrigue of space. Although few humans have gone there, millions of gamers have explored the virtual universe in games that continue to push technical boundaries.

LONGEST DEEP-SPACE RESCUE IN *ELITE: DANGEROUS*

With a Latin motto that translates as "locate and save" (*Collocare occasionem liberabuntur*), the Fuel Rats are a group of *Elite: Dangerous* pilots dedicated to rescuing stranded players in Frontier's 2014 space epic. Since the group was formed on 2 Jun 2015, more than 1,500

players have contributed to missions that have saved over 40,000 out-of-fuel gamers.

As confirmed by Frontier, the longest recovery was the Rescue of Persera, in which the Fuel Rats travelled 65,659.04 light years – over half the length of the Milky Way! The feat finished on 23 Dec 2017 and took a whopping 75 hours.

372 M

The Hull E specialized freighter is the **largest flyable ship in *Star Citizen***. At 372 m (1,220 ft 5 in) long and 104 m (341 ft 2 in) high, the freighter dwarfs the vast majority of available ships in Cloud Imperium Games' space-faring MMO. A lack of manoeuvrability might hamper it in a fight, but its cargo capacity gives it an advantage in the game's interstellar trading market.

Exploring the universe in style...
As of 20 Mar 2018, the **most expensive spaceship in *Elite: Dangerous*** was the Imperial Cutter (left), yours for a mere 208,969,451 in-game credits. The **most expensive spaceship in *Star Citizen*** was the "Origin 890 Jump" interstellar yacht (right). It was available on 29 Nov 2017 for a very real $1,068 (£802) from the game's store (though, as of 20 Mar 2018, it was listed as "not available").

LONGEST-RUNNING CONVENTION FOR A SINGLE GAME

Since its first staging in 2004, EVE Fanfest has been bringing fans of CCP Games' *EVE Online* together on an almost annual basis in Reykjavik, Iceland. As of its 2018 event, held on 12–14 Apr, it had been running for 14 years – only skipping a year in 2011.

First open-world game
In the hugely influential space-trading game *Elite* (Ian Bell/David Braben, 1984), players assumed the role of pilots who were free to explore the vast openness of space. In all, eight galaxies and more than 2,000 planets constituted the game's "open world", as players fought with pirates and traded in commodities to earn a living.

FACT!

As of Feb 2018, *Elite: Dangerous* players had travelled 20,262,978,541 light years and driven 92,322,972,771 m (302,896,892,293 ft) on planets.

MOST CONCURRENT STEAM PLAYERS FOR AN OPEN-WORLD SCI-FI GAME

When *No Man's Sky* (Hello Games) launched on 9 Aug 2016, it attracted 212,321 PC space explorers to Steam simultaneously. Hello Games founder Sean Murray later commented that he had been expecting a figure more in the region of 14,000.

GAMING GOLD

Enemy unknown?
In 2017, *Elite: Dangerous* pilots reported seeing mysterious flower-shaped craft (left). These were later confirmed to signal the return of *Elite*'s (1984) bad guys, the Thargoids!

Most crowdfunded game
The appeal for public support from publisher Cloud Imperium Games for its *Star Citizen* project began in Sep 2012, but it has continued to make headlines and generate funds. As of 19 Mar 2018, the space-faring sim had raised a remarkable $180,386,613 (£129,326,000) from 1,997,150 backers (referred to as Star Citizens). This figure secures *Star Citizen*'s place as not just the most

crowdfunded videogame, but the **most crowdfunded project overall.**

Most systems discovered in *Elite: Dangerous*
As of 16 Mar 2018, intrepid space explorer "Allitnil" had discovered 99,128 systems in the 2014 space-farer, according to the game's website (www.edsm.net). He has tracked his progress in charting the game's unknown regions since 17 Jan 2016.

Most downloaded mod for *No Man's Sky*
HytekGaming's "LowFlight" mod for *No Man's Sky* lets players fly their spacecraft as close to the surface of a planet as they want. It also adds a hover feature to the ships and allows them to explore underwater. It was released for PC in Aug 2016 and had been downloaded 86,265 times as of 20 Mar 2018, making it the most popular mod in the community.

Most fuel delivered on a single rescue in *Elite: Dangerous*
The Fuel Rats – the same group of space-based rescuers featured in our lead record (left) – had an earlier mission in Jul 2015. In a rescue that was dubbed "Operation: Neospike", the group responded to a distress call from a commander who had been stranded 3,600 light years from civilization. A huge consignment of 500 units of fuel was delivered to the stricken craft.

FANTASY

Open-world fantasy games take us inside the magical realms of folklore and fairy tale. On your journey, don't be surprised if you bump into knights, wizards, elves, dwarfs and more. Just make sure you're armed with the game's sharpest sword when it comes to taking on the inevitable evil sorcerer…

Farthest distance in *Breath of the Wild* Ridgeland Tower Gliding Challenge
Players who chance upon *The Legend of Zelda: Breath of the Wild*'s Ridgeland Tower will discover a hang-gliding mini-game. Brazil's Rodrigo Lopes is the master of the sky, staying airborne for a distance of 2,912.1 m (9,554 ft) on 10 Sep 2017, as verified by Twin Galaxies.

FIRST 100% COMPLETION OF *BREATH OF THE WILD*

Before this record could even be attempted, speed-run enthusiasts had to decide on exactly what qualified as a 100% completion of Nintendo's action-adventure title. Treasure chests, armour upgrades, puzzle shrines and Divine Beasts were all topics for discussion – as was the small matter of 900 Korok seeds.

Once it was decided that all of the above must be solved, discovered or defeated, French Twitcher "Xalikah" leapt in head first, taking 49 hr 9 min 41 sec to achieve absolutely everything in an attempt that ended on 17 Apr 2017. His record-breaking run even included a nap break. "When I hit 30 hours, it was hard for me," he admitted on his Speedrun post.

His run led to swift competition, with "SpecsN_Stats" (USA) posting the **fastest 100% completion of *Breath of the Wild*** in 32 hr 15 min 18 sec on 30 Dec 2017.

YOUR NEW FAVOURITE GAME

VAMPYR
Platforms: PS4, Xbox One, PC
Dr Jonathan Reid faces a terrible dilemma in Focus Home Interactive's blend of open-world action and RPG. After being turned into a vampire, he must satisfy his thirst for human blood, while keeping his oath to save lives.

125 BETRAYALS

In *Middle-earth: Shadow of War* (Warner Bros., 2017), your army of orcs is always on the lookout to make a play for the top job. When this happens, it's called a "betrayal". The only way for Talion to survive the crisis point is to show the orc who's boss with the sharp end of his sword. As of 13 Mar 2018, Xbox One gamer "bottomshelfbob" had experienced the **most betrayals in *Middle-earth: Shadow of War***, with 125 orcs rising up against him, as verified by TrueAchievements.

First open-world survival game
The second decade of the new millennium has witnessed an explosion of open-world survival games, particularly on the Steam platform, with the success of PC titles such as *DayZ* (2013), *Ark: Survival Evolved* and *PLAYERUNKNOWN'S BATTLEGROUNDS* (both 2017). The genre's roots can be traced back to the indie sandbox RPG *UnReal World*, which was released in 1992. Set in Iron Age Finland, its harsh environments tested players' capacity to survive. The game was still receiving updates in Apr 2018.

Fastest any% completion of *Middle-earth: Shadow of War*
"Gaius_Ultima" (DEU) did not simply walk into Mordor, they sprinted. On 28 Jan 2018, the PC player brought chaos to Sauron's ranks in 3 hr 50 min 37 sec, pinning his fast time on his "levelling-up strategy".

Most popular mod for *The Witcher III: Wild Hunt*
With a commanding 426,935 unique downloads and 23,884 endorsements since being released on 26 Nov 2015, *The Witcher III HD Reworked Project* was the most popular mod for the sprawling RPG epic as of 13 Mar 2018. It was created for PC gamers by modder "Halk Hogan" to improve the game's visuals through the addition of enhanced models and textures.

Fastest any% completion of *Dragon's Dogma: Dark Arisen*
On the PC version of Capcom's acclaimed action role-player – itself an expanded release of 2012's *Dragon's Dogma* – American gamer "glasnonck" recorded a rapid completion time of 1 hr 11 min on 4 Mar 2017. Of his record-setting run, "glasnonck" said that "a crash during the Greatwall and a bad Eyeball fight" stopped him from setting an even better time.

109 RECIPES

If *Final Fantasy XV*'s photo-realistic dishes made you hungry, you're not alone. The in-game grub inspired "Tsubasa" (HKG) to recreate all 109 recipes for her blog, *Honey and Toast*, in Nov 2017 – the **most meals created from recipes in a game**. She made all the recipes freely available in English, Mandarin and Japanese. The ingredients cost "Tsubasa" HK$31,500 (US$4,035; £3,011).

EXPANDED FRANCHISE

The Witcher's Geralt is donning his armour for his live-action debut on Netflix in, we think, 2019. The new show will look to capitalize on the success of Andrzej Sapkowski's fantasy novels and the trilogy of videogames.

ZOMBIES

Zombies have been stalking after gamers almost since the dawn of pixels. However, the current explosion of open-world survival games has given those stumbling, groaning hordes a new platform on which to make their menacing way towards us. Eek!

MOST VALUABLE VIDEOGAME PACKAGE

$10M

In Feb 2016, publisher Techland released a $10-m (£7.2-m) version of its standalone expansion *Dying Light: The Following*, entitled the "Spotlight Edition". This solitary bundle was available exclusively through British retailer GAME.

It included a supporting role in a proposed film adaptation of the game (yet to be confirmed), professional acting lessons, stuntman/parkour training, an off-road driving course, an FX make-up session, a personal on-set trailer, a screening tour with first-class accommodation and flights, 10 VIP tickets for the film's opening night, an original copy of the film script, the chance to voice a future character in the series and four copies of *Dying Light: The Following* itself, each signed by the development team.

145,259

As of 3 Aug 2017, ruthless Xbox One gamer "CotJocky466" (USA) was way out in front when it came to the **most zombies killed in *State of Decay: Year-One Survival Edition***. According to Xbox site TrueAchievements.com, he'd slaughtered 145,259 undead denizens. Undead Labs' zombie-filled open-world survival game challenges players to stay alive by building and maintaining bases, scavenging for items and trading with fellow survivors. We suppose that it can't hurt if you can also manage to wipe out over 145,000 of the game's undead horde while you're at it!

EXPANDED FRANCHISE

Dead Rising: Watchtower (2015) and *Endgame* (2016) are spin-off flicks from Capcom's comedic zombie-splatterer. Jesse Metcalfe stars as a journalist caught up in a viral outbreak.

FASTEST COMPLETION OF *DEAD RISING 4*

On 6 Jan 2018, Xbox One speed-runner "kadennoh" (JPN) punched, kicked and blasted his way through the "normal difficulty" option on Capcom's madcap zombie open-worlder *Dead Rising 4* (2016) in 2 hr 0 min 3 sec, as verified by Speedrun.com. In the guise of series icon Frank West, "kadennoh" chopped 1 min 3 sec off the run time that had been set by previous record holder "Zimmycakesrtg".

12,320 HOURS

As of 16 Jan 2018, PC gamer "ʃªⲧáᏞᎥⲦⲧ" had spent the **greatest aggregate time playing** *DayZ* (Bohemia Interactive, 2013), according to Steam-tracking site SteamLadder. That's nearly 17 months! Amazingly, the gamer had spent even more time playing *CS:GO, Garry's Mod* and *Arma III*!

YOUR NEW FAVOURITE GAME

DAYS GONE
Platform: PS4

Sony's post-apocalyptic horror hurls hundreds of infected humans at us all at once. Referred to as "Freakers" (rather than zombies), they can actually be used to your advantage, as clever players can lure them into enemy camps to wreak havoc.

1 HOUR 5 MINUTES 4 SECONDS

Fastest completion of *Red Dead Redemption: Undead Nightmare*
Xbox 360 player "Joshimuz" (UK) cleansed *Red Dead*'s wild west of undead in 1 hr 5 min 4 sec, as verified on 29 Oct 2015 by Speedrun.com.

Undead Nightmare was a 2010 standalone expansion for Rockstar's western that saw hero cowboy John Marston seeking out a cure for the undead blight infecting the land.

29 YEARS

Longest time between games in a zombie series
The release of *Zombi* for PS4, Xbox One and PC on 18 Aug 2015 meant that there was a gap of 29 years between Ubisoft's entries in its horror series. The debut, also titled *Zombi*, was a first-person point-and-click adventure based on George A Romero's 1978 movie *Dawn of the Dead*. First released for the Amstrad CPC in France in 1986, the game also has the distinction of being French publisher Ubisoft's first-ever title.

Most viewed fan film based on a zombie videogame
Ampisound's live-action video "Dying Light – Zombie Parkour POV", based on Techland's *Dying Light* (2015), had picked up 21,765,277 views as of 16 Jan 2018. Shot in Cambridge, UK, and first published on 9 Jan 2015, the video follows a parkour runner from a first-person perspective as he takes to the rooftops to flee the eerily athletic undead.

Fastest completion of *Dying Light*
US gamer "TheFuncannon" laid waste to the PC version of Techland's *Dying Light* by recording an any% run of 1 hr 44 min 28 sec (in-game time). His time, verified by Speedrun on 18 Oct 2017, pipped fellow speed-runner "Wolfe87" (UK) to the post by just 7 sec.

First zombie videogame
US Games' *Entombed* (1982) for the Atari 2600 was the first game to feature our undead friends. Players assumed the role of an archaeologist who had to navigate a vertically scrolling maze of catacombs, while trying to avoid zombies and dead ends. The game pre-dates Bram Software's *Zombies*, released for the Atari 800 in 1983.

Most zombies killed in *How to Survive 2*
As of 9 Mar 2018, Xbox One player "Henry the Ugly" had slain 49,526 infected zombies in 505 Games' top-down survival game, according to the Xbox tracking site TrueAchievements.

If animal zombies are more your thing (or nightmare), then spare a thought for Xbox One player "invader nug" (USA), who'd achieved the **most animal zombies killed in *How to Survive 2*** as of 7 Aug 2017. According to TrueAchievements, he had slayed 5,675 infected alligators, pigs, rabbits and giant turkeys.

GRAND THEFT AUTO

Speed, growling supercars, leaving cops in the dust and a whole lot of law-breaking might be what made Rockstar's *Grand Theft Auto* (*GTA*) famous. But it's the open, anything-can-happen nature of its gameplay – whether going solo or online – that keeps gamers hooked.

MOST CASH EARNED IN *GTA ONLINE*
The richest crimelord of all is "RaquelRJ" (BRA), who had amassed over GTA$17 trillion of in-game cash in *GTA Online* (2013) as of 8 Mar 2018, according to Xbox tracking site TrueAchievements. The precise figure was actually GTA$17,068,000,028,900, but we don't think she would quibble over a measly few billion...

800,000 LINES
GTA: Chinatown Wars (2009) was created using the **most lines of code in a Nintendo DS game** – 800,000 of them all told. The game reportedly has more code than *GTA: San Andreas* (2004), despite the PS2 title being a 3D open-world game. The record-breaking amount of programming was necessary to create *Chinatown Wars'* huge playable environment.

MOST CARS STOLEN
As of 27 Feb 2018, the world's most successful virtual car thief was "Ferguson010886", who had taken illegal possession of 3,182 cars in the Xbox One version of Rockstar's *GTA V* (2014), as verified by TrueAchievements.

A one-person crime wave, "Ferguson010886" is clearly not being pursued successfully by Los Santos' police force. But he is within the sights of a rival gamer, "Ce11Ph0nzR0ck3r", who, as of the same date, had car-jacked and hot-wired 3,127 automobiles.

FIRST HOLLYWOOD MOVIE REMADE IN AN ACTION-ADVENTURE GAME

Using a modded version of *GTA V*, YouTuber "KRAMER'S MEDIA" (RUS) recreated *Terminator 2: Judgment Day* (1991) within the game. A video published on 11 Apr 2017 contains all of the film's key scenes, including the apocalyptic opening and the motorcycle chase (left).

Most expensive vehicle in *GTA Online*
Released on 10 Jun 2015 as part of the "Ill-Gotten Gains Part 1" DLC, the gold-painted Buckingham Luxor Deluxe private jet was priced at a wallet-crippling GTA$10,000,000.

Looking for something cheaper? The Dec 2015 "Executives and Other Criminals" DLC offered the Aquarius Galaxy Super Yacht for GTA$8,000,000 – **most expensive yacht in *GTA Online***. For that, you get a 64-m (210-ft) yacht with sundeck and your own helipad.

Greatest aggregate time playing *GTA V* (PC)
According to SteamLadder.com, the Latvian PC gamer "iiiiiiiiiiiiiii" had recorded 24,259 hr of full-throttle, gun-toting gameplay across *GTA V* and its *GTA Online* multiplayer component, as of 22 Mar 2018. That's equivalent to 2 years 280 days!

Most Golden Joystick "Best Game" awards won by a gaming franchise
The *Grand Theft Auto* series has won four of the prestigious awards voted for by gamers and handed out at the London-based ceremony. The first award was for *GTA III* in 2002, the second for *GTA: Vice City* in 2003, the third for *GTA: San Andreas* in 2005 and the fourth for *GTA V* in 2013.

Most followed game developer on Twitter
Rockstar Games had a staggering 9,215,012 followers on Twitter as of 22 Mar 2018. Across the whole of the industry, PlayStation (15,472,188) and Xbox (12,693,119) exceeded that figure, but they are console makers as well.

London calling
GTA: London 1969 (1999) contains a little bit of gaming history. The London-based caper for PS One was the **first console videogame expansion** – it required the original *GTA* (1997) game disc to function.

Largest stunting crew in *GTA*
Thanks to its huge open world, *GTA V* has been perfect for gamers looking to test themselves in death-defying virtual stunts. Videos have been posted of characters parachuting from buildings, launching themselves off mountains and even performing BMX stunts from planes (above). The largest *GTA* daredevil crew – with 30 members as of 5 Apr 2018 – is Evolve Stunting, specializing in amazing team montages.

Most played *GTA Online* playlist
Playlists are sets of jobs that multiple gamers can tackle simultaneously online. The most popular is "Venture Off-Road", which lets groups of players test their off-road racing skills on rough terrain across hilly deserts, rural lands and mountains. As of 8 Mar 2018, it had been tackled 745,940 times.

TOP 10

MOST SUBSCRIBED YOUTUBERS

Star gamers are riding high on the explosion in popularity of YouTube and Twitch (see pp.92–93). Broadcasters such as El Salvador's "fernanfloo" – who has the **most subscribers for a YouTube channel dedicated to gaming** – have millions of followers clamouring for their latest posts.

1 FERNANFLOO (SLV)

27,479,422 SUBSCRIBERS

Most played: PLAYERUNKNOWN'S BATTLEGROUNDS

"fernanfloo" is more than partial to the odd round of PLAYERUNKNOWN'S BATTLEGROUNDS.

4 MARKIPLIER (USA)
20,137,202 SUBSCRIBERS
Most played: *Various*

7 POPULARMMOS (USA)
14,207,434 SUBSCRIBERS
Most played: *Minecraft*

10 ALI-A (UK)
12,741,426 SUBSCRIBERS
Most played: *Fortnite*

3 VEGETTA777 (ESP)
21,850,747 SUBSCRIBERS
Most played: *Minecraft*

6 DANTDM (UK)
18,515,008 SUBSCRIBERS
Most played: *Minecraft*

9 AUTHENTICGAMES (BRA)
13,428,410 SUBSCRIBERS
Most played: *Minecraft*

2 VANOSSGAMING (CAN)
22,760,058 SUBSCRIBERS
Most played: *Garry's Mod*

5 JACKSEPTICEYE (IRL)
18,672,906 SUBSCRIBERS
Most played: *Various*

8 THEWILLYREX (ESP)
13,792,181 SUBSCRIBERS
Most played: *Various*

All data as verified by SocialBlade.com on 11 Apr 2018. YouTubers must be included in Social Blade's gaming category.

WWII D-DAY GAMES

6 Jun 2019 marks the 75th anniversary of the D-Day Normandy landings. Over the years, game developers have revisited WWII operation time and again to celebrate the Allies' successful invasion of Normandy – as our selected visual history shows…

1984

1988

1993

1994

2000

2001

2002

2003

2004

2005

2006

2007

2008

2009

As of the release of *Call of Duty: WWII* in Nov 2017, at least 55 videogames had based all or part of their gameplay on the events of D-Day – the **most videogame re-enactments of a real-world military campaign.**

The Allied invasion of Normandy – also known as Operation Overlord – began with the D-Day beach landings in northern France on 6 Jun 1944. The loss of life was considerable, but this, and the campaign that followed, proved to be turning points for WWII in Europe, resulting in the eventual Allied victory of 1945.

2017

2016

2013

2011

2010

2014

ADVENTURE

Discovering mythical cities, battling terrifying monsters and running from shuffling zombies is all in a day's work for gamers. Adventure games allow us to explore worlds that are as perilous as they are wondrous – and let us play the hero while we're at it...

LONGEST VIDEOGAME MARATHON ON A SURVIVAL HORROR GAME

Italian gamer Lorenzo Ramondetti decided to brave the horrors of Capcom's *Resident Evil* (*RE*) series for his marathon stint. On 20–22 Sep 2016, he played the PC versions of *RE 4* (2005) and *RE 5* (2009) for a confirmed 36 hr 29 min 40 sec, stopping only for the odd comfort break – as even heroes need to visit the bathroom every now and then!

Unfortunately, a tech problem stopped him from setting an even more formidable benchmark. Lorenzo claimed a total playing time of 50 hr, but the supporting video evidence failed at the above mark. But even his curtailed time was enough to set both the survival horror marathon record and the **longest videogame marathon on a *Resident Evil* game**.

We asked him what the most difficult aspect of his attempt was. "After many hours, your reflexes are slowed, and beating the bosses becomes really difficult," he answered. And his advice for anyone else looking to survive a similar gaming marathon? "Organize the attempt well, drink lots of water and avoid coffee. But, above all else, the most important thing is to hold on!"

> **"I DECIDED TO PLAY RESIDENT EVIL FOR MY MARATHON RUN BECAUSE IT'S SCARY ENOUGH TO KEEP ME AWAKE!"**
>
> LORENZO RAMONDETTI

ACTION ADVENTURE

If you have a thirst for adventure and yearn for a life less ordinary, then you've come to the right place. Action-adventure games recreate the kinds of scenes that you'd usually find only in Hollywood blockbusters. But this time, *you're* the one being dropped into the middle of the danger zone.

LARGEST COLOSSUS IN *SHADOW OF THE COLOSSUS*

Sony's touching and atmospheric adventure *Shadow of the Colossus* was deservedly praised as an all-time classic when it first hit the PS2 in 2005. Now, some 13 years later, the game has been remade for the PS4. The visuals and controls received an overhaul, but, crucially, the story and the colossi remained intact.

The much-improved graphics allow us to marvel once more at the magnificence of the 13th colossi, Phalanx, who remains the largest beast in the game. As is clear from our main image, it's more daunting in appearance than ever. Essentially a gigantic flying armoured snake, Phalanx has a total body length that's estimated at 200 m (656 ft). It's capable of giving the game's hero, Wander, more than a run for his money as he looks to dispatch the giant in his quest to revive his sweetheart.

9.95 MILLION

Developed by US studio Naughty Dog, Sony's *Uncharted* series has been gaming royalty since 2007. Its fifth main series title, *Uncharted 4: A Thief's End* (2016), is the **best-selling PS4-exclusive game**, having sold 9.95 million copies as of 20 Mar 2018, according to VGChartz. It's the sixth-best-selling PS4 title overall, with sales topped only by multi-platform blockbusters *GTA V* (17.43 million), *Call of Duty: Black Ops III* (15 million), *Call of Duty: WWII* (11.86 million), *FIFA 17* (10.89 million) and *FIFA 18* (10.58 million).

FASTEST COMPLETION OF *THE LAST GUARDIAN*

Appreciating the beauty and emotional impact of the story in *The Last Guardian* (Sony, 2016) was clearly not a priority for speedster "satsu". On 25 Nov 2017, the Japanese gamer led Trico, the part-bird, part-dog creature, to his destination in just 3 hr 18 min 2 sec.

30 MINUTES 32 SECONDS

"bjurnie" (NLD) set the fastest no-powers completion of *Dishonored 2* (Bethesda, 2016) on 11 Aug 2017. Playing as Emily Kaldwin – but being sure to ignore her supernatural powers – the gamer sprinted through the single-player campaign in 30 min 32 sec. Just two days later, "cearadeth" (FIN) equalled that time.

Fastest completion of
Batman: Arkham Knight
On 24 Feb 2018, speed-runner "Feanorus" (RUS) seized control of *Arkham Knight*'s leaderboard with an "Easy" difficulty run of 2 hr 41 min 37 sec, as verified by Speedrun. "Overall mediocre run but without big failures," commented the record-breaker.

The **fastest completion of** *Batman: Arkham Knight* **on "Nightmare" mode** was made by "Psychotik", aka Ricardo Cardenas (CAN). He battled his way through the ordeal in 2 hr 48 min 40 sec on 3 Sep 2017.

Most enemies stealth-killed in
Rise of the Tomb Raider
Quietly did it for US Xbox One player "shadowmarrba", who, in the guise of Lara Croft, had killed 39,275 enemies in *Rise of the Tomb Raider* (Square Enix, 2015) without any of them raising the alarm. His stealthy achievement was verified by TrueAchievements on 24 Apr 2018.

Longest-running consistent game universe
With interlinked stories that span more than five decades of narrative, Hideo Kojima's iconic stealth series *Metal Gear* had entertained and perplexed gamers for a total of 30 years 222 days. That span of time covers the period between the MSX2 computer debut of *Metal Gear* on 13 Jul 1987 and the release of *Metal Gear Survive* on 20 Feb 2018. The in-game events of the new release explore the gap between the *Metal Gear Solid V* releases *Ground Zeroes* (2014) and *The Phantom Pain* (2015).

Fastest completion of
***Gravity Rush 2's* Freestyle Race II**
Kat, the main character in Sony's 2017 gravity-defying adventure, has plenty of tricks up her sleeve to help her get around Neu Hiraleon. PS4 gamer "mute101416" used a few of those to place first in the Freestyle Race II with a record time of 16.23 sec on 4 Jan 2018.

YOUR NEW FAVOURITE GAME

THE LAST NIGHT
Platforms: Xbox One, PC
Odd Tales' sci-fi cyberpunk adventure uses beautiful *Blade Runner*-style aesthetics to bring its world to life. Players assume the role of Charlie, a lowly cog in a future society where technology reigns supreme – but at what cost to humanity?

To coincide with the release of new movie *Tomb Raider* (2018), Square Enix created a light-gun arcade game that was available exclusively in Dave & Buster's videogame arcade/restaurants in North America.

Most liked action-adventure game on Steam
Square Enix's 2013 reboot of the origins of archaeologist adventurer Lara Croft in *Tomb Raider* was clearly met with approval. As of 20 Mar 2018, 77,285 PC players had given the game the thumbs up on Steam.

GAMING GOLD

You enjoy role-playing games.

In love with a Psycho
Few gamers will forget the moment they first encountered Psycho Mantis in *Metal Gear Solid* (1998). The psychic villain could tell you what other games you owned and make your control pad move all on its own.

Whether they focus on the mysteries of ancient worlds, twisted tales of high-school life or eerie journeys into outer space, the storylines of narrative adventures are every bit as compelling and rewarding as anything you'd find in a good book...

FASTEST 100% COMPLETION OF *WHAT REMAINS OF EDITH FINCH*

On 25 Dec 2017, PC gamer "Duders" (USA) completed everything you can possibly complete in Giant Sparrow's 2017 adventure game in the rapid time of 1 hr 2 min 17 sec, as verified by Speedrun. His nearest rival was "Scuqualo" (ITA), whose latest time of 1 hr 3 min 50 sec, set on 16 Jan 2018, was still a margin of 1 min 33 sec behind the record set by "Duders".

A 100% run of *What Remains of Edith Finch* involves braving every inch of the Finchs' labyrinth-like home as each family member's strange tale unfolds. Gamers have to look into all peepholes, peer through every telescope, allow the drunken sailor to finish his song, walk on both paths to the house, pot the balls on the pool table (trick shots optional), knock every letter into the bath and do many more weird and wonderful things besides.

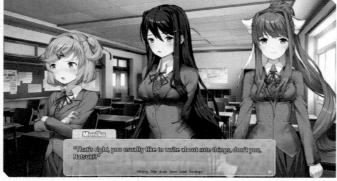

Monika

"That's right, you usually like to write about cute things, don't you, Natsuki?"

History Skip Auto Save Load Settings

HIGHEST USER-RATED ADVENTURE ON STEAM

Team Salvato's twisting (and twisted) tale of life in a Japanese high school has made *Doki Doki Literature Club!* (2017) a hit with just about anybody who plays it. According to Steam Database, the visual novel had a user rating of 95.63% as of 7 Feb 2018, placing it higher than any other narrative adventure. Its nearest rival was Telltale Games' *The Wolf Among Us* (2013), with a user rating of 95.21%.

GOLD

GAMING

I'M A ROCKER!

DISCO SUCKS!

Maniac Mansion
LucasArts' first full point-and-click adventure saw the SCUMM engine make its debut. It would be used to create the studio's stellar line-up of future classics.

Highest-rated visual novel (PS4)
Danganronpa V3: Killing Harmony (NIS America) tells a darkly comic tale about unlucky teenagers who are kidnapped and imprisoned by the evil (but cute) teddy bear Monokuma (right) and his mysterious master. As of 7 Feb 2018, it had an aggregate review score of 82.10%.

Most liked adventure game on Steam
The gripping episodic adventure *Life is Strange* (2015) had been awarded positive reviews on the PC distribution platform by 104,571 players as of 28 Feb 2018. Its puzzles, solved by rewinding and fast-forwarding time, have proven a hit with gamers, making it the 12th most liked PC game on Steam.

FASTEST COMPLETION OF *TACOMA*

Mexican speed-running specialist "SirArthvr" spared no time trying to find out what had happened to the absent crew on the deserted space station *Tacoma*. Instead, as verified by Speedrun on 4 Aug 2017, he raced and glided through Fullbright's 2017 sci-fi adventure, paying absolutely no heed to the game's thought-provoking story, to set a record run that stopped the clock at 13 min 41 sec.

YOUR NEW FAVOURITE GAME

IN THE VALLEY OF GODS
Platform: PC
For its second game, Campo Santo moves from *Firewatch*'s rural America to 1920s Egypt. Expect adventure, secret chambers and the chance of untold riches as we join film-makers Rashida and Zora in unravelling the riddles of ancient Egypt.

Most full-motion video footage in a game
D'Avekki Studios' indie mystery *The Infectious Madness of Doctor Dekker* (2017), which challenges players to solve a murder while interviewing patients of the deceased doctor, features 7 hr 11 min 58 sec of full-motion video (FMV).

First game rated "18" by the BBFC
CRL's text adventure *Jack the Ripper* – based on the unsolved murders of the notorious 19th-century serial killer who stalked London's East End – was awarded an "18" rating by the British Board of Film Classification on its release on 11 Dec 1987. The text-based adventure cast players in the role of a suspect looking to clear his name of any guilt, but it was the game's gory images that caused the furore. One retailer reportedly refused to stock the title as a consequence of its unprecedented age rating.

Fastest-selling Limited Run Games game
According to the specialist game publisher as of 7 Feb 2018, the narrative adventure *Night Trap: 25th Anniversary Edition* for PS4 (2017) sold all 8,000 available copies in less than one minute. The remaster of Sega's *Night Trap*, which was first released for the Sega CD console in 1992, is an interactive movie in which players take on a role of a secret agent whose unlikely job is to guide to safety a group of women as they are attacked by vampires.

Most critically acclaimed adventure game for eighth-gen platforms
The emotional storytelling of Giant Sparrow's *What Remains of Edith Finch* (2017) resonated with reviewers. As of 1 Mar 2018, it enjoyed a GameRankings score of 89.52% based on 43 reviews. It was also the third most critically acclaimed adventure game ever.

PLATFORMERS

Ever since Mario first took on Donkey Kong in 1981, platformers have supplied us with endless thrills and spills. These days, they provide the literal platform for speed-runners to show off their moves, which is why we've concentrated on those gamers who can leave even Sonic in the dust...

GAMING GOLD

Early girl power
Nintendo turned gender-based assumptions on their head in 1986 by revealing that *Metroid*'s hero, Samus Aran, was in fact a woman.

SONIC MANIA'S FASTEST FINISH

After chasing the acclaim of his glory days, everyone's favourite hedgehog was suddenly hot again with the release of *Sonic Mania* (Sega, 2017). Players could choose to speed through Sega's iconic landscapes as Sonic, Tails or Knuckles (or a combination), leading to many chances for speed-running records.

Playing on the PS4 on 6 Nov 2017, "GamerYogi" set the **fastest completion of *Sonic Mania* with Knuckles (any version)**, the US speed-runner whizzing through the game in 1 hr 8 min 39 sec, as verified by Speedrun.

Gameplay was even more of a blur in the company of "joeybaby69". On 22 Feb 2018, the US gamer took 49 min 17 sec to achieve the **fastest completion of *Sonic Mania* with Sonic and Tails (any version)**. Pairing Sonic with the flying fox is clearly a quicksilver combo.

FASTEST COMPLETION OF *METROID: SAMUS RETURNS*

Japan's "KazamidoriGanma" blazed a trail through Nintendo's 2017 *Metroid 2* 3DS remake in 1 hr 35 min 33 sec, as verified by Speedrun.com on 5 Jan 2018. Bounty-hunting legend Samus Aran could not have done it any better herself.

YOUR NEW FAVOURITE GAME

YOSHI
Platform: Switch
Nintendo's cutesy dinosaur will soon be heading to a Switch near you in a platformer simply called *Yoshi*. The twist here is that the game takes place upon paper-made dioramas that can be twisted and folded like a giant pop-up book.

2 HOURS 28 MINUTES 3 SECONDS

PS One classics *Crash Bandicoot* (1996), *Crash Bandicoot 2: Cortex Strikes Back* (1997) and *Crash Bandicoot: Warped* (1998) were all given a facelift before being crammed into *Crash Bandicoot N. Sane Trilogy* (Activision, 2017). The platforming *tour de force* was soon tamed, with "gabriel-batista9" (BRA) achieving the **fastest completion of *Crash Bandicoot N. Sane Trilogy*** in just 2 hr 28 min 3 sec, as verified by Speedrun.com on 18 Jan 2018.

FASTEST COMPLETION OF *STEAMWORLD DIG 2* ON PC

In a blur of pickaxe-wielding, "youpalaa" (FRA) finished *SteamWorld Dig 2* on PC in 25 min 13 sec on 12 Feb 2018, as verified by Speedrun. The **fastest completion of *Steamworld Dig 2* on Switch** – or on any console for that matter – was by "GooberShadow" (USA), who completed an any% play-through in 36 min 20 sec on 6 Oct 2017.

Fastest 100% completion of *Little Nightmares*
Twitch user "AlyssaMintChip" (USA) tried not to look over her shoulder as she braved the entirety of the PC version of Bandai Namco's creepy 2017 platformer in a mere 52 min 57 sec, as set on 25 May 2017 and verified by Speedrun. Her run was a little slower than her **fastest any% completion of *Little Nightmares***, achieved in 39 min 35.42 sec on 23 Jan 2018.

Highest-rated platformer on Steam
As of 8 Jan 2018, *A Hat in Time* (Gears for Breakfast, 2017) had a user-approval rating of 95.09% on PC distribution platform Steam. A total of 6,046 players had liked the 3D platformer, with 85 giving it the thumbs down. "The music, characters, story, feel, design, genius writing... It all meshes into one cute and adorable, loveable game," mused one happy PC gamer after purchasing the platformer.

Farthest distance travelled in *Inside*
Traversing the trap-filled corridors of Playdead's puzzle platformer of 2016 is an eerie experience. But that didn't put off Xbox One player "Renanvsk", who had travelled a total of 4,002.5 km (2,487 miles) while playing the game, as of 23 Feb 2018. His record was verified by TrueAchievements and is nearly twice as far as nearest rival "Lukizta", who had covered 2,200.7 km (1,367 miles).

Fastest 100% completion of *Super Mario Odyssey* (no assists)
"hazeruin" (JPN) hotfooted his way through the 2017 blockbusting platformer on Nintendo Switch in just 11 hr 50 min 40 sec on 23 Feb 2018. For the Japanese speedster, that meant collecting all 999 power moons, every hat and all of Mario's costumes. He also had to possess all of the 52 enemy types, unlock every song and pick up every souvenir. Phew!

FACT! Kirby might be a Nintendo superstar now, but that wasn't the plan. The character's creator, Masahiro Sakurai, recently admitted that the fluffy pink cloud was merely a placeholder that then stuck!

SURVIVAL HORROR

DON'T go into that spooky basement on your own. DON'T ever assume the boogeyman is really dead. And DEFINITELY DON'T take vacations in remote areas where "seven people disappeared last summer". These are just a few of the rules of horror that the scariest games force you to ignore...

SCREAMING THROUGH *RESIDENT EVIL VII*

More enemies, tougher boss fights, fewer checkpoints, helpful items being moved around and, to top it all, Jack Baker popping up to terrify you at awkward moments – all in all, these obstacles make playing with the "Madhouse" difficulty setting turned on in Capcom's gruesome survival horror a rough ride. But Ireland's "JigzawTwitch" raced through the **fastest completion of *Resident Evil VII: Biohazard* ("Madhouse" difficulty)** in 1 hr 39 min 31 sec on 30 Apr 2017, as verified by Speedrun.com.

French gamer "Psarthex" saw no reason to spend any longer than necessary in the company of murderers, especially armed with only a knife. On 14 Aug 2017, he completed the game with "Easy" difficulty enabled to set the **fastest knife-only completion of *Resident Evil VII: Biohazard*** in 1 hr 46 min 49 sec, a time also verified by Speedrun.

5,044

Most camp counselors killed in *Friday the 13th: The Game*
Playing as movie boogeyman Jason Voorhees, "GLASSYBOWL 3D" had despatched 5,044 camp counselors in the Xbox One version of the multiplayer survival horror as of 28 Feb 2018. In the game, up to seven players, in the guise of those counselors, try to escape the axe-wielding clutches of Jason, who is controlled by one bloodthirsty player.

GAMING GOLD

A murder of crows?
"It looks like he was killed by a CROW – or something!" says *Resident Evil*'s Barry Burton upon finding his dead colleague Forest Speyer (left). It's a gruesome sign of things to come...

MOST ENEMIES KILLED IN *THE EVIL WITHIN 2*

As of 1 Feb 2018, merciless Xbox One gamer Chris "sxy BEAST1974" Russo had slain 5,266 of the nightmarish mutations that inhabit Bethesda's 2017 survival shooter, according to TrueAchievements. The similarly ruthless, but not quite as prolific "DanielBent" had wiped out 4,946.

YOUR NEW FAVOURITE GAME

MOONS OF MADNESS
Platforms: PS4, Xbox One, PC
What's real and what's in the mind is the central theme of Rock Pocket Games' psychological horror. The influence of H P Lovecraft's story *At the Mountains of Madness* should be felt strongly in what promises to be a mind-bending experience.

Most watched video on Twitch
On 25 Jul 2017, Twitch confirmed that a video of "JurassicJunkieLive", aka Tom Wheldon (UK), being jump-scared by his young daughter while playing *Outlast 2* had become the platform's most watched video of all time, just four days after the broadcast was live-streamed on 21 Jul. The video, called "Streamer daughter walks in on him while playing a scary game", had accrued over 1.5 million views in that time, and as of 15 Mar 2018 had been watched 2,549,675 times. "JurassicJunkieLive" had around 100 Twitch followers at the time of broadcast; that number had grown to 4,921 as of 15 Mar 2018.

Fastest "Insane" completion of *Outlast 2*
On 17 May 2017, UK gamer "ItsJabo" completed Red Barrels' intense survival horror in the game's toughest mode, which has no checkpoints and sends the player back to the beginning if they die. Despite all these barriers, the PC gamer finished the terrifying horror in just 1 hr 58 min 45 sec, as verified by Speedrun.

Most viewed YouTube channel for horror games
Especially renowned for his *Five Nights at Freddy's* gaming videos, YouTuber "Markiplier", aka Mark Edward Fischbach (USA), had 8,970,596,758 views of his channel as of 28 Feb 2018. Although "Markiplier" covers several genres, his channel has a clear focus on horror games. His top 10 most popular gaming broadcasts are dominated by Scott Cawthon's creepy indie series and include "WARNING: SCARIEST GAME IN YEARS | Five Nights at Freddy's - Part 1", which had 65,721,179 views.

Lowest-rated horror videogame
Garnering a score of just 25.81% across 26 reviews on GameRankings.com, *Amy* (VectorCell, 2012) is the most critically panned survival horror ever. "There is not one gimmick, not one mechanic, not one technical element of *Amy* that isn't wrong in some way," said one reviewer.

FACT!

Of all the characters in the *Resident Evil* franchise, none has featured more frequently than Chris Redfield, with 14 appearances as of 5 Mar 2018 – the **most playable character in the *Resident Evil* game series.**

161,590 PLAYERS

In Dec 2013, Valve's co-op zombie shooter *Left 4 Dead 2* (2009) recorded a peak of 161,590 simultaneous players, a figure that stood as of 28 Feb 2018. It was the ninth-most-recorded by any videogame on Steam and the **most concurrent players for a survival horror game**.

EXPANDED FRANCHISE

Including 2016's *Resident Evil: The Final Chapter*, American actress Milla Jovovich has played Alice in six *Resident Evil* films in 14 years, making her the **most prolific live-action videogame movie star**.

THE LEGEND OF ZELDA

What's truly staggering about Nintendo's fantasy adventure series is just how different every entry is. Each Link is a little bit different, too, with one playing the ocarina while another is able to turn into a wolf. Only one thing remains constant: that he's our hero!

GOLD GAMING

Being Zelda
A classic it ain't, but *Zelda: The Wand of Gamelon* (1993) for the Philips CD-i was the first *Legend of Zelda* videogame to make Princess Zelda a playable character.

MOST EQUIPPABLE WEAPONS IN A *LEGEND OF ZELDA* GAME
From Savage Lynel Crushers to Royal Claymores, *The Legend of Zelda: Breath of the Wild* (Nintendo, 2017) features 153 equippable weapons. This total is made up of 127 hand weapons and 26 bows, plus seven items that can be accessed only with specific *Zelda* amiibos. Of course, it's the unique Master Sword (above) that Link truly has his eye on.

FASTEST TIME TO COMPLETE *THE WIND WAKER HD*
The open seas and puzzle-filled dungeons of *The Wind Waker HD* (2013) tend to take most people days, not hours, to negotiate on their way to thwarting Ganondorf. Not so Sweden's "Linkus7", who completed Nintendo's Wii U title in just 1 hr 3 min 18 sec – speeding through faster than Link in a pair of Pegasus boots. His successful bid, achieved on 9 Mar 2018 and verified by Speedrun, was just 12 sec faster than "gymnast86" (USA), who was hot on his heels with a time of 1 hr 3 min 30 sec.

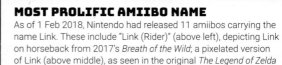

MOST PROLIFIC AMIIBO NAME
As of 1 Feb 2018, Nintendo had released 11 amiibos carrying the name Link. These include "Link (Rider)" (above left), depicting Link on horseback from 2017's *Breath of the Wild*; a pixelated version of Link (above middle), as seen in the original *The Legend of Zelda* (1986); and "Toon Link" (above right) from 2002's *The Wind Waker*.

Highest attach rate for a videogame
The attach rate is the number of copies of a game sold versus the number of consoles in people's homes. *The Legend of Zelda: Breath of the Wild*'s reputation as a must-have game for the Nintendo Switch was confirmed in Mar 2017 by the game's remarkable attach rate of 102%. Switch owners had bought 925,000 copies of the game, despite only 906,000 Switch consoles having been sold. Industry analysts put this down to gamers buying both the regular version and the collector's edition,

collectors purchasing it despite not yet owning a Switch and private sellers stocking it in bulk to resell online.

Fastest 100% completion of
The Legend of Zelda: A Link Between Worlds
On 14 Jun 2017, speed-runner "romulostx" (BRA) completed the 3DS adventure *A Link Between Worlds* in 3 hr 4 min 59 sec, as verified by Speedrun. He collected every heart, fully upgraded the Master Sword and obtained every item.

Fastest footrace in
The Legend of Zelda: Breath of the Wild
As verified by Twin Galaxies on 8 Sep 2017, Rodrigo Lopes (BRA) is the most fleet-footed *Breath of the Wild* player. He posted a time of 46.99 sec in the Nintendo title's footrace mini-game, which can be found in Hyrule's Ridgeland region. To complete it, players have to follow a route set out by flags on a mountain and all the while stay ahead of the Hylian traveller Konba. Beating him carries a reward of 50 rupees.

Lowest-rated *Legend of Zelda* game
It's testament to the strength of *The Legend of Zelda* series that even its lowest-rated entry, *Tri Force Heroes* (2015) for the 3DS, still scored a respectable 72.01% on GameRankings as of 9 March 2018. It was based on *Zelda* titles with a minimum of 20 reviews.

LARGEST NINTENDO-MADE WORLD
Using Link's height as a guide, Reddit user "EngineeringHyrule" determined that the kingdom of Hyrule, as seen in *The Legend of Zelda: Breath of the Wild*, covers an area of approximately 62.1 km^2 (24 sq mi). In 2016, Nintendo stated that the open-world map is 12 times bigger than Hyrule as it is in *The Legend of Zelda: Twilight Princess*, released for the Nintendo Wii in 2006.

BEST-SELLING *ZELDA* GAME

In 2018, *The Legend of Zelda: Ocarina of Time* marks its 20th anniversary after being originally released on N64 on 21 Nov 1998. Link's debut for the 64-bit system – the first time we'd seen Hyrule with 3D visuals – has not just become the top-selling game in the *Zelda* series, but also the **best-selling**

action-adventure game on any Nintendo platform, with 7.6 million copies sold as of 12 Mar 2018, according to VGChartz.

The title was later ported to the Nintendo 3DS handheld in 2011, and it was a sign of the adventure's long-lasting popularity that it sold an additional 5.18 million copies.

FACT!

The Legend of Zelda: Breath of the Wild overflows with beautiful images. In May 2017, Japanese gamer NV/Ju compiled his pictures of the kingdom of Hyrule and made them into a book.

2017'S MOST ACCLAIMED ANIMAL ICONS

What unites Sonic, Yoshi and Pikachu? They all owe their origins to the animal kingdom, however loosely. Of all the titles released in 2017, these are the most critically acclaimed games that put our furry friends centre stage...

10
YOOKA-LAYLEE
72.22%
Team17;
Xbox One (also on
PS4, Switch, PC)

9
POOCHY & YOSHI'S WOOLLY WORLD
77.04%
Nintendo;
3DS

8
THE DISNEY AFTERNOON COLLECTION
78.96%
Capcom;
PS4 (also on
Xbox One, PC)

7
MONSTER HUNTER STORIES
79.15%
Capcom/Nintendo;
3DS (also on iOS,
Android – JPN only)

6
POKKÉN TOURNAMENT DX
80.10%
Nintendo;
Switch (also on Wii U)

Ratings correct as of 9 Mar 2018 and based on a minimum of 20 reviews, as verified by GameRankings.

As of 6 Feb 2018, the **most critically acclaimed game of all time featuring an animal hero** was the original *Okami* (2006) for PS2, with a rating of 92.65%.

5

CRASH BANDICOOT N. SANE TRILOGY

81.28%

Activision; PS4

4

POKÉMON ULTRA MOON

83.07%

Nintendo; 3DS

3

POKÉMON ULTRA SUN

84.59%

Nintendo; 3DS

2

SONIC MANIA

87.02%

Sega; PS4 (also on Xbox One, Switch, PC)

1

ŌKAMI HD

88.15%

Capcom; PS4 (also on Xbox One, PC)

THE SOUND OF GAMING

In the late 1980s, when the popularity of the Nintendo Entertainment System (NES) was at its height, videogame music was as limited as the graphics of the games. But now, just as the pixel art visual style used in those '80s and '90s games is back in vogue, so too is the music. Chiptune artists are musicians who use clever programming and sheer musical talent to create new tracks from the sound chips of consoles – especially Famicoms (the Japanese version of the NES) and Game Boys. The result is original music inspired by the gaming soundtracks of the past.

MOST VIEWED CHIPTUNE VIDEO ON YOUTUBE

Swede Linus Åkesson's self-made "chipophone" 8-bit synthesizer proved to be an internet sensation. An amazing video demonstration, first published on 21 Jul 2010, of Åkesson replicating classic gaming soundtracks – from *Super Mario Bros.* to *Tetris* – had 2.3 million views as of 9 Apr 2018.

FIRST GAME BASED ON A CHIPTUNE ARTIST'S SONGS

UK chiptune artist "Chipzel", aka Niamh Houston, holds a unique record – a game was created that was based on her music (rather than vice versa). *Spectra*, issued in May 2015 for Xbox One and PC, is a 3D racer in which players guide a car down a track to the rhythm of the beat.

MOST SONGS TO REFERENCE A VIDEOGAME FRANCHISE

Q&A: MEGA RAN

Raheem "Mega Ran" Jarbo (USA) has recorded and released 130 songs that pay homage to Capcom's robotic superhero Mega Man – a character that's inspired his music and his recording alias.

Why did you pick *Mega Man* as your game to sample?

It's my favourite game by far. In the beginning, it was the bright colours, the great soundtracks, awesome gameplay and crazy difficulty. I keep coming back to these games, even now. I couldn't get the music out of my head, so that inspired me to work it into my own music.

What did Capcom say to you when it heard your music?

Well, I immediately thought the worst was to come, like a lawsuit... But the guys there actually enjoyed and appreciated my tunes and asked me to work with them. They invited me to my first Comic Con to sign autographs. Later, we partnered up for some great projects and I'm extremely thankful to the guys at Capcom for their open-mindedness.

How much are you looking forward to *Mega Man 11*? Are you involved?

Oh man, you have no idea! I love the new 2.5D style and the subtle changes to Mega Man's armour when he gets a new weapon. I'm so stoked for this game and would love to assist with music. If I get that call, I'm there in a flash! Let's hope the classic composers are all involved to bring back that old-school feel.

Which Mega Man bad guy is your favourite?

Man, they're all so cool in their own way. I change my mind every time I play any of the games. Right now, I'm feeling *Mega Man 2*'s Guts Man (left). As a super-strong construction bot, he's like the one robot that makes the most practical real-world sense, I think. I'd love to have a Guts Man robot in my back yard, helping me with the yard work!

MOST VIEWED CHIPTUNE COVER ON YOUTUBE

A 2013 cover by Rakohus (USA) of Imagine Dragons' 2012 track "Radioactive" had amassed 1,758,331 views as of 10 Apr 2018. Titled "Radioactive (8-Bit NES Remix)", it recreates the hit song as it might have sounded on an NES as an 8-bit dancer (below) bops along.

The **most viewed original song on YouTube by a chiptune artist** is Anamanaguchi's "Miku" (2016), with 2,971,086 views.

MOST STREAMED CHIPTUNE ARTISTS ON SPOTIFY (2017)*

1. Anamanaguchi (USA, right)
2. Disasterpeace (USA)
3. she (POL)
4. I Fight Dragons (USA)
5. Dj Cutman (USA)
6. Sabrepulse (UK)
7. Stamp (THA)
8. Dubmood (SWE)
9. Shirobon (UK)
10. Chipzel (UK)

* As verified by Spotify on 15 Jan 2018

ROLE-PLAYING

There are few gaming genres that pull us into their stories as well as RPGs. From the high fantasy of, well, *Final Fantasy*, to the planet-hopping sci-fi of *Mass Effect*, RPGs let us explore living, breathing new worlds – and break records while we're at it.

LARGEST COLLECTION OF *FINAL FANTASY* MEMORABILIA

Tai-Ting Tseng (TPE) owns a treasure trove of games, toys, statues, keychains, books, soundtracks, clothes, videos and plenty more besides relating to Square Enix's famous RPG. His collection of 3,782 unique items takes up "every corner" of his home in San Jose, California, USA.

This chocobo-tastic medley of curios includes 239 videogames from around the world, 130 soft toys – featuring 23 moogles and 32 chocobos – and four pairs of underpants!

"I've been a fan of the franchise since 1992," Tai-Ting told us. "*Final Fantasy* has been my passion ever since."

"MY MOST TREASURED COLLECTABLE IS A COMPOSER-SIGNED VINYL RECORD. IT'S A KEEPSAKE FROM THE *FINAL FANTASY* CONCERT WHERE I PROPOSED TO MY WIFE!"

TAI-TING TSENG ON HIS HOUSE-FILLING COLLECTION

MMORPGs

From gloomy dungeons in fantasy lands to gleaming cities on alien worlds, MMORPGs provide intrepid gamers – and their friends – with a breathtaking assortment of environments to explore, enemies to vanquish and loot to plunder...

YOUR NEW FAVOURITE GAME

BLESS ONLINE
Platform: PC
Fantasy lands, huge bosses and much levelling-up. Sound familiar? Perhaps, but Neowiz's MMORPG promises deep character customization and a twisting plot as players choose a side in a war between the nations of Hieron and Unión.

6,142 SHIPS

Star-trekking *EVE Online* pilots usually content themselves with exploring star systems and getting involved in political tussles. But, on 23 Jan 2018, a total of 6,142 pilots converged to take part in the "Siege of Keepstar 9-4R" – the **most players in a single solar system in EVE Online**. Experts were expecting the ensuing battle to be the largest (and most expensive) yet in the game's history, but, in the end, server problems prevented the attacking force from dealing enough damage to the Keepstar, thus ending the encounter before it could begin.

MOST UNIQUE PETS COLLECTED IN WOW
European gamer "Ryzølda", of the "Hyjal" realm, had collected 954 of *World of Warcraft's* 963 unique pets as of 8 Feb 2018 (with 934 of the pets being at maximum power). The **oldest *World of Warcraft* gamer to collect 850 unique pets** is Donna Glee Reim (USA), also known as "GrannyGlee", who was aged 86 years 198 days when she achieved the feat on 3 Sep 2017.

Lord British RIP
The assassination of *Ultima Online*'s supposedly invulnerable Lord British (developer Richard Garriott) in 1997 remains one of the most memorable events in any MMORPG.

MOST POPULAR MOUNT IN *THE ELDER SCROLLS ONLINE*

As of 6 Feb 2018, the swift-of-hoof Palomino Horse had been chosen as the trusty steed of 2,563,695 characters, as confirmed by *ESO*'s developer, ZeniMax. Vermilion Scuttler was the **most popular pet in *The Elder Scrolls Online***, with 1,604,757 characters adopting the familiar reptilian.

FIRST GUILD TO BEAT ARGUS THE UNMAKER

You have to be either brave or crazy to take on Argus the Unmaker. He is the final and most formidable boss of the "Antorus, the Burning Throne" raid from *World of Warcraft: Legion*. Argus can be faced only when playing the Mythic-difficulty version of the raid. Even then, taking him on is possible only once all the other bosses have been felled.

Fighting him definitely isn't easy. It took Method (one of *WoW*'s most famous guilds) 320 attempts before it was able to triumphantly announce Argus's demise via Twitter at 8:27 a.m. (GMT) on 13 Dec 2017. Method's members were finally able to take Argus down by developing survival strategies that were successful against his Sweeping Scythe, Death Fog and Tortured Rage attacks.

Most achievements in *Guild Wars 2*
In NCSOFT's 2012 fantasy role-player, achievements are awarded for completing tasks across all game types (PvE, PvP and WvW). "Malediktus.9250", as of 8 Feb 2018, had stacked up 37,288 achievements.

Top-rated world in *Guild Wars 2*
As of 8 Feb 2018, the Blackgate server was rated at 1943.1328, as verified by NCSOFT – 25 points higher than its nearest rival, Sea of Sorrows. Players in *Guild Wars 2* (2012) must choose a world when initially registering their character, with each world being hosted on a separate server. In total, there are 51 worlds/servers across North America and Europe (Blackgate is on a North American server). Each server's rating is calculated using an in-game algorithm that averages players' skill levels, giving perhaps the truest indication of which world's players are best.

Most updated MMORPG
Initially released in Jan 2001, Jagex's *RuneScape*, set in the medieval fantasy realm Gielinor, had, on average, been updated once a week. As of 25 Jul 2017, that amounted to 1,014 updates.

Highest-scoring player in *Star Wars: The Old Republic*
In BioWare's 2011 title, teams of players aligned to the Sith or the Old Republic battle each other in player-versus-player areas for the glory of appearing on the Ranked Warzone Arena Leaderboards. As of 26 Jan 2018, the highest-scoring player in any season or class was the Sith Sorcerer "Never Back-down", who scored 4,247 points in the Warzone Arena's eighth season.

Most followed MMO on Twitter
As of 22 Feb 2018, the official Twitter account for Blizzard's iconic *World of Warcraft* (@Warcraft) had 1,451,464 followers. It ranked as the most for any MMO on the social-media platform. Behind *WoW* in the Twitter rankings were the likes of *The Elder Scrolls Online*, with 848,758 followers, *Guild Wars 2*, with a following of 335,656, and *Star Wars: The Old Republic*, which had 291,224 Twitter followers.

FACT! Released in Apr 2004, the **first superhero MMORPG** was NCSOFT's *City of Heroes*. It ran until 30 Nov 2012, when it – and its legion of heroes – was finally taken offline.

JRPGs

The genre of Japanese role-playing games (JRPGs) is a quintessential mainstay of gaming, with a heritage that's as important to videogames as Super Mario or *DOOM*. Whichever game you decide to take on, be prepared to be swept along on an epic and emotional roller-coaster...

PERFECTION *PERSONA*-FIED

As of 28 Mar 2018, *Persona 5* (Atlus, 2016) for the PS4 was the **most critically acclaimed RPG for an eighth-generation home console**. Enjoying a GameRankings score of 93.36% based on 57 reviews, the JRPG outscored all other RPGs for current home consoles (PS4, Xbox One, Switch), including *The Witcher III: Wild Hunt* (92.23%) and *Diablo III: Ultimate Evil Edition* (91.25%). One reviewer called it "astounding", saying it offered "an experience that's perfectly realized from the moment it begins".

The **most critically acclaimed RPG for an eighth-generation handheld console** was another Atlus title, *Persona 4 Golden* (2012). The PS Vita title – a re-release of the PS2 game *Shin Megami Tensei: Persona 4* (2008) – scored a huge 94.16% across 43 reviews.

First *Final Fantasy VII* player to hit level 99 before fighting any boss
On 8 Apr 2017, "CirclMastr" uploaded to YouTube a 52-min sliver of the 500 hours he'd spent since Jan 2015 taking *Final Fantasy VII* (Square Enix, 1997) characters Cloud and Barret to level 99 without leaving the initial Reactor area. He did it to "prove to myself that I can persevere".

GAMING GOLD

♫ We must part now.
My life goes on.
But my heart won't give you up.

On song in *FFVI*
In one of *Final Fantasy*'s most famous moments, players had to be word perfect to guide Celes (left) through an operatic number in order to recruit gambler (and future hero) Setzer.

LONGEST-RUNNING JRPG SERIES

With the Japanese release of Square Enix's *Dragon Quest XI: Echoes of an Elusive Age* for the PS4 and 3DS on 29 Jul 2017, the *Dragon Quest* series had been running for 31 years 63 days. It began with *Dragon Quest*, released for the NES in Japan on 27 May 1986.

The series remains immensely popular in Japan, with *Dragon Quest XI* selling around two million copies in its first few days on sale. It was due to receive a worldwide release on 4 Sep 2018.

YOUR NEW FAVOURITE GAME

KINGDOM HEARTS III
Platforms: PS4, Xbox One
Square Enix and Disney's crossover continues as Sora returns, alongside Donald Duck, Goofy and friends. Once more, our heroes will do battle across iconic Disney-inspired environments, this time from *Monsters, Inc., Toy Story* and more.

880,000

Best-selling RPG for Nintendo Switch
As of 20 Mar 2018, *Xenoblade Chronicles 2* had shifted a total of 880,000 copies on Nintendo Switch, according to VGChartz. Developed by Monolith Soft, the 2017 sequel to the 2010 original outperformed its predecessor by a wide margin, with gamers enticed by the scale of its ambition.

LONGEST REPLICA WEAPON BASED ON A JRPG

In Feb 2017, "Killer 927" (JPN) built a replica of *Monster Hunter*'s Aquamatic "Longshot" sniper rifle. The model measured 2.5 m (8 ft 2 in) long. It took the *Monster Hunter* enthusiast two months to make the weapon from PVC pipe, wood and metal fittings. He used his own height of 1.8 m (5 ft 10 in) as a guide to replicating the weapon's in-game scale.

Most JRPGs released for one console
No fewer than 118 JRPGs have been released for the PlayStation 2 console since its 2000 launch. This figure includes contributions to the successful *Final Fantasy*, *Kingdom Hearts* and *Persona* series. The most recent was *Sakura Wars: So Long, My Love* (2009). Close behind in second place are the 114 JRPGs for the Nintendo DS, including *Pokémon* and *Dragon Quest* games.

Largest JRPG cartridge
In terms of file size, the largest cartridge for a JRPG is *Xenoblade Chronicles 2* (Monolith Soft, 2017) on the Nintendo Switch console. Switch cartridges currently come in 1-GB, 2-GB, 4-GB, 8-GB, 16-GB and 32-GB sizes. According to the official Nintendo eShop, *Xenoblade Chronicles 2* takes up 13 GB of space, so needs a 16-GB cartridge. By contrast, 3DS cartridges had a maximum capacity of 8 GB.

Most powerful boss in *Persona 5*
In the well-received JRPG from 2016, the main in-game character, Joker, has been sent to Tokyo's fictional Shujin Academy after being falsely accused of assault. There, he eventually encounters the wardens. Though Caroline and Justine look innocent, these twin jailers are the formidable guardians of the Velvet Room and are both ranked at level 99, the game's highest possible rating.

Longest localization delay for a JRPG
Romancing SaGa 2 (Square), telling the stories of emperors through the ages, had been released for the Super Famicom (the Japanese version of the Super NES) on 10 Dec 1993 and was popular in its native Japan. But it was not until 26 May 2016 that the JRPG was finally made available in English for Android and iOS. That's a delay of 22 years 168 days!

FACT!

Spanish Twitch streamer "Elboddy" is trying to speed-run three *Final Fantasy* games (*VII*, *VIII* and *IX*) at the same time! In his first "Tri-Fantasy" attempt on 20 Dec 2017, he lasted 7 hr 9 min 35 sec before being killed.

ACTION RPGs

Who wants to wait? Action RPGs forgo turn-based action in favour of flowing combat that keeps the number-crunching of traditional RPGs under the bonnet. That's not to say that hit points and damage done aren't important, but the stats don't get in the way of the action.

MONSTER HUNTER: WORLD'S MOST DEADLY...

Pummelling a paolumu and jousting with a great jagras is all in a day's work for the heroes of Capcom's *Monster Hunter: World* (2018). The mightiest monster-hunter of them all was Xbox One gamer "Sleepfuture". The American had tracked, targeted and then taken down no fewer than 5,734 of the game's largest, ugliest and deadliest beasts as of 11 Apr 2018 – the **most large monsters hunted in *Monster Hunter: World***. TrueAchievements also confirmed that the second most deadly was "Kisialos Z" (FRA), who, with 2,997 kills, had plenty of catching up to do. Time to sharpen that sword and get back out there!

3 HOURS 19 MINUTES 17 SECONDS

The *Mass Effect* series' "Insanity" modes test the resilience of even the most determined spectres and pathfinders, and *Mass Effect: Andromeda*'s (2017) mode is no different. Undaunted, the fearless "Besrodio" (USA) took EA's RPG to task, recording the **fastest any% completion of *Mass Effect: Andromeda*'s "Insanity" mode** in 3 hr 19 min 17 sec on 10 Apr 2017, as verified by Speedrun. "Could definitely get this under 3 hours," the PC player commented.

YOUR NEW FAVOURITE GAME

CODE VEIN
Platforms: PS4, Xbox One, PC
The aim for you and other vampire-like Revenants in this apocalyptic action RPG is not to save society, but just to survive. Bandai Namco used the line "Prepare to dine" in promoting *Code Vein* – a nod to the game's *Dark Souls* influences.

First upside-down completion of *Dark Souls*
"LobosJr" (aka Mike Villalobos) explored another angle when he took on FromSoftware's famous 2011 title using a mod that turned it literally on its head. The upside-down run took the American three days before he finally finished it on 9 Jul 2015.

13 YEARS

Team Ninja's samurai epic *Nioh* had endured the **longest development period for an action RPG videogame** when it was finally released for the PS4 on 7 Feb 2017 – 13 years after work on it began in 2004 (when it was intended as a PS3 title). Just to prove that good things do come to those who wait, the game, despite its lengthy development, was a hit.

RAREST NON-PLATINUM TROPHY IN *NIER: AUTOMATA*
As of 13 Mar 2018, only 10.5% of PS4 players had earned the seldom-seen "Supreme Support Weapons" trophy, according to PSNProfiles. If you want to prove your worth in Square Enix's 2017 action RPG, the key is to upgrade all of your character's robotic support pods to their max level.

FACT! On 24 Jan 2018, Capcom introduced *Monster Hunter: World* with a huge *Monster Hunter*-themed BBQ in London, UK. A mountain of meat and 50 kg (110 lb) of cheese were consumed over four days.

Fastest any% completion of *Nioh*
On 8 Mar 2018, German gamer "DenZve" sliced through all of *Nioh*'s main missions to defeat the arduous samurai survival game in exactly 53 min. "Nerve-wrecking" was the player's verdict.

First action RPG
Released for the NEC PC-88, an early home computer sold only in Japan, *Dragon Slayer* (1984) was the first true action RPG. The game has the hallmarks of the genre, such as an emphasis on combat and a limited inventory that forces players to think hard about what they carry.

Fastest time to level 70 in *Path of Exile*
In a solo run on 14 Apr 2017, the Canadian gamer "Havoc616" took a total of 5 hr 53 min 40 sec to rush his Templar from base character to level-70 veteran. The run was made even more perilous by the fact the player had subjected his character to the game's hardcore league.

Most popular romantic partner in *Mass Effect: Andromeda*
In Mar 2017, more than 10,000 players cast their vote at GamesRadar in a poll intended to establish which of the game's companions they romanced first. Cora Harper, the human biotic commando, snuck into first place with 29% of the votes, followed by asari academic "Peebee" B'Sayle (28%) and the turian mercenary Vetra Nyx (18%). Crisis specialist Liam propped up the table with just 6% of the vote.

Most viewed trailer for an action RPG
As of 13 Mar 2018, the trailer for Bethesda's *Fallout 4* had drawn 21,628,206 views on YouTube, plus 315,000 thumbs-up approvals.

ELDER SCROLLS ONLINE

On the continent of Tamriel, danger lurks around every corner. Trolls, vampires, harpies and plenty more ferocious creatures wander its wilds – and they all want to take a bite out of unsuspecting travellers. Wherever you roam, make sure your wits are as sharp as your sword...

MOST POPULAR RACE IN *THE ELDER SCROLLS ONLINE*

One of the most important decisions that players must make before they begin their adventures in *The Elder Scrolls Online* (ESO) is which of the game's fantastical races they want to be.

Known for their magical powers – as much as their arrogance – the High Elves, the Summerset Isles' golden-skinned people, have been the most commonly chosen race for players of the MMORPG since its release for the PC (Apr 2014) and then the Xbox One and PS4 (Jun 2015). As of 1 Feb 2018, gamers opted for the High Elves (also known as the Altmer) on 4,253,713 occasions. That's equal to 14.98% of total selections. Behind them are the Nords (3,804,581/13.39%) and the Dark Elves (3,473,675/12.23%), as confirmed by *ESO*'s publisher, Bethesda.

As of the same date, the **most popular character title in *The Elder Scrolls Online*** was "Volunteer", a title given to gamers who fight rival players in the Alliance War. This favoured character title had been used by 612,756 players and was followed by "Master Wizard" (374,373) and "Fighters Guild Victor" (290,663).

POKÉMON

ROLE-PLAYING

A phenomenon, an obsession or simply a way of life? Call it what you will, there's no doubting that *Pokémon* has moved beyond gaming into mainstream culture. *Pokémon GO* continues to make headlines, while toys, games and players keep on breaking records.

1,006
EPISODES

As of 12 Mar 2018, the **most prolific Pokémon in anime** is Ash's Pikachu, who has appeared in all 1,006 episodes of the *Pokémon* anime, beginning with the show's debut in Japan on 1 Apr 1997. If all 21 of the *Pokémon* films (including *Pokémon the Movie: Everyone's Story* in 2018) were added, that figure would rise to a total of 1,027 appearances.

Largest attendance for a mobile videogame event
An estimated 20,000 gamers attended the first *Pokémon GO* Fest in Chicago's Grant Park, Illinois, USA, on 22 Jul 2017. Tickets for the inaugural live event reportedly sold out in minutes. See p.8.

First "legendary" obtained in *Pokémon GO*
On 2 Aug 2016, software developer Niantic made headlines when, by mistake, it sent an Articuno to *Pokémon GO* gamer Kaitlyn Covey (USA).
The first legendary-type officially available for capture was Lugia. The half-bird, half-dragon was launched at the *Pokémon GO* Fest on 22 Jul 2017.

POKÉMON WORLD CHAMPIONSHIPS 2017

WHICH NATION RULES AT *POKÉMON?*

The USA is the **most successful nation in the *Pokémon* World Championships**. American Zachary Bokhari's victory in the Senior Division at 2017's *Pokémon* Trading Card Game (TCG) World Championships sealed the 15th victory for the USA in that tournament. American competitors have also triumphed on 14 occasions at the *Pokémon* Video Game World Championships, making a total of 29. Japan – the home of *Pokémon* – is the second most successful nation, registering a combined 21 victories.

GOLD

GAMING

Water, Fire or Grass? *Pokémon Red* and *Blue* players had to think carefully before committing themselves to their first Pokémon – Squirtle, Charmander or Bulbasaur – when offered the choice by Professor Oak.

First videogame franchise store
After being introduced to the world in 1996, the *Pokémon* franchise had grown in popularity to such an extent that in 1998 a dedicated store was opened in Tokyo, Japan. The Pokémon Center – similar to the Disney Store – has sold *Pokémon* merchandise that included limited-edition Game Boy consoles and plush toys, as well as figurines, backpacks, clothing and soundtrack CDs. More Pokémon Centers have since opened in major cities across Japan and the USA.

Longest (suspended) prison sentence for playing a videogame
On 11 May 2017, Russian YouTuber Ruslan Sokolovsky was sentenced to 3.5 years of jail time. His crime was playing the mobile AR game *Pokémon GO* in a church in Russia. The court found him guilty of "inciting hatred, violating religious feelings and illegal possession of special technical means" (a pen with a video camera). Thankfully for the *Pokémon GO* player, his term was suspended.

Best-selling Game Boy videogame
Pokémon Red and *Blue* (Nintendo, 1996) had shifted 31.37 million copies as of 9 Mar 2018, according to VGChartz. Breaking that figure down into different markets around the world, it sold the most in North America (11.27 million), closely followed by Japan (10.22 million).

Most common Pokémon type
Out of the 807 currently known Pokémon, 65 are classified as "Normal" types. The second most common type is "Water", with 62 examples. Of those with combined types, the most common cross is "Normal"/"Flying", with 26 instances.

ILLUSTRATOR
ポケモンイラストレーター

ピカチュウ　HP40

MOST EXPENSIVE *POKÉMON* TRADING CARD AT AUCTION

On 18 Nov 2016, a "Pikachu Illustrator" Trainer Promo Hologram trading card (above left) from 1998 sold at auction in California, USA, for $54,970 (£44,175). The **most expensive *Pokémon* trading card at retail** was a limited-edition, solid-gold re-issue of the first Pikachu card (above right), made to mark *Pokémon*'s 20th anniversary in Oct 2016. It was priced at 216,000 Yen ($2,061; £1,690).

MOST POKÉMON EVOLUTIONS

As this montage shows, the changeable Eevee (centre) has a total of eight evolutions. From left to right, these comprise dark-type Umbreon, ice-type Glaceon, water-type Vaporeon, fairy-type Sylveon, psychic-type Espeon, grass-type Leafeon, fire-type Flareon and electric-type Jolteon. Eevee had just three evolutions in *Pokémon Red* and *Blue*, but has gained five more since.

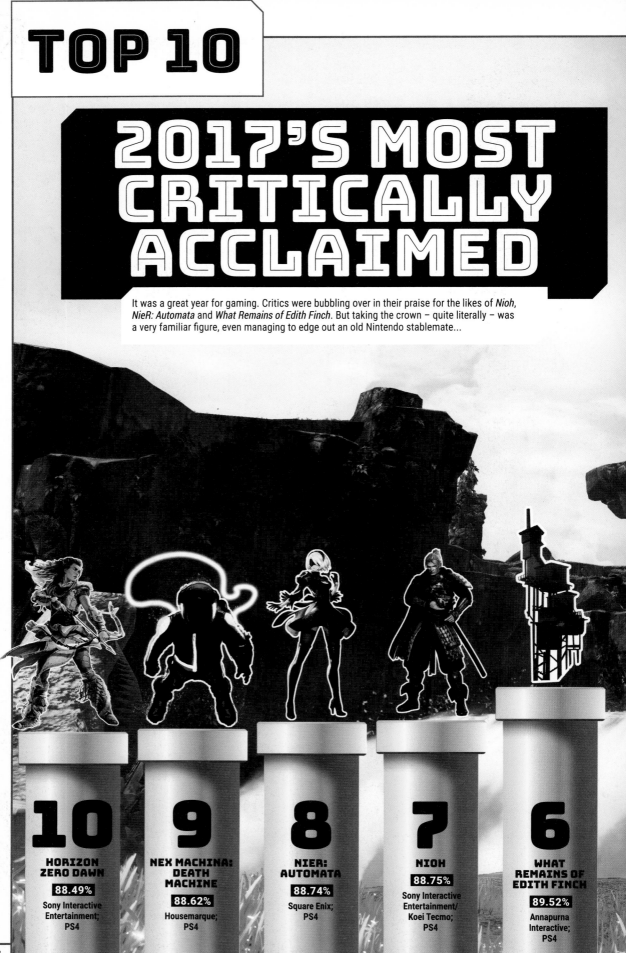

2017'S MOST CRITICALLY ACCLAIMED

It was a great year for gaming. Critics were bubbling over in their praise for the likes of *Nioh*, *NieR: Automata* and *What Remains of Edith Finch*. But taking the crown – quite literally – was a very familiar figure, even managing to edge out an old Nintendo stablemate...

10
HORIZON ZERO DAWN
88.49%
Sony Interactive Entertainment; PS4

9
NEX MACHINA: DEATH MACHINE
88.62%
Housemarque; PS4

8
NIER: AUTOMATA
88.74%
Square Enix; PS4

7
NIOH
88.75%
Sony Interactive Entertainment/ Koei Tecmo; PS4

6
WHAT REMAINS OF EDITH FINCH
89.52%
Annapurna Interactive; PS4

Ratings correct as of 2 Mar 2018 and based on a minimum of 20 reviews, as verified by GameRankings.

As of 17 Apr 2018, Sony's *God of War* was the most critically acclaimed game of 2018 (94.84%, based on 46 reviews). But can any of 2018's titles top *Super Mario Odyssey*'s score?

5
MARIO KART 8 DELUXE
92.39%
Nintendo; Switch

4
DIVINITY: ORIGINAL SIN II
92.94%
Larian Studios; PC

3
PERSONA 5
93.36%
Atlus/Atlus USA/ Deep Silver; PS4

2
THE LEGEND OF ZELDA: BREATH OF THE WILD
97.28%
Nintendo; Switch

1
SUPER MARIO ODYSSEY
97.38%
Nintendo; Switch

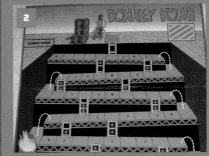

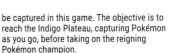

1 PAC-MAN (1982)
2–4 players

The goal here is to collect the most pellets. Players roll two dice, then choose one to move their PAC-Man figure and one to move a ghost. If you manage to trap a rival with a ghost, the unlucky player must give you two of their pellets!

2 DONKEY KONG (1982)
2–4 players

To mimic the coin-op's gameplay, the board game comes with two dice. The white one indicates how many spaces the player must move, while the red dictates how many spaces Donkey Kong's barrels move. The winner is the player who has gained the most points – by leaping barrels – at the time any player reaches the top of the board.

3 THE LEGEND OF ZELDA: THE HYRULE FANTASY (1986)
2–4 players

The *Zelda* board game was released in Japan at nearly the same time as *The Legend of Zelda* videogame. Its board is a like-for-like representation of the videogame's overworld. Its familiar-sounding goal is to unite all the pieces of the Triforce and defeat Ganon.

4 SONIC THE HEDGEHOG GAME (1992)
2–4 players

The goal here is to collect more rings than the other players. But the clever bit is that the board is split into four unique levels, each based on the videogame's zones. There's even a showdown with Dr Robotnik at the end!

5 POKÉMON MASTER TRAINER (1999)
2–6 players

All of the first-generation Pokémon (excluding Mew) can

be captured in this game. The objective is to reach the Indigo Plateau, capturing Pokémon as you go, before taking on the reigning Pokémon champion.

6 DOOM: THE BOARDGAME (2004)
2–4 players

Tabletop *DOOM* is a tactical, scenario-driven game in which one player controls the demonic invaders and everyone else plays as a space marine. To win, the marines must find weapons and key cards to push back the hellish hordes and complete their objectives.

7 WORLD OF WARCRAFT: THE BOARD GAME (2005)
2–6 players

With an average game time running at around four hours, this adaptation of the hugely popular MMORPG asks a lot of its players. After choosing a character and a faction (either the Horde or the Alliance), players compete to overthrow one of the game's overlords – the lich Kel'Thuzad, the demon Kazzak or the dragon Nefarian.

8 STARCRAFT: THE BOARD GAME (2007)
2–6 players

With 180 plastic figures in the box, this is one of the more complex games in our selection. In the fight for galactic supremacy, each player controls a faction representing *StarCraft's* classic races – the Terrans, Zerg and Protoss. The last faction standing is the winner.

9 HALO INTERACTIVE STRATEGY GAME (2008)
2–10 players

Drawing on elements from the first three *Halo* videogames, this turn-based game lets players re-enact the war between the human UNSC army and the invading alien force, the Covenant.

First it was board games that inspired videogames. Then the favour was returned, with many of the biggest videogames spawning successful tabletop alternatives. Here, we roll the dice on some old-school adaptations that let you play your favourite games… with no console required.

10 SID MEIER'S CIVILIZATION: THE BOARD GAME (2010)

2–4 players

Taking its cues from *Civilization IV*, players begin the game with a city, a scout and one army figure. They then have to wage war or make peace with other players as they forge their way through the ages to secure one of four possible victories.

11 GEARS OF WAR: THE BOARD GAME (2011)

1–4 players

Instead of dividing players between the COG marines and Locust hordes, a deck of cards is used to govern the actions of the Locust soldiers. Players must make effective use of cover as they tackle the seven missions on offer.

12 BIOSHOCK INFINITE: THE SIEGE OF COLUMBIA (2013)

2 or 4 players

In this game, one player (or team of players) controls the evil Founders, while the other takes charge of the Vox Populi. Building on the story of the *BioShock Infinite* videogame of the same year, the aim is to raise an army to take control of the floating city, Columbia.

13 ASSASSIN'S CREED: ARENA (2014)

2–4 players

Cards drive the action in this *Assassin's Creed* adaptation. You must commit cards to attack and progress, but also manage them wisely. Once your deck is spent your character dies, meaning you must return to the starting point.

14 THE WITCHER ADVENTURE GAME (2014)

2–4 players

Up to four players assume the roles of Geralt

of Rivia, Triss Merigold, Yarpen Zigrin and Dandelion. The goal is to obtain more Victory points than your rivals by completing quests.

15 XCOM: THE BOARD GAME (2015)

1–4 players

As an alternative to poring over the included rulebook, this board game can be played with a free companion app. This selects from five invasion plans, which dictate the movements of the alien threat on the game board. As with the videogame, players will need to plan their resistance carefully to repel the invaders.

16 PORTAL: THE UNCOOPERATIVE CAKE ACQUISITION GAME (2015)

2–4 players

The tabletop take on Valve's *Portal* franchise just had to be different, and sure enough it is. The objective of this game is to acquire the most cake. As you'd imagine, the way to do so is by the clever use of your portal gun.

17 DARK SOULS: THE BOARD GAME (2017)

1–4 players

With £3,771,474 ($5,417,610) raised, this game holds the record for the **most money pledged to a Kickstarter board game based on a videogame**. Many of the series' wicked bosses are here, including *Dark Souls'* Ornstein and Smough, the Pursuer from *Dark Souls II* and the Dancer of the Boreal Valley from *Dark Souls III*.

18 RESIDENT EVIL 2: THE BOARD GAME (2018)

1–4 players

This co-operative survival horror game sees its players venture into the zombie-infested streets of Raccoon City. Your objective is to survive the t-Virus outbreak and escape in one piece.

SHOOTERS

Shooters aren't just about guns and ammo. They can educate new generations about the horrors of history's worst wars, teleport us into the realms of sci-fi or even find ways to circumvent the tropes of the genre by replacing guns with oversized paint rollers...

> " HALO IS MY ABSOLUTE FAVOURITE FRANCHISE. I PLAYED NOTHING BUT HALO 2 MULTIPLAYER FOR OVER A YEAR! "
>
> RAYMOND "STALLION83" COX

HIGHEST XBOX GAMERSCORE

For every Xbox Achievement a player unlocks on Xbox 360 and Xbox One games (as well as on select PC and mobile titles), he or she is awarded GamerScore points. As of 26 Feb 2018, Raymond "Stallion83" Cox (USA) had amassed a massive 1,746,820 points, as verified by TrueAchievements.

It was on 13 Mar 2014 that he achieved the landmark of becoming the **first gamer to achieve a million Xbox GamerScore**. The moment – while playing *Titanfall* – was streamed live on Twitch, attracting over 10,000 viewers. "During my run to a million GamerScore, there were some months that I would play up to 16 hours a day," he told us. "[Microsoft] flew me out to New York City. They had me on TV talking about my accomplishment. They also gifted me the one and only Xbox Live lifetime gold membership card and a white, limited-edition, employee-only Xbox One console and several launch games. What a cool and unforgettable experience that was!"

MILITARY SHOOTERS

From World War I to the Vietnam War, just about every modern-day conflict has been used as the setting for a first-person shooter (FPS). And, just as there are heroes in war, so too are there heroes in war games. Here we celebrate the biggest games and the best eSports stars...

BEST-SELLING FPS SERIES

Since its 2003 debut, Activision's military juggernaut *Call of Duty* has topped gaming sales charts all over the world. According to VGChartz, the series had shifted 276.25 million physical units across all platforms as of 18 Jan 2018.

The series has dominated the charts to the extent that six of the 10 all-time best-selling shooters are *Call of Duty* games. Of those, *Modern Warfare 3* (2011) is the **best-selling first-person shooter ever**, having shifted 30.98 million copies across Xbox 360, PS3, PC and Wii.

VGChartz estimates that, as of 18 Jan 2018, *Call of Duty: WWII* (2017) – the latest entry in the series – had sold 10.87 million copies. This puts it well on course to top 2016's *Infinite Warfare*, which had sold 12.63 million since its release. Experts have put this down to the series' return to its World War II roots.

LONGEST-RUNNING FPS

BJ Blazkowicz has been taking on the worst of the Nazi army for over 25 years in *Wolfenstein* shooters. His first appearance in an FPS was in id Software's *Wolfenstein 3D*, released for home computers on 5 May 1992. His most recent outing was in Bethesda's *Wolfenstein II: The New Colossus*, released on 27 Oct 2017.

Over the years, BJ has faced enemies much more dangerous than mere humans. Counted among his wide and varied foes were undead super-soldiers, cyborgs (above), robot cats and dogs, walking tanks, black knights and even the ghosts from *PAC-Man*.

YOUR NEW FAVOURITE GAME

BATTALION 1944
Platforms: PS4, Xbox One, PC
First-person shooters usually favour arcade thrills over realism, but not so Bulkhead Interactive's *Battalion 1944* (due late 2018). In its close-knit five-on-five encounters only teamwork and tactics – not gung-ho charging in – will win the day.

MOST "BEST PLAYER" AWARDS IN *BATTLEFIELD 1*

As of 18 Jan 2018, super-trooper "FluMusic" (USA) had been awarded the tag of "Best Player" in 3,714 *Battlefield 1* multiplayer skirmishes on the Xbox One, as verified by TrueAchievements. To secure the award, players must be the most effective at securing their team's objective, reviving team-mates, repairing vehicles and giving orders.

First gamer to achieve Level 2,000 on Steam

In early Jul 2017, the somewhat mysterious and keen *Counter-Strike: Global Offensive (CS:GO)* player "St4ck" became the first to achieve a landmark level of 2,000 on Steam – putting him ahead of all other Steam users.

A gamer's Steam level is determined by their Experience Points (XP), which are increased by owning badges and games, and participating in Steam events. Knowing this, "St4ck" purchased huge quantities of special holiday badges during 2017's Steam Summer Sale in order to up his level. He reportedly spent thousands of dollars.

Most valuable *CS:GO* weapon skin

According to YouTuber and *CS:GO* expert "McSkillet" (USA), an anonymous devotee of Valve's tactical shooter reportedly paid more than $100,000 (£74,634) in Jun 2016 for the incredibly rare Karambit Case Hardened Factory New Blue Gem combat knife. The blue-hued, sickle-shaped blade might look deadly, but the weapon skin is purely cosmetic and offers no advantage in combat.

First *Call of Duty* videogame with female soldiers

Call of Duty: Ghosts, released on 5 Nov 2013, wasn't just notable for being the first *CoD* on the PS4 and Xbox One generation of consoles, but also for including female troops for the first time. A selection of women footsoldiers were available in the game's multiplayer mode.

Most followed FPS on Twitter

As of 18 Jan 2018, Activision's @CallofDuty Twitter channel had 3,464,991 followers. It was the 12th most followed gaming channel overall and the most for any shooter – ahead of *Overwatch* (2,729,419), *Destiny* (2,314,684) and *Battlefield* (1,523,065).

$286,300

HIGHEST-EARNING *CALL OF DUTY: INFINITE WARFARE* PLAYER

As of 20 Oct 2017, USA's Matthew "FormaL" Piper (inset) had won $286,300 (£217,209) from competing in Activision's *Call of Duty: Infinite Warfare* (2016), according to eSportsearnings.com. In 2017, he led the OpTic Gaming team to victory at the *Call of Duty* World League Championship and also won Console Player of the Year at the Esports Industry Awards.

MOST REGISTERED PLAYERS FOR AN FPS

Smilegate's tactical shooter *CrossFire* had approximately 900 million registered players worldwide as of Oct 2017. Launched in South Korea in early 2007, it was the **top-earning free-to-play PC game of 2013** – largely due to players buying modified weapons and items with real currency. Its comparatively low system requirements ensure it can be played on most PCs. It's also widely praised for its smooth online gameplay.

GAMING GOLD

D-Day landings
Activision's *Call of Duty 2* (2005) used the Xbox 360's graphical power to recreate the WWII D-Day landings as we'd never seen, or played, before.

SCI-FI SHOOTERS

Spare a thought for the poor aliens, robots and evil future dictatorships that routinely play the part of cannon fodder in the world of sci-fi shooters. Yes, they might be bent on world domination or have plans to destroy the universe, but are they really all that bad? Of course they are!

14 SECONDS

Budding *Titanfall 2* (2016) pilots barely have time to strap on their jump kits before they're facing a timed assault course that doubles as the tutorial in EA's first-person sci-fi shooter. On 10 Feb 2018, Xbox One gamer "Rbrite" (USA) recorded the **fastest completion of *Titanfall 2 Gauntlet***, speeding through the course in just 14 sec.

HIGHEST-RATED VIDEOGAME ON STEAM

As of 5 Mar 2018, Valve's brain-bending 2011 puzzler *Portal 2* carried an approval rating of 97.27%, with 117,966 players giving it the thumbs up and only 1,540 players disliking the title. It edged out *Factorio* (96.55%), *The Witcher III: Wild Hunt* (96.41%) and *Counter-Strike* (96.22%).

FIRST TEAM TO BEAT A *DESTINY 2* RAID

PS4 fireteam "The Legend Himself" became the first clan to conquer *Destiny 2*'s (Activision, 2017) inaugural raid "Leviathan" – less than six hours after it had first opened. The speedy conquest was announced by developer Bungie via Twitter at 11:47 p.m. (BST) on 13 Sep 2017. By comparison, the original "Vault of Glass" raid in *Destiny* (2014) took around 10 hr to conquer – eventually being overcome by the fleet-footed players of the "PrimeGuard" clan.

On 8 Dec 2017, players "TryHardJoe", "bran", "Meowlight", "MikeE", "Edwardc4" and "SpRoKiTs24" became **the first team to beat the Eater of Worlds raid lair in the *Destiny 2: Curse of Osiris* expansion**, taking just 2 hr to complete it.

330 ATTACK

Added on 5 Dec 2017 in the *Destiny 2: Curse of Osiris* (Activision, 2017) DLC, the trace rifle laser "Prometheus Lens" had the **highest attack rating for a *Destiny 2* weapon**, as verified by DestinyTracker.com. With an attack rating of 330 and a firing rate of 1,000 rounds per minute, the "Prometheus Lens" was deemed so powerful that it was nerfed soon after.

Splatoon 2 causes a splash

As of 31 Dec 2017, Nintendo's *Splatoon 2* had sold 4.13 million copies worldwide to become the **best-selling Switch shooter**, according to VGChartz. Approval for the paint-sloshing combat game was also reflected in its review scores. As of 5 Mar 2018, it was the **most critically acclaimed Switch shooter**, with a GameRankings aggregate score of 82.84%, based on a total of 54 reviews.

YOUR NEW FAVOURITE GAME

METRO EXODUS

Platforms: PS4, Xbox One, PC

Following *Metro: Last Light* and *Metro 2033*, this post-apocalyptic shooter is the latest instalment in Deep Silver's sci-fi series. Players resume the role of Artyom as he looks to make a fresh start – pity he didn't inform the game's deadly mutants...

MOST DOWNVOTED COMMENT ON REDDIT

The Force was definitely not with EA when the games publisher responded to player complaints about Luke Skywalker, Darth Vader and other *Star Wars Battlefront II* (2017) heroes being locked behind hours of grinding, or paid-for loot boxes. As of 5 Mar 2018, EA's reply had achieved 683,000 downvotes.

First cover-based shooter

Namco's *Kill Switch* (2003) was the first game to let players snap to cover at the press of a button. It also introduced gameplay elements – such as blind firing while behind cover – that are still used to this day in titles such as Sony's *Uncharted 4* (2016) and *Gears of War 4* (Microsoft, 2016).

First team to beat every *Destiny* raid boss without dying or using guns

On 14 May 2017, a team of raiders led by Redditor "GladHeAteHer182" (aka "Gladd") completed this epic quest, which required "meticulous planning" and "careful strategy". In total, 12 players contributed to the attempt as participants swapped with each other for a much-needed rest over the 60-hr ordeal. "Gladd" announced the achievement, saying: "We had come so close SOOO many times, but failed in one way or another. However, persistence led us down the road to victory... FINALLY!"

Longest time to complete a *Halo 3* "tricking challenge"

On 28 Apr 2017, in a demonstration of the value of patience, the *Halo* collective "Termacious Trickocity" finally opened "The Cage", a seemingly impossible mission devised by other *Halo 3* players, nearly nine years after it had been set. Players had to break into a room, situated at the end of level Sierra 117, that was sealed off behind metal bars. Achieving the feat required an incredibly elaborate solution, where enemies had to be taken out in a specific order, cutscenes activated at certain times and players positioned at particular points. It reportedly took the group hundreds of hours of playing time – and head-scratching – to solve.

Fastest completion of *Prey*

On 23 Jun 2017, PC player "seeker_" (FRA) took on the Typhons from Bethesda's *Prey* (2017) and emerged victorious in just 6 min 59 sec, as verified by Speedrun.

In 2017, German gamers got the chance to play an uncensored version of 1998's *Half-Life* for the first time. The free download made in-game blood red again and humans were no longer replaced by robots.

SHOOT-'EM-UPS

Demanding lightning-quick reactions and an itchy trigger finger, shoot-'em-ups – or "shmups" to those who know – are the ultimate tests of skill, not to mention patience. Players revel in the genre's vast range of styles, from futuristic settings to the classic cartoon beauty of *Cuphead*.

MOST HAND-DRAWN FRAMES OF ANIMATION IN A VIDEOGAME

It seems that the only thing more difficult than playing *Cuphead* – StudioMDHR's beautiful but notoriously tough shoot-'em-up – was creating it in the first place! According to StudioMDHR, its art team hand-drew close to 45,000 individual frames of animation to create the game's vibrant visuals, which pay homage to classic 1930s-era cartoons. In contrast, the number of frames used in Cinematronics' similarly hand-drawn arcade games *Dragon's Lair* (1983) and *Space Ace* (1984) is 31,431 and 34,116 frames, respectively.

StudioMDHR estimated that it took an average of 25 min to draw, ink, scan, colour and finalize each frame, putting the total time to complete all 45,000 frames at around 18,738 hr – or two years and seven weeks!

As if animating *Cuphead* wasn't enough work, the studio filled it with 36 fiendish bosses – the **most boss fights in a run-and-gun shoot-'em-up** – then created a combined 43 additional forms the bosses could transform into, resulting in the **most boss transformations in a run-and-gun shoot-'em-up**.

Most played Xbox One shoot-'em-up
Top-down shooter *Halo: Spartan Assault* (Microsoft, 2013) had been played by 94,055 blast-happy gamers as of 2 Feb 2018, according to TrueAchievements. Set between *Halo 3* and *Halo 4*, it follows the events of the Great War as players pick up arms to battle Covenant forces once again.

HOUSEMARQUE HIGH SCORERS

As verified on 7 Dec 2017 by Finnish shmup specialists Housemarque, "tallamon" (ITA) grabbed the **highest score on *Nex Machina's* "Hero" difficulty mode** on 31 Aug 2017 with 9,161,555,030 points.

Fellow Italian "baudone" holds the **highest score for *Resogun's* Arcade mode on "Hero" difficulty**. He took Housemarque's 2013 shmup to task, scoring 21,328,589,030 on 2 Jul 2017.

Housemarque also verified the **highest score on *Super Stardust HD*** (2007) for PS3. On 9 Mar 2010, Finland's "TLO-MEK" scored 2,016,958,340 points on the timeless shoot-'em-up.

33 YEARS

LONGEST TIME FOR A GAME RE-RELEASE

On 20 Oct 2017, 33 years after it launched in 1984, the Commodore 64 shoot-'em-up *Revenge of the Mutant Camels* enjoyed a limited re-release. It was packaged with *Llamatron: 2112* (Atari ST, 1991) on an Atari Jaguar cartridge titled *Jeff Minter Classics* (AtariAge, 2017) and sold on AtariAge's website and at the Portland Retro Gaming Expo (USA).

FASTEST COMPLETION OF *ENTER THE GUNGEON*

This top-down blaster's roguelike format means that levels vary slightly with every play-through, but that did not impede the progress of Russia's "Wonderis_". As verified by Speedrun.com, he demolished all in his path as the game's Convict character, completing the task in 13 min 1 sec on 13 Nov 2017.

MOST CRITICALLY ACCLAIMED TWIN-STICK SHOOT-'EM-UP (PS4)

Housemarque's sci-fi shoot-'em-up *Nex Machina: Death Machine* (2017) had a GameRankings.com rating of 88.62% as of 30 Nov 2017. It's the joint-third-highest-rated shmup ever, behind Sega's *Panzer Dragoon Orta* (2002) and Microsoft's *Geometry Wars: Retro Evolved 2* (2008).

First player to obtain a Platinum trophy on *Helldivers*
All you need to do to get *Helldivers'* "The epitome of Super Earth" Platinum trophy is to unlock the game's 30 other trophies. Sounds easy, right? Wrong! As of 2 Feb 2018, only 23 players had managed to get their hands on it. According to PSNProfiles, the first to accomplish this fiendish feat was China's "Warlord0601", who did so on 11 Oct 2016.

Highest cumulative total score on *Battle Garegga Rev.2016*
Repeat play-throughs of the Xbox One's acclaimed bullet hell shooter had taken Japan's "SatoSato310" to a cumulative score of 4,596,305,940 as of 2 Feb 2018, according to TrueAchievements. His exploits didn't end there: in his quest to be the best, he had also collected 92,570 10,000-point medals, defeated 3,849 bosses and "roasted" 2,126,363 pink flamingos.

Highest Story Mode score in *Raiden V*
As of 2 Feb 2018, "dotk3" (JPN) held the record high score for top-down space shooter *Raiden V* (Moss Co., 2016) on Xbox One. His total of 110,324,300 points in a single play-through of the game's Story Mode was 907,800 higher than the second-placed score of 109,416,500 by "TAITOAPLAN" (JPN), as verified by TrueAchievements.

Fastest all-bosses completion of *Cuphead* with a dance pad
For most of us, eliminating all of *Cuphead's* dastardly bosses is plenty hard enough. Doing so while using two connected *Dance Dance Revolution* dance mats as the only means to control the titular character is unthinkable. According to TwinFinite, extreme Australian gamer "PeekingBoo" took just 1 hr 24 min 40 sec to do exactly that on 9 Oct 2017. Funky!

Dragon-filled fantasy shooter *Panzer Dragoon Orta* (Sega, 2002) boasted a GameRankings rating of 90.36% as of 5 Feb 2018, making it the **most critically acclaimed on-rails shooter.**

SPLATOON 2

Inklings the world over have been donning their coolest threads and grabbing their favourite paint rollers to once more return to the ink-splatting fray. Nintendo's paint-'em-up has proven a particular hit online, where Nintendo Switch gamers have been setting splat-tastic new records...

MOST INK PAINTED IN A VIDEOGAME

The minuscule Inklings of *Splatoon 2* (Nintendo, 2017) like nothing better than spending their days shopping for cool clothes and painting the turf of rival gangs with gallons of ink. According to Nintendo, if Inklings were scaled up to the size of an average human being, then as of 22 Jan 2018 *Splatoon 2* players would have covered 6.12 million km² (2.36 million sq mi) of turf with ink in online battles across the world since the game's launch on 21 Jul. That's enough ink to cover two-thirds of the USA, or three times the whole of France, Spain, Germany, Italy and the UK combined (with ink to spare). Imagine cleaning all that up!

WHO WANTS EGGS WITH THEIR SALMON?

Things get even more wonderfully messy (if that's possible) in Salmon Run mode. These frantic 100-sec co-op battles (for up to four players) involve splatting Boss Salmonids to release Golden Eggs, which must be picked up and deposited to complete each round. Nintendo told us that, since Jul 2017, *Splatoon 2* players had collected a whopping 3.3 billion Golden Eggs.

OVERWATCH

Blizzard's squad shooter crashed the gaming scene in 2016. Since then, its cast of colourful characters and reliance on teamwork have struck a chord with its growing community. It has also established itself as an important part of the eSports world, with its best players pocketing huge prizes.

THE STORY SO FAR...

Overwatch's seasons are ticking by at pace, with seven having been completed as of 20 Feb 2018. Updates to the game might have changed it slightly between each season but, as verified by Blizzard itself, some areas of player expertise can still be compared to once and for all settle the debates over who the best players ever really are.

For example, the player who dished out the **most hero damage** was the USA's "Colton", who dealt 4,509,948 points of damage to rival players in Season Four. It was in Season Five that "도도이" (KOR) – pronounced "Dodoyi" – scored the **highest healing total**, benevolently healing 22,390,446 points of his team-mates' damage. Elsewhere, "BATMAN" (USA) landed the **most final blows** with 55,777 in Season Four, and the same player went on to score the **most eliminations**, dealing death to 120,745 players during Season Five of *Overwatch*.

HIGHEST-EARNING *OVERWATCH* PLAYER
Ryu "Ryujehong" Je-hong is a vital member of Lunatic-hai, *Overwatch*'s top eSports team, as well as a core player in South Korea's all-conquering, World Cup-winning national squad. As of 21 Feb 2018, he had earned more from *Overwatch* events than anyone else. eSportsearnings confirmed that he'd pocketed $52,546 (£37,569) from the 13 pro events in which he had competed. His nearest rival was fellow countryman Gong "Miro" Jin-hyuk, who had career earnings of $46,010 (£32,896) as of the same date.

First official *Overwatch* League match
On 10 Jan 2018, the first official *Overwatch* League (OWL) match took place as San Francisco Shock (SFShock) faced Los Angeles Valiant (LAValiant), both from California, USA. LAValiant won 4–0. The game followed qualifying to establish the 12 inaugural teams. Concurrent viewers on the League's official Twitch channel topped 415,000 on the first day of play. On 11 Feb 2018, London Spitfire defeated New York Excelsior 3–2, after being 2–0 down at one point, to become the League's initial Stage One champions.

First *Overwatch* world champions
The inaugural tournament in Blizzard's newest eSport game was staged at the Anaheim Convention Center as part of the 2016 BlizzCon in the USA (29 Oct–5 Nov), with 16 nations represented. South Korea became the first world champions. They did so without losing a single map and thrashed Russia 4–0 in the final, inspiring the website Mashable to comment that they "utterly destroyed everyone".

South Korea hold the **most wins of the *Overwatch* World Cup**, having won the event both times since the eSports tournament's inauguration in 2016. After going through the debut event with an unblemished record, it was more of the same from South Korea in 2017, defeating Canada 4–1 to retain the crown.

Longest winning streak of pro *Overwatch* matches
According to GosuGamers, the USA's Team EnVyUs won 59 matches in a row on Blizzard's vibrant shooter. The unbeaten run was achieved between 13 Feb and 9 Apr 2016 and still stood as the longest streak as of 20 Feb 2018.

The winding streets and narrow passages of the Mexico-themed escort map Dorado are perfect for launching deadly attacks or demonstrating your team's steadfast defence. Dorado's popularity has made it the **most played map in competitive** **Overwatch tournaments**, as verified by GosuGamers.com. As of 24 Jan 2018, the map had been played 2,204 times in pro events.

Overwatch is famous for its Pixar-like animated videos. In late 2017, its director Jeff Kaplan commented that he "would really love" to bring a feature film based on Blizzard's smash-hit shooter to the big screen.

TALLEST MOBILE VIDEOGAME COSPLAY

Heads were turned at New York Comic Con in Oct 2016 as an attendee in a gigantic suit standing 8 ft 4 in (2.54 m) tall strutted his stuff. Observers were stunned to be in the presence of *Overwatch*'s wandering knight Reinhardt, courtesy of an outfit designed and built by cosplayer Thomas DePetrillo (USA) of Extreme Costumes. Thomas's creation, as measured in the USA on 7 Dec 2017 in his own workshop, is something to behold – especially when he's swinging his fearsome hammer!

SPOTIFY SOUNDTRACKS

The best soundtracks stir the soul as they add atmosphere, tension and excitement to the action happening on screen. Some are so good that they're worth listening to outside the game. Here, we reveal 2017's most streamed soundtracks on Spotify, according to the streaming service itself.

1

THE WITCHER III: WILD HUNT
Composers: Percival, Marcin Przybyłowicz, Mikolai Stroinski
Release: 11 May 2015
Label: CD Projekt Red

2

HORIZON ZERO DAWN
Composers: The Flight, Niels van der Leest, Joris de Man, Jonathan Williams
Release: 10 Mar 2017
Label: Sony Interactive Entertainment Europe

3

THE ELDER SCROLLS V: SKYRIM
Composer: Jeremy Soule
Release: 11 Nov 2011
Label: Bethesda Softworks

4

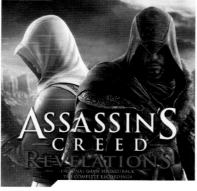

ASSASSIN'S CREED: REVELATIONS
Composers: Lorne Balfe, Jesper Kyd
Release: 15 Nov 2011
Label: Ubisoft Music

5

THE ELDER SCROLLS ONLINE
Composers: Brad Derrick, Malukah, Rik Schaffer, Jeremy Soule
Release: 4 Apr 2014
Label: Bethesda Softworks

6

FALLOUT 4
Composer: Inon Zur
Release: 6 Nov 2015
Label: Bethesda Softworks

7

THE LAST OF US
Composer: Gustavo Santaolalla
Release: 7 Jun 2013
Label: Sony Computer Entertainment America

8

BATTLEFIELD 1
Composers: Patrik Andrén, Johan Söderqvist
Release: 28 Oct 2016
Label: Electronic Arts Music

9

DRAGON AGE: INQUISITION
Composer: Trevor Morris
Release: 17 Nov 2014
Label: Electronic Arts Music

10

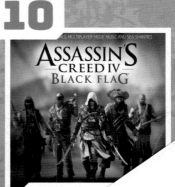

ASSASSIN'S CREED IV: BLACK FLAG
Composer: Brian Ty
Release: 14 Oct 2013
Label: Ubisoft Music

PLANET COSPLAY

Cosplay is not simply about dressing up as your favourite characters from popular entertainment – it's also about embodying their spirit. Gamers have been quick to jump on board the craze with designs that have become a colourful focal point of gaming events all across the world...

WORLD COSPLAY SUMMIT

Location: Nagoya, Japan
Inaugural year: 2003
Attendance: 200,000

First held in 2003, the annual World Cosplay Summit is the **longest-running dedicated cosplay event**. Participants from all over the world cosplay as characters from Japanese videogames, manga, anime and tokusatsu (live-action film and TV). Since 2005, the show has climaxed with the World Cosplay Championship, in which cosplay teams representing their countries compete to become Grand Champion. As of 2017, Italy and Brazil had the **most World Cosplay Championship victories** – three wins each.

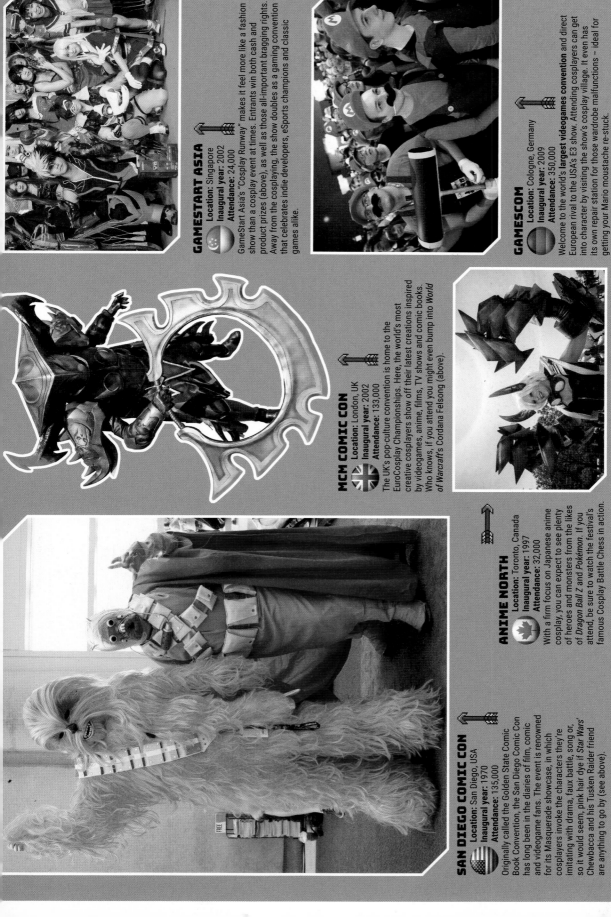

GAMESTART ASIA

Location: Singapore
Inaugural year: 2002
Attendance: 24,000

GameStart Asia's "Cosplay Runway" makes it feel more like a fashion show than a cosplay event at times. Entrants win both cash and product prizes (above), as well as those all-important bragging rights. Away from the cosplaying, the show doubles as a gaming convention that celebrates indie developers, eSports champions and classic games alike.

GAMESCOM

Location: Cologne, Germany
Inaugural year: 2009
Attendance: 350,000

Welcome to the world's **largest videogames convention** and direct European rival to the USA's E3 show. Attending cosplayers can get into character by visiting the show's cosplay village. It even has its own repair station for those wardrobe malfunctions – ideal for getting your Mario moustache re-stuck.

MCM COMIC CON

Location: London, UK
Inaugural year: 2002
Attendance: 133,000

The UK's pop-culture convention is home to the EuroCosplay Championships. Here, the world's most creative cosplayers show off their latest creations inspired by videogames, anime, films, TV shows and comic books. Who knows, if you attend you might even bump into *World of Warcraft's* Cordana Felsong (above).

ANIME NORTH

Location: Toronto, Canada
Inaugural year: 1997
Attendance: 32,000

With a firm focus on Japanese anime cosplay, you can expect to see plenty of heroes and monsters from the likes of *Dragon Ball Z* and *Pokémon*. If you attend, be sure to watch the festival's famous Cosplay Battle Chess in action.

SAN DIEGO COMIC CON

Location: San Diego, USA
Inaugural year: 1970
Attendance: 135,000

Originally called the Golden State Comic Book Convention, the San Diego Comic Con has long been in the diaries of film, comic and videogame fans. The event is renowned for its Masquerade showcase, in which cosplayers invoke the characters they're imitating with drama, faux battle, song or, so it would seem, pink hair dye if *Star Wars'* Chewbacca and his Tusken Raider friend are anything to go by (see above).

VIRTUAL REALITY

Don't understand what all the fuss is about when it comes to VR? Just strap on a PS VR, an Oculus Rift or a HTC Vive and prepare to have your mind expanded. VR adds a whole new dimension to gaming, letting us explore in-game worlds in a truly amazing new way.

> **" VR IS A PLACE WHERE YOU CAN BE WHO YOU WANT TO BE AND STEP INTO PORTALS THAT TAKE YOU INTO DIFFERENT WORLDS. "**
>
> NATHANIËL "NATHIE" DE JONG

1987
The actual phrase "virtual reality" is coined by American computer scientist, visual artist and music composer Jaron Lanier (above). It emerges from Lanier's partnership with a former Atari colleague, Thomas Zimmerman, and their company, called VPL (Virtual Programming Language) Research.

1987
SegaScope launches for the Sega Master System console. Although not true VR, the peripheral invented by Mark Cerny displays 3D in full colour. Rapidly moving shutters in its lenses create a 3D effect when playing games.

1989
VPL Research debuts its EyePhone at the Texpo telecommunications show in San Francisco, California, USA. It has a head-mounted display and DataGlove, the latter tracking movement and orientation. EyePhone has the ability to move objects in a computer-generated environment.

1991
The British VR company Virtuality, led by Jonathan Waldern, introduces its 1000 Series pods (below). The VR pods feature LCD screens with a resolution of 276 x 372 pixels, four speakers and a microphone. They're sold with standing or sitting configurations.

1993
Sega showcases its VR headset at the Consumer Electronics Show (CES) in Las Vegas, Nevada, USA. The three-dimensional virtual realities explored via its "binocular parallax" viewer and head-tracking never make it to market.

2015
The Kickstarter campaign for FOVE is launched on 19 May, achieving its funding goal three days later. FOVE is billed as "the world's first eye-tracking virtual reality headset". It takes its name from the fovea, the part of the eye with the highest visual acuity. It doesn't harm its chances that it sounds like "love".

2015
Microsoft reveals its HoloLens augmented reality headset in a press conference at the Electronic Entertainment Expo (E3) in Los Angeles, USA. It allows users to observe virtual objects overlaid on the real world, which can be manipulated by hand gestures and the user's voice.

2016
Sony brings PlayStation VR to PS4. Its head-mounted visor has a 5.7-inch (14.4-cm) OLED panel and a display resolution of 1080 p. It has over 40 games at launch, a mix of dedicated and partly compatible titles.

2016
HTC Vive is launched. It's a collaboration between Taiwanese electronics firm HTC and games developer/videogame distribution company Valve (USA). It's primarily a gaming device, but features space-tracking tech that allows users to see real-life obstacles while wearing the headset.

VR ROUND-UP

We've introduced you to VR's most popular YouTuber and taken you on a tour through VR's past and present. Now it's time to put on your headset and embark on Guinness World Records' first-ever round-up of the biggest and best achievements in virtual reality…

2.84 MILLION

As of 9 Apr 2018, the 2.84 million sales of *Resident Evil VII: Biohazard* on PS4 ensured it was the **best-selling PS VR game fully playable in VR**. In an impressive feat of programming, Capcom managed to make its survival horror fully VR-enabled when it launched on 24 Jan 2017. This meant that PS4 owners who also had a PlayStation VR (PS VR) headset were able to brave the game's house of horrors in this even scarier manner… if they dared!

FIRST VR GAME TO TOP THE STEAM CHARTS

Raw Data's gameplay, which sees players destroying futuristic enemies with all manner of sci-fi weaponry, clearly appealed to VR fans. On 14 Jul 2016, it became the first VR game to top Steam's sales charts when it was released on the distributor's Early Access program. The accolade was recognized by Valve, the owner of the Steam platform, in a congratulatory tweet.

YOUR NEW FAVOURITE GAME

ACE COMBAT 7: SKIES UNKNOWN
Platforms: PS4, Xbox One, PC
High-altitude dogfights will get some extra bite when Bandai Namco's *Ace Combat 7* takes to the skies. PS VR-owning pilots will be able to get closer to the action by donning their headsets to fight through a series of exclusive missions.

First device to bring everyday objects into virtual reality
Released in Dec 2017, HTC's Vive Tracker allows developers to turn ordinary objects into positionally tracked devices. The 10-cm (3.9-in) accessory can be attached to tennis rackets, golf clubs and similar items. They can then be monitored by HTC's Lighthouse tracking system, so that their movement and position can be replicated in VR games as they're used.

First eSports tournament broadcast in VR
Hosted in Seattle, Washington, USA, on 3–13 Aug 2016, the sixth staging of Valve's *Dota 2* world championship – The International – was the first eSports tournament to be broadcast in VR. VR viewers were required to have a SteamVR-capable headset. Those who wished to watch the stream had to install Steam and *Dota 2*, then access *Dota 2*'s VR Hub.

Highest virtual slide
Visitors to the Shard skyscraper in London, UK, could test their nerve through two VR experiences in 2017. The virtual games were located on the open-air Skydeck of the building, which added to the sense of immersion.

In *The Slide*, participants were sat down in a sled as it whizzed along a virtual helter-skelter slide 800 ft (243 m) above London. In *Vertigo*, players had to tip-toe along thin girders with the terrifying view of the city far below.

First player to fully complete *RIGS: Mechanized Combat League*
According to PSNProfiles, "norcalpville" (USA) was the first person to accomplish everything in Sony's futuristic PS VR sports combat game. He managed to collect the game's 33 trophies by 17 Oct 2016, just four days after the game's release.

First VR theme park
THE VOID opened its doors on 1 Jul 2016 in New York, USA. Visitors are kitted out with a haptic feedback vest (that vibrates if you get hit) and a VR headset to experience virtual worlds like never before.

THE VOID's attractions combine camera-tracking with real-world obstacles to create the illusion that players really are in the game, be that while blasting stormtroopers in *Star Wars: Secrets of the Empire* or getting slimed in *Ghostbusters: Dimension*.

FIRST CROSS-PLATFORM VR GAME
Released on 26 Sep 2017, *EVE: Valkyrie – Warzone* is an updated version of the VR shooter *EVE: Valkyrie* (CCP Games, 2016). Among its features is a mode that allows players using different VR headsets to converge on the same online match. This includes players using the Oculus Rift, PS VR and HTC Vive – and even players on PC and PS4 without a headset.

FACT!

The first virtual reality "pods" by the Virtuality Group (UK) started popping up in arcades and city centres in 1991 – they were basic, colourful examples of flying, driving, shooting and puzzle-solving games.

MOST CRITICALLY ACCLAIMED VR GAME

In 2001, shoot-'em-ups took a huge leap forward with the release of rhythm shooter *Rez* (Sega). Its clever – and psychedelically hypnotic – use of graphics and music drew praise from all quarters. In Oct 2016, a VR re-imagining arrived for Sony's PS VR, published by Enhance Games. *Rez Infinite* proved to be every bit as good as its predecessor and was similarly acclaimed.

As of 9 Apr 2018, *Rez Infinite* boasted a GameRankings score of 89%, which was based on 23 reviews. The manner in which it used VR to let its players view its stages in 360° – something that wasn't possible in previous *Rez* games – drew particular praise. *Rez Infinite* was also awarded the Best VR Game prize at 2016's The Game Awards ceremony.

8 MINUTES 1 SECOND

Fastest time to complete *SUPERHOT VR*
On 22 Jan 2018, Vive player "Qwhilla" (USA) practically sprinted through Superhot Team's time-slowing 2016 shooter. The blazing run took a mere 8 min 1 sec, as verified by Speedrun.

FIRST VR PLATFORM GAME
On 27 Nov 1995, *Virtual Boy Wario Land* gave gamers their first taste of VR platforming. Created for Nintendo's ill-fated Virtual Boy console, it starred the money-grabbing Wario in a (very red) side-scrolling adventure. It featured stereoscopic 3D elements that were unique to the console.

twitch

MOST FOLLOWED TWITCHERS

The total number of followers of "Ninja" (below) – owner of the **most followed Twitch channel dedicated to gaming** – ballooned by around two million in the weeks after his famous all-star stream with musician Drake. His success is as much down to his skill as his special guests.

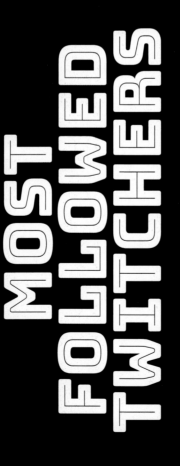

A *Fortnite* Twitch stream by the USA's "Ninja" (aka Richard Tyler Blevins) on 14 Mar 2018 featured superstar rapper Drake (right). The stream had the **most concurrent viewers for a Twitch stream by an individual.** It attracted around 628,000 concurrent viewers, according to figures from Twitch.

1 NINJA (USA)

5,144,968 FOLLOWERS

Most played: *Fortnite*

2
SUMMIT1G (USA)

3,059,477
FOLLOWERS

Most played: *Fortnite*

3
SHROUD (CAN)

2,933,291
FOLLOWERS

Most played: *League of Legends*

4
SYNDICATE (UK)

2,577,535
FOLLOWERS

Most played: *Fortnite*

5
IMAQTPIE (USA)

2,236,618
FOLLOWERS

Most played: *League of Legends*

6
NIGHTBLUE3 (USA)

2,195,250
FOLLOWERS

Most played: *Fortnite*

7
DRDISRESPECTLIVE (USA)

2,145,058
FOLLOWERS

Most played: *Fortnite*

8
LIRIK (USA)

2,064,654
FOLLOWERS

Most played: *Fortnite*

9
SODAPOPPIN (USA)

1,844,161
FOLLOWERS

Most played: *World of Warcraft*

10
LOLTYLER1 (USA)

1,580,001
FOLLOWERS

Most played: *League of Legends*

All data for Twitch accounts of individuals only and as verified by SocialBlade.com on 8 Apr 2018. NB: "shroud" was formerly known as "mEclipse".

GAMERS GIVING BACK

From *Super Mario* marathons to *World of Warcraft* sprints, gamers have found inventive ways to turn their hobby into charitable fundraising. Over the years, they've collected millions for charities such as Child's Play, which donates toys and games to hospitals. Here are just a few of the ways gamers are giving back...

200

HOSPITALS AROUND THE GLOBE THAT RECEIVE GRANTS AND DONATIONS THROUGH THE CHILD'S PLAY CHARITY

MARIO MARATHON

Every year, the team behind the Mario Marathon (mariomarathon.com) put Nintendo's plumber through his paces in support of Child's Play. Over the past 10 years, the streamers have played virtually every *Super Mario* title to raise a total of $630,000 (£445,681) from donors.

Q&A: MATT WIGGINS

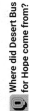

Desert Bus for Hope co-founder and special guest coordinator.

Q Where did Desert Bus for Hope come from?

A It was originally founded by members of comedy troupe LoadingReadyRun in 2007. We wanted to contribute to the Child's Play charity when we got our hands on *Desert Bus* [a game by magician duo Penn & Teller designed to be purposely boring]. We got the idea of a marathon fundraiser where people could donate to force us to play it. The result

was more successful than we considered possible.

Q Why are games charities like this important?

A Everyone likes to play. Play is joyful, social and relatable across all generations – and it has the ability to ease pain and improve quality of life.

Q What makes this fundraiser unique?

A Many videogame charity marathons involve playing good and entertaining games. *Desert Bus* doesn't have a lot of entertainment value, so we - have to bring our own fun.

It acts as a centrepiece around which we put on skits, costumes, singalongs and lots of social interaction. This gives Desert Bus for Hope a flavour unlike other charity marathons.

Q How much have you raised so far?

A $4,468,779 (£3.17 m). We had $22,805 (£11,417) in 2007 and had grown to over $654,000 (£484,665) by 2017.

$3.6 M/£2.6 M

AMOUNT CHILD'S PLAY RAISED IN DONATIONS IN 2017

GAMING FOR GOOD

Extra Life is a gaming charity that was set up in 2008. It was a way for founder Jeromy Adams to honour his friend Victoria Enmon, who passed away from cancer, and the Texas Children's Hospital where she was treated. In its first two years, it raised $302,000 (£189,603). That figure had risen to over $11 million (more than £8 million) in 2017. Says Mike Kinney, the director of Extra Life: "The passion and dedication of those who participate is an inspiration to all of us. We're all excited to see Extra Life continue to grow."

50,000

NUMBER OF GAMERS REGISTERED WITH EXTRA LIFE TO PLAY GAMES AND RAISE MONEY FOR THEIR LOCAL CHILDREN'S MIRACLE NETWORK HOSPITAL

RUNNING OF THE GNOMES

Once upon a time, Ashleigh Ayn Sult invited *World of Warcraft* team-mates to race in-game as pink-haired gnomes for Breast Cancer Research. In 2017, *WoW* developer Blizzard helped by setting up the Great Gnomeregan Run micro-event. Combined, the events have raised over $16,000 (£12,038) for cancer vaccine development.

SMASH THE RECORD

This *Super Smash Bros.* and speed-running marathon fundraiser (smashtherecord.com) was founded in 2014 by students at the University of Central Florida. The rules are that there are no rules, with unique match-ups, make-your-own guidelines and dance parties to raise money for the St Jude Children's Research Hospital. It has generated over $150,000 (£105,610).

GAMERS FOR GIVING

After a *Halo 2* event was shut down on the grounds of gaming's negative effects, a group of students wanting to show it as a force for good formed Gamers for Giving. They raise funds via gaming tournaments and streaming marathons (gamersoutreach.org), an organization providing therapeutic recreation to children in hospitals.

GAMES DONE QUICK

Twice each year, Games Done Quick (gamesdonequick.com) invites top speed-runners to showcase their skills. In its latest Awesome Games Done Quick event, held on 7–14 Jan 2018 in Herndon, Virginia, USA, $2,295,190 (£1,615,970) was raised for the Prevent Cancer Foundation. Over its seven-year run, it has collected more than $14 m (£9.9 m).

WORLD BUILDERS

This year's *Guinness World Records* book has a section dedicated to "Makers" – inventors who build amazing new things. In *Gamer's*, we've gone one better by dedicating this chapter not *just* to makers of things, but also to gamers who build entire worlds!

FASTEST TIME TO BUILD A CASTLE IN MINECRAFT SURVIVAL MODE

During a visit on 21 Mar 2018 to the Guinness World Records HQ in London, YouTuber and *Minecraft* buff "SeaPeeKay", aka Callum Knight (UK), built a custom castle – designed by GWR – in *Minecraft*'s Survival mode in 4 min 20 sec (the fastest time of three attempts).

Ever the perfectionist, he'd already thought of even quicker ways to build it when we spoke to him after the attempt: "I was being very careful to not misplace blocks, which I think slowed me down," he said. "I feel I could've knocked more time off if I'd worked out the quickest and most efficient way to place the blocks."

You can see Callum lording it up in his castle in our main picture, but you could knock him off his throne. Turn to pp.104–05 to find out all the details you'll need to build Callum's castle for yourself. You'll also find three other awesome *Minecraft* record attempts – featuring rocket launches, igloo building and horse corralling – to try at home!

"THE POSSIBILITIES IN MINECRAFT ARE LIMITLESS. THERE ARE ALWAYS NEW THINGS TO DO EVERY TIME YOU LOAD UP THE GAME.

CALLUM "SEAPEEKAY" KNIGHT

LONGEST JOURNEY IN *MINECRAFT*

In Mar 2011, Kurt J Mac (USA) took his first steps on a journey to *Minecraft*'s fabled Far Lands – and we've been following his adventure ever since. For those new to his quest, the Far Lands are roughly 12,500 km (7,767 mi) away from where *Minecraft* players first appear when they start a game.

Kurt documents his journey on his YouTube channel "Far Lands or Bust!", raising money for charity as he goes. As of 6 Mar 2018, exactly seven years into his trek, he'd walked 3,280,569 blocks (3,280 km; 2,038 mi), which equates to 26% of his journey.

He's already having strange experiences. "The most noticeable effect of going this far is the jittery player movement," he said. "As the coordinate number gets larger, it gets more imprecise, causing the world to appear to skip underneath us while travelling. The effect is already somewhat nauseating to some viewers. It will only get worse."

MINECRAFT

We've constructed six entire pages to celebrate the world's most popular build-'em-up! Keep reading to meet the people playing *Minecraft* in ways never thought possible, see the amazing things that have been built, and find out about Stampy Cat's very special record…

First *Minecraft* mob voted for by players

Activities at MineCon Earth on 18 Nov 2017 included an online vote for a new mob (the collective name for monsters in *Minecraft*). From four candidates, The Monster of the Night Skies – which attacks players who are short of sleep – won the vote. It will be added as part of the Update Aquatic.

First live play performed in a videogame
Playcraft Live is a theatre production with a twist. As the actors are on stage, their performance is re-enacted within *Minecraft*. The project made its debut at The Playhouse Theatre in Derry, Northern Ireland, on 14 Oct 2017. The first play performed was written by Alex Scarrow and was based in the same universe as the author's *TimeRiders* sci-fi novels.

Fastest no-glitch completion of *Minecraft*
On 28 Mar 2017, "TheeSizzler" completed *Minecraft* (which means defeating the beastly Ender Dragon, above) in 7 min 16.88 sec. After beating his own record, the Canadian gamer took to Speedrun to promise he would "come back to try to get sub 7 [min]".

First MineCon wedding proposal
On 18 Nov 2011, Matt Dunn proposed to his girlfriend Asia Ramirez. A happy event, for sure, but not ordinarily something that would make it into our book. What made the proposal special was that it took place on stage in Las Vegas at MineCon 2011, in front of 5,000 people and millions of viewers! For *Minecraft* fans Matt and Asia, what could be more fitting than giving their wedding a *Minecraft* theme? Decorations at the ceremony in Sacramento, California, USA, included *Minecraft* creations from artist Greg Aronowitz.

First high-definition *Minecraft* makeover
During its E3 2017 press event, on 11 Jun, Microsoft announced that *Minecraft* would receive a graphical overhaul. Dubbed the "Super Duper Graphics Pack", the update promised 4K graphics, improved lighting, shadows, water effects and more – see the before (left) and after (right) images above. However, the planned 2017 launch was delayed, with the update now due for release at some point in 2018.

First *Minecraft*-branded videogame console
Unveiled in Japan on 6 Dec 2016, the "Minecraft Special Edition" PS Vita (left) was a white version of Sony's handheld that was decorated with *Minecraft* artwork. It was bundled with the game, a special pouch and a custom theme.
　　Not to be outdone, in Aug 2017 Microsoft unveiled an Xbox One S console with dirt, grass and redstone decorations (right).

WORLD BUILDERS

FASTEST TIME TO MAKE AND DISPLAY 10 CAKES IN *MINECRAFT* SURVIVAL MODE

If you love playing *Minecraft*, then the chances are you'll know exactly who "Stampy Cat" is. The YouTuber, aka Joseph Garrett, is a UK-based *Minecraft* streamer who just loves cake – especially the cake to be found in his favourite game.

Several of his cake-tastic videos, such as "The First Cake" (2013) and "Cake Thief" (2014), have racked up many millions of views. Given his confectionery craving and *Minecraft* fixation, it's no wonder that his unique record combines his two favourite things!

On 3 Apr 2018, at Guinness World Records' HQ in London, UK, "Stampy Cat" made short work of his cake-creating task, taking 3 min 51 sec to make 10 cakes on the PC version of *Minecraft*. His culinary creations are on display in the main picture. Key to his fast time was finding novel ways to make wheat grow as quickly as possible. We won't give his secret away, but suffice it to say that many skeletons were sacrificed!

" I PLAY MINECRAFT ALL THE TIME, BUT IT WAS REALLY EXCITING DOING IT TO SET A WORLD RECORD! "

JOSEPH "STAMPY CAT" GARRETT

WORLD BUILDERS

First Atari 2600 emulator in *Minecraft*
Jaws dropped on 6 Dec 2016 as YouTuber "SethBling" unveiled an Atari 2600 emulator created within *Minecraft*. To get the classic 1977 gaming console running required "a couple [of] thousand command blocks" – objects that modify the game world. There were limits though, as *Space Invaders* and *Donkey Kong* ran at only 60 frames per hour! There was no way to control the emulated games, either.

LARGEST UNDERWATER CITY IN *MINECRAFT*

Minecraft master builder and YouTuber "Jeracraft", aka Jeremy Sanchez (GIB), had a very good day on 29 Jul 2017. Not only was he celebrating the milestone of achieving 300,000 YouTube subscribers, but he also posted a video showing off his amazing Lost City of Atlantis build.

He constructed the ocean out of blue stained glass, something he told us was the "most challenging part of the project". It then took him two weeks to piece together the fortress city (main picture), a structure that was built using five million blocks!

He then added statues, hillside dwellings, ornate bridges, soaring towers and underwater vegetation to bring his vision of the fabled sunken city to life. "Jeracraft" topped his creation off with a statue of the Greek god Atlas, who can be seen supporting Earth (far right). It was an imposing final flourish to his "underwater paradise".

3 MINUTES 54 SECONDS

Fastest time to build a house in *Minecraft* Survival mode
Scaling down a little from his castle (see p.96), "SeaPeeKay", aka Callum Knight (UK), took just 3 min 54 sec to construct a house. Callum completed the challenge as part of our "GWR Gamer's: The Showdown" live stream on 28 Nov 2017.

First working mobile phone in *Minecraft*
On 1 Dec 2015, "CaptainSparklez" (USA) hosted a demonstration of a working mobile phone network in *Minecraft*, created by communication technology company Verizon.

The phone could send texts and surf the web. Even more incredibly, the in-game device had the ability to make calls (even video calls) to real-world phones. It used specially designed software to recreate images and video using blocks (see above).

Largest LEGO® *Minecraft* set
Launched in mid-2017, The Mountain Cave presents builders with a 2,863-brick task, which easily tops the previous largest set – the 1,600-brick The Village. Once built, it measures 31 cm (12 in) high, 53 cm (20 in) wide and 29 cm (11 in) deep. Some of its cooler features include a rotating cave-spider spawner and a minecart track.

First *Minecraft* mini-game
On 21 Jun 2017, Battle Mode became *Minecraft*'s first official mini-game. Created by Mojang, the console-exclusive mode embraces the battle royale formula from games such as *Fortnite*, but boils down the usual 100-player scraps to just eight players. The winner is, of course, the last person standing – usually the gamer who most successfully uses the various weapons, armour and health-restoring snacks to their advantage.

Largest MMORPG built in *Minecraft*
Wynncraft is a free-to-play MMORPG that was created within *Minecraft*. Released on 29 Apr 2013, it consists of a sprawling fantasy overworld that covers approximately 22 km²/8.49 sq mi (around 4,000 x 5,500 blocks) – and that's not including other explorable areas such as dungeons. "The landscape was custom-designed and every building and feature was completely hand-built," said Francis Mailloux, one of the game's designers.

READER CHALLENGES

Here's where we invite you to step into the spotlight. We've designed four very special *Minecraft* records just for the launch of this book. Choose any (or all!) and make your attempt on either PS4, Xbox One, Switch or PC. With "SeaPeeKay" encouraging you from the sidelines, you're in good hands.

FASTEST TIME TO BUILD A CASTLE IN *MINECRAFT* CREATIVE MODE
FOR CONSOLE AND PC PLAYERS

To get our challenges up and running, we've let "SeaPeeKay" have a go at this one already (pp. 96–97). He set a time of 4 min 20 sec, but we know you can do better! Your task is to build the same castle as in our main picture. It must have four walls, four turrets with battlements, an opening to the castle with a portcullis, a water-filled moat and a wooden bridge. Your last act before the clock stops is to make the castle your own by placing a coloured banner (any colour will do) at the top of it.

Fastest time to build a rocket in *Minecraft* Survival mode
FOR CONSOLE AND PC PLAYERS

To prepare for this one, create a superflat world in Creative mode, then stack blocks of ice into a tower until the coordinate readout says Y: 50 – this is the point your rocket has to reach.

Break all the blocks (except the one at Y: 50), fill your hotbar only with the material for your rocket, then switch to Survival mode. Start timing and build a rocket of any design (the one pictured is just an example). With the rocket built, get in and launch it. Stop the clock after you reach the ice block and break it with your fist.

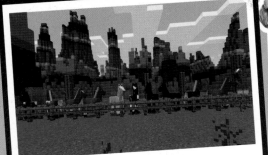

Fastest time to saddle and stable 10 horses in *Minecraft* Survival mode
FOR CONSOLE AND PC PLAYERS
Howdy, pardners! Before you can channel your inner cowboy or cowgirl, you'll need to prepare. To start with, create an enclosure of 50 x 20 blocks. Use fence blocks at the four corners of the enclosure and create a fence gate wall every 12 blocks (to create three jumps). Finish the structure by building 10 stables at one end of it (see above).

Next, spawn 10 horses and tame them using golden apples. Once that's done, empty your inventory of everything except for 10 saddles and then switch to Survival mode. Start the clock, grab the first horse and bring it back to your stable – leaping the three fences as you go. The clock stops once all of your horses have been stabled.

HOW TO APPLY

To make sure your best time qualifies as an official GWR attempt, you must set up the game according to our exact specifications. You'll find detailed instructions (including videos that show you exactly what to do) at **www.guinnessworldrecords.com/minecraft** We'll also explain how to find out what the current best time is for all of these challenges and what to do with your video evidence once you've beaten the record. Good luck!

Fastest time to build an igloo in *Minecraft* Survival mode
FOR CONSOLE PLAYERS ONLY
Before you build your very own igloo, you'll need to create a superflat world with layers of snow, oak wood, cobblestone, coal ore, white wool, black wool and bedrock (make sure you create them in that order). Once you're done, load the world in Survival mode. Then, with the clock ticking, mine the necessary resources to create your igloo, which must include a bed, a crafting table, a furnace and four torches.

Your igloo must be 7 blocks wide x 5 deep x 4 high (see above). Once it's built, cover the floor with black carpet and add the bed, crafting table, furnace and torches.

ROBLOX

Why build something within a game when you can build a game instead? *Roblox* has been letting gamers do just that since 2006. That was when publisher Roblox Corporation renamed its *DynaBlocks* game-creation platform as *Roblox*. The rest, as they say, is history...

$41 MILLION

Most money paid to developers on a game-making platform
According to Roblox Corporation's statistics, as of 29 Mar 2018 it had paid out around $41 m (£29 m) to those users who had made and shared games on the platform.

Most watched *Roblox* video
A video of YouTuber "DanTDM", aka Daniel Middleton (UK, left), playing the quirky *Roblox* game *The Normal Elevator* had 19,282,228 views as of 29 Mar 2018. The 14-min video, uploaded on 27 Feb 2016, shows Dan's giant-headed avatar riding an elevator that ends up in strange locations, such as a seemingly unescapable cave and an eerie, abandoned campsite.

Highest-earning game created in *Roblox*

Welcome to Bloxburg by "Coeptus" had made more money than any *Roblox* creation as of 29 Mar 2018. In the money-spinning RPG, players can build their dream house, go to work, get together with friends and explore the city of Bloxburg.

Fastest completion of *Cleaning Simulator*

On 20 Jul 2017, budding superstar janitor "videm" (USA) completed a solo run of *Roblox*'s *Cleaning Simulator* (without moon gravity enabled) in just 22 min 45.96 sec, as verified by Speedrun.

MOST CONCURRENT PLAYERS FOR A GAME-MAKING PLATFORM

As of 28 Mar 2018, the massively multiplayer online (MMO) game-creator *Roblox* more than justified its claim to be a "social platform for play" by recording a peak of 1.7 million people playing at the same time.

On 13 Aug 2017, the user-made game *Jailbreak*, created by "badcc", aka Alex Balfanz, and "asimo3089" (both USA), had 103,000 gamers playing it at once – the **most concurrent players for a game made in *Roblox***. That's one heck of a game of cops and robbers! See below right for more on *Jailbreak*.

Most visited game created in *Roblox*

As of 29 Mar 2018, *MeepCity* by "alexnewtron" had welcomed 1,242,773,297 visitors through its doors, as verified by the official *Roblox* site. It was just ahead of *Jailbreak* (with 1,149,021,912 visitors).

Most likes for a game made in *Roblox*

Jailbreak's players have a choice: they can turn to a life of crime or choose to uphold the law. But whichever decision they take, they've clearly been arrested by the title's winning gameplay. As of 29 Mar 2018, *Jailbreak* had 1,574,303 likes and its players had logged on to play it over 100 million times. "MASSIVE!" was how *Jailbreak*'s co-creator Alex Balfanz described hitting that latter figure.

WORLD BUILDERS

1995
LEGO Fun to Build is one of the first titles released for Sega's education-focused, child-friendly Pico console. *Fun to Build* features several action-oriented mini-games that take place in a castle, under water and in space.

1997
LEGO Island (Mindscape) for the PC is an open-world game released many years before the genre really takes off. It encourages building and exploration across a variety of missions and is an early indicator of how the LEGO games of the future will play.

1998
LEGO establishes LEGO Media to publish the company's games. Under this new label, *LEGO Loco* and *LEGO Chess* are released for the PC. The former is a *Sims*-style game based around railways, while the latter weaves fantasy elements into the traditional rules of chess.

2011
A year of heavy hitters, with three releases capitalizing on huge movie franchises: *LEGO Harry Potter: Years 5–7*, *LEGO Star Wars III: The Clone Wars* and *LEGO Pirates of the Caribbean: The Video Game*.

2010
TT Games oversees the release of *LEGO Harry Potter: Years 1–4*, which also comes to mobile devices. And there's more wizardry as *LEGO Universe* (below right) arrives as the first LEGO-themed Massively Multiplayer Online (MMO) title.

2009
The relic-hunter returns in *LEGO Indiana Jones 2: The Adventure Continues*. Elsewhere, *LEGO Rock Band* rocks out, while *LEGO Battles* is LEGO's take on the real-time strategy genre.

2008
Warner Bros. Interactive Entertainment publishes *LEGO Batman: The Videogame*. Sales of 13.54 million as of 19 Apr 2018 make it the **best-selling superhero game**. *LEGO Indiana Jones: The Original Adventures* sees another icon, Indy, given the same LEGO treatment.

2012
The partnership between Warner Bros. and TT Games continues to produce well-received titles. *LEGO Batman 2: DC Super Heroes* and *LEGO The Lord of the Rings* come to every major gaming platform. The former also signifies an important LEGO debut on Nintendo's Wii U console.

2013
A bumper year for LEGO games. It displays confidence in home-grown titles such as *LEGO City Undercover* (below) for Wii U and *LEGO City Undercover: The Chase Begins* for the new and exciting Nintendo 3DS. There is only one character-licence release this year but it's a big one, as the legends of the Marvel Universe come to *LEGO Marvel Super Heroes*.

2014
The year of *The LEGO Movie* also means *The LEGO Movie Videogame*! But that's by no means all. There is *LEGO Ninjago: Nindroids*, *LEGO The Hobbit*, *LEGO Star Wars: Microfighters* and *LEGO Batman 3: Beyond Gotham*. Funcom also brings its MMO *LEGO Minifigures Online* to PC and mobile platforms.

2015
The headline-making title is the ambitious toys-to-life *LEGO Dimensions* (above), developed by TT. The console-only game mixes real-world building with in-game escapades using a "magical portal".

EVOLUTION OF LEGO® GAMES

Improvements in technology have led to huge strides in how LEGO-themed games have looked and played across the years – so much so that it's hard these days to tell the company's games and animated movies apart. Nevertheless, the LEGO philosophy of learning and development through play has prevailed across every game based on the famous building bricks. Here, we take a trip through the history and highlights of our favourite LEGO videogames from 1995 to 2018.

1999
LEGO Media enters the console market, bringing *LEGO Rock Raiders* (above) and *LEGO Racers* to the PS One. A new arrival for the PC is *LEGO Friends*, following the fortunes of a girl band called Tuff Stuff.

2000
The start of the new millennium marks the end of LEGO Media, but it goes out with a bang, releasing five PC games: *LEGO Alpha Team* (above), *LEGO My Style: Preschool*, *LEGO My Style: Kindergarten*, *LEGOLAND* and *LEGO Stunt Rally*.

2001
LEGO Software rises from the ashes of LEGO Media to release *LEGO Island 2: The Brickster's Revenge* and *LEGO Racers 2* (above) for PC, PS2 and Game Boy Advance. *LEGO Creator: Harry Potter* is LEGO's first licensed title.

2002
EA partners with LEGO to release soccer title *Soccer Mania* and vehicle stunt game *Island Xtreme Stunts*. *LEGO Creator: Harry Potter and the Chamber of Secrets* continues the new direction of games based on licensed characters.

2004–05
THQ enters the fray, publishing two Game Boy Advance titles: *LEGO Knights' Kingdom* (2004) and *Bionicle: Maze of Shadows* (2005). But the big news is the arrival of *LEGO Star Wars: The Video Game* (2005) that recreates *Star Wars* episodes 1–3. Developed by TT Games and published by Eidos, it becomes the blueprint for almost every LEGO game that follows.

2003
Argonaut, noted UK developer of *Star Fox* (*Starwing* in Europe), develops *Bionicle: The Game*, based on the *Bionicle: Mask of Light* movie. The title hits every console of the time, but is met with indifference.

2007
LEGO Star Wars: The Complete Saga is let loose: 15.33 million sales as of 19 Apr 2018 make it the **best-selling Star Wars videogame**. With a winning formula, LEGO starts looking for other popular franchises.

2006
LEGO's fruitful relationship with TT Games continues with the eagerly awaited *LEGO Star Wars II: The Original Trilogy* (LucasArts). It goes on to sell more than 7 million copies.

2016
A landmark year for blockbuster franchises as *LEGO Star Wars: The Force Awakens* and *LEGO Marvel's Avengers* both appear. The latter reaches slightly beyond its age rating to include Jessica Jones (right) in the form of a mini-figure.

2017
As well as *The LEGO Batman Movie Videogame* and *The LEGO Ninjago Movie Videogame*, *LEGO Marvel Super Heroes 2* is warmly welcomed, upping the ante with its action-packed missions and wisecracking figures.

2018
Warner Bros. announces the release of *LEGO The Incredibles*, which is timed to coincide with the opening weekend of the film *The Incredibles 2* at theatres (15 Jun in the USA, 13 Jul in Europe). *LEGO The Incredibles* is the 34th game for TT Games – the **most prolific developer of toy videogames**.

LEGO® WORLDS

What more apt a game title could there be for our World Builders chapter than *LEGO Worlds*? Warner Bros.' build-'em-up lets you unleash your inner master builder to recreate just about anything you can imagine with the world's most famous building blocks...

First completion of *LEGO Worlds*
When *LEGO Worlds* was first released to the PS4 on 7 Mar 2017, there were 62 trophies on offer, from "Pirate Playground Professional" to the holy-grail Platinum trophy "Master of Master Builders!". According to PSNProfiles, player "przondziono" (DEU) was the first to earn them all, doing so just after midnight on 21 Mar 2017, only two weeks after the game's release. The German was roughly eight minutes ahead of Brazilian gamer "leoxp2016".
Two later expansion packs, *Classic Space* and *Monsters*, raised the trophy count by another 10, and on 26 Oct 2017, "taku0123456789" (JPN) was the **first to complete *LEGO Worlds* (72 trophies)**.

Largest brick in *LEGO Worlds*
On 28 Jan 2018, the LEGO brick turned 60 years old. To celebrate this landmark, *LEGO Worlds* created a huge replica of the iconic 2 x 4 LEGO brick. At an estimated real-world size of 10 ft (3.04 m) high, 1,200 lb (544.3 kg) in weight and consisting of 133,000 pieces, the red brick – given the codename "Showcase Model (62)" – was made available for all players of the game to download.

LARGEST RECONSTRUCTION OF A REAL-WORLD STRUCTURE IN *LEGO WORLDS*

Among the world's greatest wonders are the Pyramids of Giza, the imposing resting places of the pharaohs of ancient Egypt. In Jan 2017, UK design studio Gazamo Ltd – Edward Revill-Johnson (UK), Jonas Walter (DEU) and Ushio Tokura (JPN) – scaled a new peak of achievement when recreating it virtually with a remarkable 123,000 bricks. Their tribute to Khufu's Great Pyramid – the **tallest pyramid** in the real world – was calculated to stand at around 125 m (410 ft), slightly less than the original (146 m/479 ft).

The same team used 82,448 bricks to recreate Rome's Colosseum – the **largest 1:1 reconstruction of a real-world structure** in *LEGO Worlds*. Its dimensions were 189 x 156 x 48 m (620 x 511 x 157 ft)!

First to skydive the farthest possible distance in *LEGO Worlds*

YouTuber "Sketch" and a colleague dug to the lowest point in *LEGO Worlds* (0.256 units) and built a tower to the highest point (131.040 units). On 25 Mar 2017, the pair leapt off the peak to fall the farthest possible distance. They then uploaded their free-falling accomplishment to YouTube.

2 MINUTES 36 SECONDS

"TehAwesomeGenius" set the **fastest time to achieve Discoverer Builder** in *LEGO Worlds* on 2 May 2017. The American PC gamer took 2 min 36 sec to complete the first three quests on the Pirate Playground level. By doing so, they earned the three gold bricks necessary to unlock the Steam Achievement.

Fastest land vehicle in *LEGO Worlds*

On 18 Jul 2015, Damien Fate (USA) created a flat, straight track as a way to speed-test 13 land vehicles. In a "wheelie good" run, the motorcycle was the fastest, completing the test in 4.52 sec. The tractor, steamroller and lawnmower were the slowest.

4,839 PLAYERS

MOST CONCURRENT *LEGO WORLDS* PLAYERS

When *LEGO Worlds* was first launched on Steam Early Access on 1 Jun 2015, gamers immediately took to their PCs to try it out. According to Steam Charts, as many as 4,839 players were enjoying the title at any given moment on that initial day of release. In its launch month, an average of 1,522 gamers were playing *LEGO Worlds* concurrently. This put the game among the most played LEGO titles on Steam, with only *LEGO Marvel Super Heroes* (2013) edging ahead of its figures.

MOST PROLIFIC VIDEOGAME SERIES BASED ON A TOY

The release of *LEGO Marvel Super Heroes 2* (Warner Bros.) on 14 Nov 2017 brought the total number of LEGO-based videogames to 72. LEGO first entered the gaming scene in 1995 with *LEGO Fun to Build*, a Japanese educational title for the Sega Pico – a cartridge-based computer designed for kids that was released in 1993.

Also included in the 72 were five LEGO Bionicle games, five mobile apps, numerous titles based on films and TV shows (including five *Ninjago* and six *Star Wars* games), a soccer game (*LEGO Soccer Mania*, 2002) and *LEGO Rock Band* (2009).

LEGO® ROUND-UP

With the 25th anniversary of the first LEGO title just around the corner, we pay tribute to the games that have given us the chance to re-live some of the biggest films and TV shows – enhanced by a sprinkling of the LEGO series' unique humour and gameplay.

MOST LICENCES IN A VIDEOGAME

28

Warner Bros.' *LEGO Dimensions* (2015) features 28 non-LEGO franchises: 2001: A Space Odyssey, The A-Team, Adventure Time, Back to the Future, Beetlejuice, DC Comics, Doctor Who, ET: the Extra-Terrestrial, Fantastic Beasts and Where to Find Them, The Flintstones, Ghostbusters, The Goonies, Gremlins, Harry Potter, The Jetsons, Jurassic World, Knight Rider, The Lord of the Rings, Midway Arcade, Mission: Impossible, Portal, The Powerpuff Girls, Red Dwarf, Scooby-Doo!, The Simpsons, Sonic the Hedgehog, Teen Titans Go! and The Wizard of Oz.

Most watched LEGO game video
As of 17 Jan 2018, "Izuniy"'s YouTube video "LEGO Jurassic World & Jurassic Park All Cutscenes Movie" had chalked up 61,138,438 views. It splices together the popular and comedic cutscenes from the *LEGO* adaptions of the *Jurassic Park* trilogy and *Jurassic World*.

First LEGO game made entirely from bricks
From virtual buildings and furniture to machines and vehicles, everything in Warner Bros.' *The LEGO Movie Videogame* (2014) is constructed from LEGO bricks. "We challenged ourselves to introduce a new element," said Tom Stone, Managing Director of TT Games. "[It gives] players more opportunities to interact with the world."

2 HOURS 56 MINUTES 28 SECONDS

Fastest completion of *LEGO Star Wars: The Force Awakens*
On 19 Jan 2018, France's "wRadion" completed Warner Bros.' *LEGO Star Wars: The Force Awakens* (2016) in 2 hr 56 min 28 sec, as verified by Speedrun.com. It eclipsed the mark set by "smkurki" (FIN) of 3 hr 4 min 39 sec.

MOST ACTORS REPRISING TV/FILM ROLES IN A GAME
As of 23 Oct 2017, when it was officially announced that there would be no more add-on packs, *LEGO Dimensions* had seen a total of 52 actors reprise the roles of characters who they had previously played on the big or small screen.

The stellar line-up included the 12th Dr Who Peter Capaldi (top left), original *Ghostbusters* star Dan Aykroyd (Dr Raymond Stantz, middle left) and Michael J Fox (bottom left) as *Back to the Future*'s Marty McFly.

Other notable characters were *Mission: Impossible*'s Benji Dunn (Simon Pegg), Homer Simpson (voiced by Dan Castellaneta) and LEGO Batman (Will Arnett).

Tallest mobile superhero cosplay costume
Iron Man's Hulkbuster suit – as seen in *LEGO Marvel Super Heroes 2* – was brought to life in gigantic fashion by cosplay designer Thomas DePetrillo (USA). It stood at 8 ft (2.44 m) tall when it was measured in his workshop on 6 Dec 2017. Impressively, the suit is fully mobile!

BEST OF THE REST

Here, the final pieces fall perfectly into place to close our World Builders chapter. Step this way as we unveil *Super Mario Maker*'s greatest levels, the most deadly robot in *Robocraft* and *Terraria*'s speediest player...

FIRST WINNER OF THE ROBOCRAFT SOLO LEAGUE COMPETITION

PC player "Biscuit03" swept aside fellow *Robocrafters* to be crowned victor in *Robocraft*'s (2013) inaugural Solo League Competition.

When the dust had settled on 29 Mar 2018, the Japanese gamer had achieved a Match-Making Rating (MMR) of 2,528. The figure is calculated according to the number of matches won and lost (then weighted against the skill level of fellow players) in Freejam's online robot-battler. "Biscuit03" was 73 points clear of "E2P" (CHE), who had an MMR of 2,455.

42 MINUTES 56 SECONDS

Fastest completion of *Terraria*
As well as being a world-builder, *Terraria* also has a speed-run community. On 15 Nov 2017, "BandsWithLegends" (USA) took just 42 min 56 sec to swiftly dispatch all of the Pre-Hardmode bosses (including The Twins, above), as verified by Speedrun.

Most "hearted" *LittleBigPlanet* level
"Ima_Taka" lovingly created the aquatic Bora Bora Island Water Sports level for the original *LittleBigPlanet* in Mar 2010. Receiving plaudits for its artistic merit, it had been liked by an impressive total of 328,349 players as of 3 Apr 2018.

Most blocks placed in *Trove*
When it comes to building, Thailand's "Cocoooo" is *Trove*'s (2015) numero uno. Stats supplied by Trion Worlds showed that the gamer had placed 10,821,344 blocks as of 13 Apr 2018. "Ninah" (USA) had spent the **longest time playing *Trove***, logging 10,403 hr 30 min (or 433 days) on the MMORPG!

Best-selling open-world 2D platform game
Terraria (2011) had sold over 20 million copies by the end of 2016, according to the game's official website. However, because 505 Games' 2D *Minecraft*-like adventure game is most often purchased as a digital download, the figures can't be verified through sales trackers such as VGChartz.

Even so, VGChartz still puts the number of physical copies of *Terraria* sold at a respectable 1.64 million as of 3 Apr 2018.

Most liked *Super Mario Maker* course
In the *Super Mario Maker* community, players award star ratings to levels created by others. As of 22 Feb 2018, the most popular course was "Mission: Impossible" by "MK8" (USA), with 326,921 stars. It seems gamers like their levels to be testing but not too hard, as "Mission: Impossible" had a 22.70% completion rate, earning it a difficulty rating of "Normal".

2,000 HOURS
Braden Moor (USA) created his aptly named *Super Mario Maker* stage "Trials of Death" in Jan 2016. As of 3 Apr 2018, he was still trying to beat it, despite spending over 2,000 hr on the fiendish level – the **longest time spent trying to beat a *Super Mario Maker* course**. It needs pixel-perfect precision to negotiate, and demands players use objects, such as springs, with split-second timing. Braden charts his progress on his "ChainChompBraden" Twitch channel. When – if? – he beats the stage, it will become an official *Super Mario Maker* level.

Most damage dealt in a single *Robocraft* match
As of 29 Mar 2018, PC gamer "Jiggyhound" (playing as "Jiggyhound4") inflicted 81,787 points of damage on the opposition – killing 41 enemy robots, scoring 30,000 points and topping his team's score chart, as verified by Freejam.

TOP 10

MONSTER HUNTER'S BIGGEST BEASTS

With exclusive figures provided by Capcom, we reveal the 10 tallest terrors looking to take a bite out of you in *Monster Hunter: World*. Though quite how Capcom managed to get the game's ferocious beasts to stand still while they measured them we'll never know!

1

1 ZORAH MAGDAROS
257.64 m/845 ft 3 in

Main habitat: N/A
Type: Elder dragon

2 XENO'JIIVA
45.09 m/147 ft 11 in

Main habitat: Elder's Recess
Type: Elder dragon

3 DIABLOS
20.96 m/68 ft 9 in

Main habitat: Wildspire Waste
Type: Flying wyvern

4 VAAL HAZAK
20.95 m/68 ft 8 in

Main habitat: Rotten Vale
Type: Elder dragon

5 DEVILJHO
20.63 m/67 ft 8 in

Main habitat: All over
Type: Brute wyvern

6	7	8	9	10
URAGAAN	**BAZELGEUSE**	**KUSHALA DAORA**	**NERGIGANTE**	**RADOBAAN**
20.58 m/67 ft 6 in	**19.28 m/63 ft 3 in**	**19.13 m/62 ft 9 in**	**18.48 m/60 ft 7 in**	**18.03 m/59 ft 1 in**
Main habitat: Elder's Recess	**Main habitat:** All over	**Main habitat:** Elder's Recess	**Main habitat:** Elder's Recess	**Main habitat:** Rotten Vale
Type: Brute wyvern	**Type:** Flying wyvern	**Type:** Elder dragon	**Type:** Elder dragon	**Type:** Brute wyvern

A WORLD OF GAMING

Videogame-themed museums, restaurants, bars and theme parks are opening their doors across the world. Here, we provide a guide to the venues that should be on any videogame tourist's hit list…

LOADING
Where: London, UK
Across multiple London-based venues, visitors can enjoy game-themed cocktails – how about a non-alcoholic "*Deus Ex* on the beach"? – while playing games from a range of consoles and eras. In warmer weather, guests can even carry on gaming in the garden.

NATIONAL VIDEOGAME MUSEUM
Where: Frisco, USA
After starting out as a travelling exhibition, the NVM found a permanent home in 2016 for its collection of over 100,000 games and gaming items. Among its many treasured pieces is a golden *Punch-Out!!* cartridge from 1987.

THE NATIONAL VIDEOGAME ARCADE
Where: Nottingham, UK
In 2016, the gaming community came together to save the NVA from closure. Across three floors, it houses over 70 playable games, ranging from 1970s coin-ops to *Mission Control* (above) – a game about making games.

CHUCK E. CHEESE'S
Where: San Jose, USA
Launched on 17 May 1977 by Atari co-founder Nolan Bushnell, the Chuck E. Cheese's Pizza Time Theatre was the **first game-themed restaurant**. The idea to create a venue that appealed to kids and their parents caught on – there are now over 600 branches.

DAVE & BUSTER'S
Where: Dallas, USA
In 1982, James "Buster" Corley and David Corriveau opened a revolutionary establishment that catered for appetites for both eating and gaming. The first Dave & Buster's was in Dallas, Texas, but there are now more than 110 branches across North America.

FUNSPOT
Where: Weirs Beach, USA
Founded in 1952 by Bob Lawton, Funspot is the **largest videogame arcade** currently open. As of 12 Jan 2016, its 70,000 sq ft (6,500 m^2) of gamer heaven housed 581 new and classic titles over three floors. Its Classic Arcade Museum stores a further 250 cabinets from the '70s and '80s, with games such as *Wheels II* (1975, left) and *Space Invaders* (1978, right).

BARCADE
Where: Brooklyn, USA
Opening its doors in 2004, Barcade was founded by four friends who enjoyed classic arcade games and beer. It struck a chord with like-minded people who wanted a place to revisit their favourite games. In Feb 2013, George Leutz (USA) set the **highest marathon score on arcade *Q*bert** (37,163,080) after spending hours practising in Barcade.

THE STRONG NATIONAL MUSEUM OF PLAY
Where: Rochester, USA
Opened in 1968 by collector Margaret Woodbury Strong, this museum holds 20,000 gaming items and is the home of the World Video Game Hall of Fame. The **first games inducted into the Hall of Fame** were *PAC-Man*, *DOOM*, *Pong*, *Super Mario Bros.*, *Tetris* and *World of Warcraft* – all in 2015.

COMPUTERSPIELE-MUSEUM BERLIN
Where: Berlin, Germany
The **first permanent game museum** has had a tumultuous time. It opened in 1997, closed to go online-only in 2000, then reopened in 2011. An East German *Poly-Play* arcade cabinet (above), which was built in 1985, is one of the rarest objects to be found across the museum's 300 exhibits.

ANGRY BIRDS THEME PARK
Where: Tampere, Finland
The *Angry Birds*-themed Särkänniemi adventure park (above) opened on 28 Apr 2012. Since then, 10 more *Angry Birds* attractions have opened across the world – the **most theme parks based on a videogame**.

DEMACIA
Where: Chongqing, China
Named after a kingdom in *League of Legends*, this *LoL*-themed restaurant serves food and drinks inspired by the game. Anyone for a deep-fried Skarner (scorpion)?

POKÉPARK (AKA POKÉMON THE PARK)
Where: Nagoya, Japan
The **first official theme park based on a game** was a temporary affair that was open in Mar–Sep 2005. It later appeared in Chinese Taipei in Jun 2006. Attractions included Mudkip's Big Splash and the Pichu Brothers' Rascal Railway.

8BIT CAFE
Where: Tokyo, Japan
It can be hard to find this retro gaming bar (on the fifth floor of a commercial building with only a small sign indicating its existence), but perseverance pays off. It's small but charming – and offers a game collection full of nostalgia.

CAPCOM BAR
Where: Tokyo, Japan
Sadly, this Tokyo bar closed in Feb 2018. It's a shame – its culinary highlights included a brain-shaped *Resident Evil*-themed cake, complete with knife sticking out of it (above). Visitors could also play a huge array of Capcom games.

MELTDOWN
Where: Paris, France
The first Meltdown bar opened in Paris in 2012. Since then, more have sprung up in Belgium, Canada, Germany, Hungary, Italy, Spain and the UK. With a strong focus on eSports, the venues stream live tournaments and each branch has its own eSports teams.

MUSEUM OF SOVIET ARCADE MACHINES
Where: Moscow, Russia
Across two venues – one in Moscow, the other in St Petersburg – this museum holds 40 Soviet-era games, including the submarine simulator *Morskoi Boi* (*Sea Battle*, right). Old 15-kopek coins are given to visitors as part of the entry fee.

THE NOSTALGIA BOX
Where: Perth, Australia
The focus of this museum falls on home consoles, including rarities such as 1982's Vectrex (above). Its collection is displayed in chronological order, starting with the 1970s. More than just preserving the past, it also hosts monthly game-testing events, to which local developers can bring their latest demos.

SUPER NINTENDO WORLD
Where: Osaka, Japan
Mario, Luigi, Princess Peach and Bowser will feature in this collaboration between Nintendo and Universal Studios. The plan is for Super Nintendo World to open at Universal Studios in Osaka, Japan, by 2020. Similar attractions will then open their doors at Universal's parks in Florida and California.

RETRO GAMING

Rip-roaring sales of Nintendo's Super NES Classic Mini suggest that there's a vibrant market for the iconic games of the past. Whether your thing is old arcade classics or vintage console titles, there's almost always a new high score to beat or long-lost secret to discover...

GAME
& WATCH

Nintendo

GAME A

◄ LEFT

" THE BEST RESPONSE WAS FROM ONE DAD. HE HAD AN AWESTRUCK LOOK ON HIS FACE AND JUST SAID 'IT'S BEAUTIFUL!' "

DR THOMAS TILLEY

PUS

155

GAME A

ALAR

GAME B

ACL

TIME

RIGHT ▶

E SCR

LARGEST PLAYABLE GAME & WATCH DEVICE

Now a computer scientist in Australia, Dr Thomas Tilley can still recall the excitement he felt as a kid back in the 1980s when he was given a Nintendo Game & Watch by his aunt. Memories of that gift inspired him to choose a Game & Watch – complete with the same *Octopus* game – when he began a project in May 2017 to build an oversized gaming device.

For the screen, he used the family TV and recreated the gold-coloured brushed aluminium of the device's front face with curtains his mother-in-law was throwing away. Impressively, he even translated the Polish instructions of the software used to emulate the Game & Watch's functions so he could make the device work.

"When I put the four sides together and got an idea of just how big it was, I thought: Wow! I wonder if this is big enough for a world record?" As it turns out, it was. The Game & Watch was 193 x 116 x 14 cm (75.9 x 45.6 x 5.5 in) when its dimensions were verified on 21 Oct 2017 by a qualified surveyor.

RETRO PLATFORMERS

The platformers of the 1980s and '90s were like the open-world games of today – flagship titles that pushed gameplay boundaries and let us explore gaming environments in ways we'd never done before. Their visual prowess might have faded over time, but their gameplay burns as brightly as ever.

FASTEST COMPLETION OF *SUPER METROID*

Super Nintendo player "zoast" (PLW) finished Nintendo's peerless 1994 action platformer *Super Metroid* in 41 min 23 sec on 4 Feb 2018 – paying short shrift to both space pirates and Mother Brain alike.

The run, as verified by Speedrun, took the speedster to the top of the leaderboard at the expense of UK gamer "Behemoth87", who had set a time of 41 min 33 sec on 13 Nov 2017.

First game with a grappling hook
Unable to jump, *Bionic Commando*'s (Capcom, 1987) Nathan Spencer (below) relied on his mechanical arm for navigating the gaps between platforms and pulling himself up to high ledges from the ground.

FIRST *SONIC THE HEDGEHOG* GAME FOR A NINTENDO CONSOLE

Two decades ago, it was unthinkable that Sonic would ever appear on a Nintendo console, so fierce was the rivalry between Sega and Nintendo. But the unthinkable happened on 20 Dec 2001 when Sega's 3D platformer *Sonic Adventure 2: Battle* was released for Nintendo's GameCube.

EXPANDED FRANCHISE

Netflix's four-part *Castlevania* animation, released in Jul 2017, was the **highest-rated TV show based on a game** as of 8 Mar 2018. It had a score of 8/10 from 13,184 Internet Movie Database (IMDb) reviews.

24 YEARS

Longest time to release an NES game
On 8 Apr 2017, UK developer duo The Oliver Twins released their NES platformer *Mystery World Dizzy*. This was 24 years after the game was originally due to come out. Although it had been finished in 1993, reported financial difficulties meant that it never emerged. The game was finally distributed as an online flash title by its original creators to celebrate the 30th anniversary of the *Dizzy* series.

2 HOURS 32 MINUTES

In a video uploaded on 8 May 2015, YouTuber "AuraPuffs" beat *Mega Man X* and *Mega Man X2* at the same time using one controller connected to the two games. The **fastest synchronized completion of *Mega Man X* and *X2*** took 2 hr 32 min and was performed without speed-running tools, relying solely on the gamer's talent for multi-tasking. Of the run, "AuraPuffs" said it was "something intense and challenging I wanted to put myself to the test with".

Fastest completion of *Battletoads*
Rare's 1991 action platformer is widely regarded as one of the toughest games ever made, with the majority of players failing to get anywhere close to its end and the battle with the Dark Queen and her army of mutants. American speedster "jc583" not only reached the climax, but did so in just 12 min 42.767 sec on 10 Jan 2018, as verified by Speedrun. The gamer was disappointed with the run

in a couple of sections but said "everything else decent". It shaved just over 2 sec off the previous best, set by "TheMexicanRunner", aka Piotr Delgado Kusielczuk (MEX/POL).

First Disney platform game
There are many Disney-inspired platformers, but the first was 1988's *Mickey Mousecapade* for the NES. In the side-scroller, our outsized-eared hero tries to defy the dastardly efforts of famous villains from

Disney's cinematic hits by rescuing a young girl.

First videogame with a "double jump"
Donkey Kong introduced jumping to the platforming genre back in 1981, but it was Namco's *Dragon Buster* in 1985 that took the art to the next level with "double jumping". The game's hero, called Clovis, was the first digital hero to pull off the physically impossible move, inspiring gamers to reach new heights.

Fastest blindfolded completion of *Donkey Kong Country 2*
On 29–30 Oct 2016, a blindfolded "katun24" (NLD) completed a "102%" (the game's equivalent to 100%) play-through of the 1995 Super Nintendo platformer in just 16 hr 3 min 16 sec. The Dutch gamer's achievement stood as the quickest as of 8 Mar 2018. "katun24" told us: "It was extremely exhausting, so I decided to only do any% runs after that!"

ARCADE GAMES

It isn't all that long ago that the best way to play games the way they were meant to be enjoyed was by depositing coin after coin into arcade machines. Consoles lead the way when it comes to providing our gaming entertainment now, but there are still those who feel the lure of the arcade…

MOST COLLECTED ARCADE COIN-OP

Fans of iconic games have enjoyed a long-standing love affair with *Ms. PAC-Man*. According to statistics published by the Vintage Arcade Preservation Society (VAPS, part of the Museum of the Game), there were 1,544 registered owners of original *Ms. PAC-Man* arcade cabinets as of 10 Apr 2018. That's more than any fellow golden-age games, including *Donkey Kong* (1,270), *Centipede* (1,233) and *PAC-Man* (1,084).

According to its creator, Toru Iwatani, *PAC-Man* (1980) was designed to be violence-free in a bid to attract women into arcades. On 13 Jan 1982, the trick was repeated with the debut of *Ms. PAC-Man* in the USA – the hair-bow-sporting heroine became the **first playable female character in a videogame**.

1,247,700 POINTS

No one can question the commitment of American gamer Robbie Lakeman. After being challenged by a friend to see how high he could rise in the *Donkey Kong* rankings, he embarked on a regime of intense practice that saw him surge to the top. He set his first record score in 2014. Since then, he has lost and regained the hotly contested **highest score on *Donkey Kong*** crown several times. He took back the record on 2 Feb 2018 with an outrageous score of 1,247,700 points – a total that was verified by Twin Galaxies on 23 Mar.

Longest game marathon on a classic arcade game
At an arcade in New Jersey, USA, gamer George Leutz (right) played Gottlieb's 1982 pyramid puzzler *Q*bert* for 84 hr 48 min straight. He began his multi-day marathon on 14 Feb 2013 and finally finished his stint on 18 Feb.

Longest-running series of arcade coin-op games
Almost 39 years elapsed between the release of the original *Space Invaders* coin-op in Jun 1978 and Jan 2017's launch (via many sequels) of *Space Invaders Frenzy* (above). The latest arcade cabinet was developed by Taito and Raw Thrills.

EXPANDED FRANCHISE

PAC-Man inspired the **first videogame character merchandise**. An initial range of PAC-Man products went on sale in 1981 and numbered close to 200 even as early as 1982. On the left is just a small selection…

Largest *PAC-Man* arcade machine
The aptly named *World's Largest PAC-Man*, a joint venture between Bandai Namco and Raw Thrills, was released in 2016. It has a giant screen that's 2.67 m (8 ft 9 in) tall and 1.71 m (5 ft 7 in) wide.

Longest-running pinball event
As of its most recent event, held in Chicago, Illinois, USA, on 11–15 Oct 2017, Pinball Expo had run for 32 consecutive years. According to Twin Galaxies' founder Walter Day, the event is a "pioneer for the pinball industry and was influential in bringing the pinball hobby international acclaim". After a recent dispute between its owners, the Expo has been confirmed once more. It will take place on 17–21 Oct 2018 in the same location as in previous years.

Longest-running coin-op arcade manufacturer
In Jul 1973, Taito launched its first arcade coin-op, the black-and-white, ball-and-paddle game *Elepong*. In the same month, Sega also released *Pong-Tron*. This means that both manufacturers share a 45-year history of producing arcade machines.

First television game show to involve videogames
Starcade was an American game show on the TBS network in which contestants competed against each other by playing arcade games. First aired in 1982, it continued until 1984, even surviving the famous videogames crash of 1983. There were 130 episodes over three seasons and its appeal has endured. Media company Shout! Factory acquired the rights to the show in 2017, so there remains the possibility that *Starcade* – in some form – could return to screens.

Largest arcade machine
The largest arcade machine is 4.4 m (14 ft 5 in) high, 1.93 m (6 ft 4 in) wide and 1.06 m (3 ft 5 in) deep – which means it's roughly three times larger than a standard arcade cabinet. No wonder its creator, Jason Camberis (USA), calls it his "Arcade Deluxe". Just as we were going to press, the same maker contacted us to say he'd built an even larger machine! Look out for more on that in next year's *Gamer's Edition*…

RAREST *SONIC THE HEDGEHOG* GAME
The Japan-only *Waku Waku Sonic Patrol Car* (1991) was a Sonic game built into a cartoony cop car (right). In the seldom-seen game, Sonic is a cop trying to keep the streets safe from Dr Robotnik. A version of the game was later published online by an owner of the coin-op.

FACT!

In 1984, the Grand Prix Race-O-Rama Arcade in Fort Lauderdale, Florida, USA, had 844 arcade games. That figure rose to 1,200 when the business moved to a nearby venue – making it the **largest videogame arcade ever.**

SUPER MARIO BROS.

It's-a him, Mario! Everyone knows and loves Mario, from those gamers who grew up in the 1980s and were raised on his classic arcade and NES adventures, to a brand-new generation of gamers who have been won over by his continuing series of platformers, sports games, RPGs and more...

Fastest completion of *Super Mario Bros.*
On 16 Feb 2018, as verified by Speedrun.com, "Kosmicd12" (USA) set a time of 4 min 56.462 sec. "Finally," he said, clearly relieved at shaving 0.066 sec off the previous record time set by "darbian".

Fastest 120-star completion of *Super Mario 64*
Collecting all of *Super Mario 64*'s stars inspires keenly contested speed-runs. On 8 Feb 2018, Allan "cheese05" Alvarez (ESP) sped through in a time of just 1 hr 39 min 19 sec.

Fastest completion of *Super Mario Sunshine* (120 Shines)
There's nothing ordinary at all about "AverageTrey". On 26 Jan 2018, the American was the first gamer to collect all of *Sunshine*'s Shines in a time of less than 3 hr (2 hr 59 min 58 sec).

Fastest completion of *Super Mario Odyssey*
The speediest no-assist completion of Mario's latest adventure was achieved by "Nicroveda" (CAN) on 6 Mar 2018 in 1 hr 3 min 33 sec. The Canadian gamer's time cut 14 sec off the previous record.

EXPANDED FRANCHISE

A Mario movie is in the pipeline. Nintendo has revealed it's held talks with Universal Pictures and Illumination Entertainment – the studio behind the Minions movies – to create a new big-screen animated adventure with its moustachioed mascot. Bowser better watch out!

Most expensive costume in *Super Mario Odyssey*
As of 17 Jan 2018, splashing out on a Skeleton suit in the Crazy Cap store on the Switch game would set you back 9,999 gold coins. The amount is also the most gold coins that Mario can hold at once in Nintendo's smash-hit platformer.

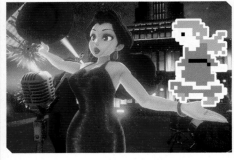

LONGEST TIME FOR A CHARACTER'S DEBUT IN A *SUPER MARIO* GAME

Despite being part of Nintendo's heritage since starring as Mario's original love interest in *Donkey Kong* (1981), Pauline waited patiently for 36 long years before appearing in a bona fide *Super Mario* game. She stars as the mayoress of New Donk City in 2017's *Super Mario Odyssey*. As you can see in the snapshots of Pauline from 1981 (inset) and 2017, the character has certainly embraced her glamorous side while waiting.

215 GAMES

Most ubiquitous game character
Proving that you can't keep a good man down, Mario had been in 215 distinct titles as of 27 Feb 2018 (excluding remakes and re-releases). How many Mario games can you name from the selection pictured below? Naturally, the answers are on p.215.

FACT!

In Nov 2017, Super Mario Cereal brought gaming to the breakfast table. The Nintendo collaboration with Kellogg's featured mushroom-shaped marshmallows, while the packaging doubled as an amiibo.

MARIO'S MOST CRITICALLY ACCLAIMED

The first *Super Mario* game to take everyone's favourite Italian plumber into outer space also received out-of-this-world review scores. The planet-hopping *Super Mario Galaxy*, released for Nintendo Wii in 2007, had an aggregate review score of 97.64% from 78 reviews, according to GameRankings. This made *Super Mario Galaxy* not only the **most critically acclaimed Mario game**, but also the **most critically acclaimed videogame ever**, as of 27 Feb 2018.

The score was all the more impressive for the fact that it's based on such a large number of reviews. One reviewer gushed: "The amount of colour, vibrancy and pure imagination literally seeping from every corner of this game is wondrous."

First perfect score on *Arcade Archives Mario Bros.*
Hamster Corporation's *Arcade Archives* series recreates iconic titles for modern gamers. The *Mario Bros.* (2017) revival for Switch was perfected by US gamer Isaiah TriForce Johnson, who registered the highest possible score ahead of anyone else, reaching 999,990 on 16 Oct 2017.

Most fan-made games based on a game universe
As of 28 Feb 2018, there were 632 "full" fan-made games based on the Mario videogame universe available

to download and play at Mario Fan Games Galaxy. The library held a wide range of genres, from puzzlers to platformers. Games included *Mario Pong, Luigi and the Quest for Nothing, First Person Mario* and the fighting game *Mario vs. Luigi*.

Fastest blindfolded completion of *Super Mario World*
Despite being blindfolded, on 24 May 2017 gamer "katun24" (NLD) successfully navigated the 1990 SNES classic in 13 min 31 sec. "katun24", who describes himself as hailing from "Northwest Quackistan" on his Twitter account

(hence the duck avatar he uses online), often streams blindfolded speed-run attempts on Twitch.

Rarest *Super Mario* game
In 1991, Nintendo toured colleges across America with the *Nintendo Campus Challenge* game as part of a national videogame competition. Following the tournament, the special cartridges created for the tour were destroyed – save one. This was retained by a Nintendo employee and sold to US collector Rob Walters in 2006. On 8 Oct 2009, the game was resold on eBay for $20,100 (£12,635).

RETRO ROUND-UP

Just as events in history have helped to shape the future, so too have the games of the past inspired the games we play today. Here, we celebrate the amazing games of yesteryear that have had an important role in perfecting the formula of the games we love today.

LONGEST TIME TO RELEASE A SUPER NINTENDO GAME

A playable demo of space-based shooter *Star Fox 2* wowed crowds at a trade show in Tokyo, Japan, in 1995. The hotly anticipated title missed its release date later that year, however, and later vanished from Nintendo's schedule. This lost classic was finally released on 29 Sep 2017, when it was included as one of the pre-loaded games bundled with the

Nintendo Super NES Classic Mini – a gap of 22 years. Despite 1993's *Star Fox* (*Starwing* in Europe) being a commercial and critical success, its sequel was cancelled by Nintendo, with the reason generally attributed to the publisher's belief that *Star Fox 2* would run the risk of being overshadowed by the imminent launch of the N64 and its higher-quality visuals.

Most prolific 8-bit game developers
From 1984 until 1992, Philip and Andrew Oliver (aka The Oliver Twins) were behind no fewer than 26 commercially released games for 8-bit computers and consoles. Taking into account the different platforms at that time, they actually created 49 8-bit games, but some of these were unreleased titles that never saw the light of day. See also p.123.

MOST PROLIFIC MOVIE-TO-VIDEOGAME STAR

As of 26 Sep 2017, 13 individual movies starring Arnold Schwarzenegger had been adapted for commercially licensed games featuring his character: 1984's *Conan the Destroyer* (loosely tied in to the 1984 game *Conan: Hall of Volta*), *The Terminator* (1984), *Predator* (1987), *The Running Man* (1987), *Red Heat* (1988), *Total Recall* (1990), *Terminator 2: Judgment Day* (1991), *Last Action Hero* (1993), *True Lies* (1994), *Batman & Robin* (1997), *Terminator 3: Rise of the Machines* (2003), *The Expendables 2* (2012) and *Terminator Genisys* (2015). When he said "I'll be back", Arnie wasn't kidding!

Fastest completion of Dam on *GoldenEye 007* (Agent difficulty)
On 27 Sep 2002, Bryan Bosshardt (USA) completed the Dam stage on *GoldenEye 007* (1997) in just 53 sec. This record remained unbeaten for the next 15 years and was thought unsurpassable. That was until Karl Jobst (AUS) posted 52 sec on 2 Dec 2017, as verified by Speedrun. "I'm just shaking, this is insane," he said after shaving 1 sec off.

Fastest doubles completion of *Tetris: The Absolute – The Grand Master 2 PLUS*
On 1 May 2017, the two-man team of "aperturegrillz" and "KevinDDR" (both USA) smashed through the arcade puzzler – an upgraded version of Arika's arcade game released in 2000 – in a time of 3 min 17.6 sec, as verified by Speedrun.

Highest score on *Nintendo Campus Challenge*
Paul J Tesi (USA) – aka "Megaretroman" – achieved a score of 18,748,000 on a reproduction of the rare NES game *Nintendo Campus Challenge*, which was originally created by Nintendo for use in a US gaming competition in 1991. His score was verified by Twin Galaxies on 8 Nov 2017.

Best-selling Super NES videogame by a second-party developer
Rare might make Xbox One games such as *Sea of Thieves* now, but before Microsoft bought Rare on 24 Sep 2002, it was closely tied to Nintendo. It operated as a second-party developer, which means its games were published by Nintendo. The Rare-developed Super NES game *Donkey Kong Country* (1994) had sold 9.3 million copies as of 22 Jan 2018, as verified by VGChartz.

Most expensive game console
Were inflation to be taken into account, the ill-fated 3DO would be the most expensive console ever. It launched in 1993 with an RRP of $699 (£464). If this price point was matched as of 8 Mar 2018, its retail value would stand at $1,199.02 (£863.36)! No wonder it was discontinued in 1996.

752,668

Highest score on *Tetris* for Game Boy
UK gamer Alex Holbrook racked up 752,668 points on the famous block-builder, as verified by Twin Galaxies on 25 Jun 2017. "Getting a bit messy. Some nice saves," he said upon hitting the 600,000 mark during his record-breaking effort. He's not done yet, either, saying: "I hope to submit an even higher score in the near future."

First Star Wars game
Based on the second film in the epic space saga, *The Empire Strikes Back* (Parker Brothers) was released in 1982 (two years after the movie) for the Atari 2600 and Intellivision.

FIRST GAME TO USE REAL-TIME SYNTHESIZED SPEECH

"It talks!" boasted the box art for Mattel's 1982 space-combat simulator *Space Spartans*. The game used the $100 Intellivoice voice synthesis module for the Mattel Intellivision console to give a voice to the ship's computer, so that it could warn players of incoming enemies.

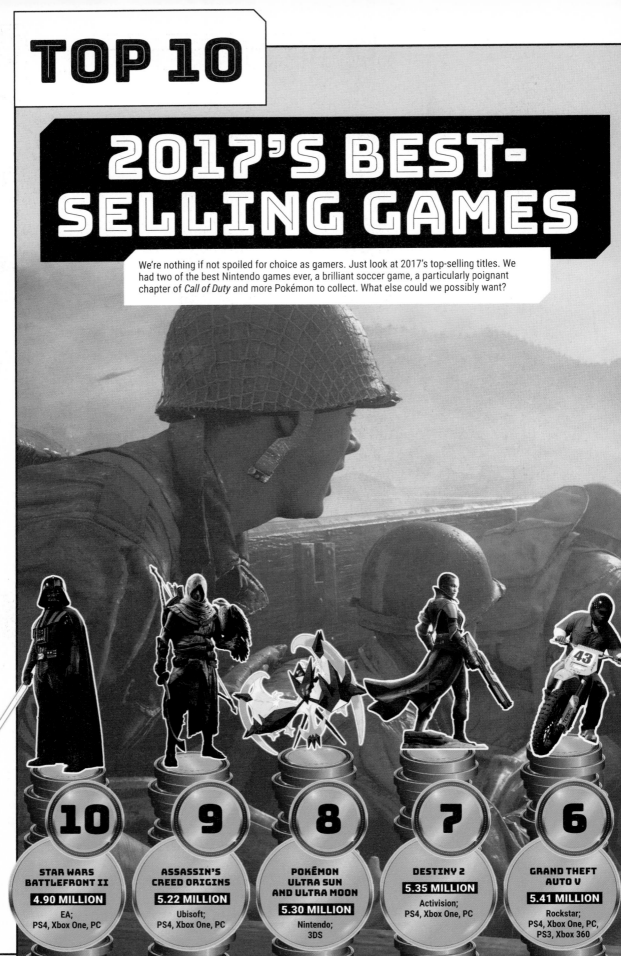

2017'S BEST-SELLING GAMES

We're nothing if not spoiled for choice as gamers. Just look at 2017's top-selling titles. We had two of the best Nintendo games ever, a brilliant soccer game, a particularly poignant chapter of *Call of Duty* and more Pokémon to collect. What else could we possibly want?

10
STAR WARS BATTLEFRONT II
4.90 MILLION
EA;
PS4, Xbox One, PC

9
ASSASSIN'S CREED ORIGINS
5.22 MILLION
Ubisoft;
PS4, Xbox One, PC

8
POKÉMON ULTRA SUN AND ULTRA MOON
5.30 MILLION
Nintendo;
3DS

7
DESTINY 2
5.35 MILLION
Activision;
PS4, Xbox One, PC

6
GRAND THEFT AUTO V
5.41 MILLION
Rockstar;
PS4, Xbox One, PC, PS3, Xbox 360

The **best-selling game ever** is Nintendo's *Wii Sports* (2006). It had sold a wholly ridiculous 82.64 million copies as of 8 Jan 2018. The fact that it was bundled with the hugely popular Wii console certainly helped.

5
MARIO KART 8 DELUXE
6.44 MILLION
Nintendo;
Switch

4
THE LEGEND OF ZELDA: BREATH OF THE WILD
7.49 MILLION
Nintendo;
Switch, Wii U

3
SUPER MARIO ODYSSEY
7.76 MILLION
Nintendo;
Switch

2
FIFA 18
13.44 MILLION
EA;
PS4, Xbox One, Switch, PC, PS3, Xbox 360

1
CALL OF DUTY: WWII
17.12 MILLION
Activision;
PS4, Xbox One, PC

ABOUT A GAME BOY

On 21 Apr 2019, Nintendo's industry-changing portable console, the Game Boy, celebrates its 30th birthday. First going on sale in Nintendo's Japanese heartlands, the handheld was a phenomenon – with amazing games, groundbreaking peripherals and brilliant successors, as our timeline shows…

1989

Videogames will never be the same, as 21 Apr marks the arrival of the Game Boy in Japan. The 8-bit portable console can display four shades of green on its 160 x 144-pixel display.

1989

The blockbuster tile-stacking game *Tetris* is among the Game Boy's North American launch titles on 31 Jul. It's compatible with the Game Link Cable that lets two players play at once.

1994

The Super Game Boy is released in Jun. The adapter allows gamers to play their Game Boy cartridges on a Super Nintendo console, letting them experience the games on the big screen.

1999

Pokémon Gold and *Silver* is the hotly anticipated, critically acclaimed and best-selling sequel to *Pokémon Red* and *Blue*. It goes on to shift a total of 23.1 million units on the Game Boy Color.

1999

The final game released for the Game Boy in North America and Europe is *Pokémon Yellow*. It's a version of *Pokémon Red* and *Blue* that allows trainers to choose Pikachu from the start.

1999

The Game Boy Transfer Pak allows data to be transferred between the Game Boy and N64. It's chief use is to transfer Pokémon between *Pokémon Red* and *Blue* and *Pokémon Stadium*.

2001

The Mobile Game Boy Adapter is a Japan-only peripheral that allows Game Boy Color and Advance owners to link their mobile phones to trade and battle in the new *Pokémon Crystal*.

2001

The Game Boy Advance (GBA) sees Nintendo's handheld enter the 32-bit era. It sells more than 81 million units to become one of the best-selling consoles ever (see pp.16–17).

2001

Going on sale on 21 Jul for the GBA, *Mario Kart: Super Circuit* is soon one of the best-selling non-*Pokémon* games on any Game Boy system. It sells nearly 5.5 million copies around the world.

2017

The groundbreaking Nintendo Switch is released on 3 Mar. It unites Nintendo's home- and handheld-console heritage by letting gamers play on the go or on a TV.

2011

On 26 Feb, Nintendo's portables embrace the third dimension with the release of the Nintendo 3DS. Game Boy and Game Boy Color games can be bought from the 3DS' online eShop.

2005

End of the line – the Game Boy Micro is the last Game Boy console to be released by Nintendo. It features changeable face plates to enable owners to customize it as they please.

GAME BOYS: BIGGEST VS SMALLEST

The **largest Game Boy**, built by Belgian tech student Ilhan Ünal (near right), measures 1.01 x 0.62 x 0.2 m (3 ft 3 in x 2 ft x 7 in). In contrast, the **smallest Game Boy**, created by Jeroen Domburg (NLD), is just 54 mm (2 in) long (far right).

1996

Almost seven years into the Game Boy's life, *Pokémon Red* and *Green* proves a huge hit. Named *Pokémon Red* and *Blue* everywhere else, it becomes the **best-selling Game Boy videogame**.

1996

The petite Game Boy Pocket is released. It cuts the battery requirements from four AAs to two AAAs and addresses the "ghosting" effect that blurred graphics on the original.

1998

Released in Japan only, the Game Boy Light has a back-lit screen so gamers can more easily play in the dark. Among the numerous versions is an "Astro Boy" model with a clear plastic case.

1998

The Japan-only Super Game Boy 2 is released. It corrects a barely perceptible fault with the original 1994 Super Game Boy that made games run 2.4% faster than they were supposed to.

1998

The Game Boy Color is the **first backwards-compatible handheld console** (in this case with the Game Boy). It's capable of showing up to 56 different colours simultaneously.

1998

The Game Boy Camera add-on can take black-and-white digital images at a resolution of 128 x 112 pixels. The Game Boy Printer can then print them on to thermal paper.

2001

The Nintendo e-Reader lets owners of the GBA scan store-bought cards to play classic NES games or find new opponents to battle in 2002's *Pokémon Ruby* and *Sapphire*.

2002

Harry Potter and the Chamber of Secrets is the last game for the Game Boy Color released in North America. It calls humans "non-magical people" rather than use the term "Muggles".

2002

Pokémon Ruby and *Sapphire* is released. Once again, the Pokémon game takes the world by storm and becomes the **best-selling GBA game**. As of 4 Apr 2018, it had sold 15.85 million units.

2004

The Nintendo DS arrives on 21 Nov. It's the first Nintendo handheld console to launch without any Game Boy branding and becomes the GBA's long-term successor.

2003

The Game Boy Player lets users play Game Boy, Game Boy Color and GBA games on the Nintendo GameCube. The peripheral connects to the bottom of the home console.

2003

Released globally in 2003, the GBA SP is an upgraded version of the GBA. It's the **first handheld console with a rechargeable battery** and it has a popular clamshell design.

SPORTS

No matter what your favourite sport is, we've got something for you. Do you like soccer? We've got you covered. American football? Yes! Basketball, baseball or ice hockey? Yes, yes and yes! Death-defying stunt-bike racing off the edges of cliffs? Of course!

MOST PS4 TROPHIES

Of all the millions of PS4 players, "DEOSS77" (RUS) had, as of 3 Apr 2018, outfought, out-thought, outplayed, outrun, outjumped, outdriven, outshot and basically out-everythinged every rival to earn 22,578 PS4 trophies – more than anyone else.

As verified by PSNProfiles, the haul was made up of 12,680 Bronze trophies, 6,113 Silver and 3,248 Gold. The gamer also had 537 coveted Platinum trophies – awards that are bestowed only once every other trophy a game has to offer has been achieved.

"DEOSS77" had accumulated them at a rate of 18.39 per day and had completed 971 of the 972 games he'd played. For the curious, Daedalic Entertainment's 2017 point-and-click adventure *Ken Follett's The Pillars of the Earth* was the only one he'd yet to finish.

The rarest non-Platinum trophy in his collection was "Is There Anything You Can't Do?", a Silver trophy from *Trials Fusion* (main picture). It's awarded to players who complete every track challenge in Ubisoft's 2014 motorcycle-stunt game. As of the above date, only 0.1% of PS4 players had achieved it.

AMERICAN FOOTBALL

Players armed with a winning mix of savvy strategy and raw power can take themselves all the way to the sport's ultimate showdown – the Super Bowl. But there can only be one winner in terms of NFL videogames – EA's mega-successful *Madden* series.

SPORTS

BEST-SELLING US SPORTS GAME SERIES

The mass appeal of the crunching action in the *Madden NFL* series had seen EA's gridiron franchise amass total global sales of 133.12 million units as of 6 Mar 2018, according to VGChartz. It's second only to EA's *FIFA Soccer* franchise as the best-selling videogame sports series.

It's also the **longest-running sports videogame series**, having kicked off with *John Madden Football* for the Apple II PC on 1 Jun 1988 and launching its latest entry (*Madden*

NFL 18) on 25 Aug 2017 – 29 years 85 days later.

The **best-selling American sports game** was *Madden NFL 07* (2006). As of 6 Mar 2018, the game had racked up Super Bowl-winning sales of 10.03 million copies across 10 platforms. *Madden NFL 07* featured new juking and spinning controls that proved a hit with fans. This meant that skilled players could spin out of tackles and evade opposing defenders in a true-to-life way.

First arcade cabinet based on EA's *Madden NFL* franchise Shipped to select arcades and bars in Aug 2004, *Madden NFL Football* supported up to four players at once and featured accurate 2004/05 rosters that could be updated online.

$370,000 WINNINGS

Madden professional eSports player Eric "Problem" Wright (USA) was the **highest-earning sports game player** as of 6 Mar 2018. As verified by eSportsearnings.com, he had won $370,000 (£267,777) in prize money. His most lucrative win was in 2013's Virgin Gaming MADDEN Challenge, when he walked away with the top prize of $140,000 (£88,859).

First TV series based on a sports videogame
Madden Nation was a 2005 TV show that focused on gamers playing against each other in *Madden NFL* in a knockout competition, with $100,000 (£57,688) to the winner. Actual NFL players occasionally competed as well. Debuting on the US cable channel ESPN 2 on 6 Dec 2005, the show ran for four seasons before being cancelled in 2008.

Most online games won in *Madden NFL 18*
As of 6 Mar 2018, Xbox One player "Crippled x Dave" had won 428 online matches of EA's American football sim, according to TrueAchievements.

First American football videogame
Atari released two titles in 1978, both of which have legitimate claims to being the first true gridiron gaming title. *Atari Football* was an arcade coin-op, played with a trackball and featuring players who, back in those simpler times, were represented by noughts and crosses. The even more plainly titled *Football* was released for the Atari 2600 console and had players that Gamespot described as closely resembling "washing machines". It pre-dated Mattel's *NFL Football* – a five-on-five gridiron sim that was first released for the Intellivision system – by nearly a year.

Most YouTube subscribers for an American sports games channel
Specializing mostly in *Madden NFL*, US gamer Chris Smoove had 3,963,251 subscribers to his dedicated gaming channel on YouTube as of 6 Mar 2018. He even gets to rub shoulders with celebrities on the US sports scene, shooting videos with San Antonio Spurs basketballer Tony Parker and retired Boston Red Sox baseball star David Ortiz.

LONGEST WINNING STREAK ON *MADDEN NFL 18* "GAUNTLET" MODE

"Gauntlet" mode, first introduced in *Madden NFL 15* (2014), challenges players to complete endless offensive and defensive scenarios to see how far they can go. The twist is that players have only four lives – once they have failed four levels, they have to start over. As of 14 Feb 2018, Xbox One gamer "KID KUDI WZRD96" had progressed through 54 levels of *Madden NFL 18*'s (2017) "Gauntlet" mode, as verified by TrueAchievements.

MOST VOICE ACTORS IN A GRIDIRON VIDEOGAME

The *Madden NFL 18* story campaign "Longshot" has a cast of 23 actors. Gamers take a role as fictional quarterback Devin Wade as he tries to play his way into the NFL. Wade is voiced by actor J R Lemon, while other stars include ex-Miami Dolphins quarterback Dan Marino (USA). It's the first time that a *Madden* game has featured such a mode, as first seen in EA's *FIFA 17* "The Journey" campaign.

GAMING GOLD

PlayStation 2

PlayStation 2

ESPN NFL 2K5

VS

MADDEN 2005

Winning takedown
Soon after *ESPN NFL 2K5* (2004) was released, EA signed a deal that made *Madden* the only licensed NFL title – the equivalent of sacking its rival's quarterback.

Rarest *Madden NFL 18* trophy
As of 14 Feb 2018, only 0.6% of PS4 players had unlocked the "Tom Brady Legacy Trophy", according to PSNProfiles. Gamers can unlock the trophy by surpassing a legacy score of 27,000 with a custom-made player, coach or owner.

FANTASY SPORTS

Why be held in check by the restrictions imposed on sport by real-world concerns such as health and safety, physics or technology? In fantasy sports, such bothersome constraints have no meaning and only the sky – unless you're playing Quidditch – is the limit...

FASTEST TIME TO SCORE THREE BASKETS WITH A PUCK IN *ROCKET LEAGUE*

Unforgiving physics and famously unwieldy cars make scoring even a solitary basket in *Rocket League*'s Hoops mode an achievement. But YouTuber and *Rocket League* maestro Ross "TommyT999" Thompson has tamed both, by scoring three baskets within exactly 16 sec of the start of a match on the PS4. To make the attempt harder still, he did it with an oversized ice hockey puck rather than the standard basketball. His attempt, on 5 Feb 2018, was verified by Twin Galaxies.

MOST POPULAR *ROCKET LEAGUE*...

Battle-Car
The Octane (above) was the most used battle-car during the first two years of *Rocket League*. Its widespread popularity was revealed by developer Psyonix on the game's two-year anniversary during Jul 2017.

DLC Battle-Car
The Dominus (above) was used by more *Rocket League* players than any other DLC battle-car during the game's first two years, as verified by Psyonix. The over-the-top muscle car was released in Aug 2015.

Import Battle-Car
Import cars are special body types found in crates or traded with other players. Psyonix revealed that the Octane ZSR (above) was the import battle-car most players turned to between Jul 2015 and Jul 2017.

MOST INJURIES INFLICTED IN *BLOOD BOWL II*

In the fantasy gridiron game *Blood Bowl II*, grinding opponents into the dust is part and parcel of the job. In fact, for the Dwarfs, Orcs, Undead (above) and other teams who favour brawn over brains, it's a bona fide strategy.

Witness to the most injuries of all coaches was Xbox One player "Hero Jones9" (USA), who, as of 5 Feb 2018, had dished out 2,095 injuries in league games, according to Xbox tracking site TrueAchievements.

YOUR NEW FAVOURITE GAME

LASER LEAGUE

Platforms: PS4, Xbox One, PC

Speedball meets *Tron* in Roll7's *Laser League* – a high-speed arena sport in which players look to frazzle the opposition using lethal walls of light. To succeed, be sure to choose your character class carefully and know when to use power-ups.

FACT!

Rocket League is actually a sequel – it's the follow-up to Psyonix's awkwardly titled *Supersonic Acrobatic Rocket-Powered Battle-Cars*, which was a PS3 exclusive, released in 2008.

Fastest time to win the Quidditch World Cup
France's "NoBallzNoCookie" lifted the Quidditch World Cup – the ultimate prize for all budding Hogwarts wizards – in a truly magical time. He took just 34 min 19 sec, making short shrift of the other 18 teams he faced in the PC version of EA's *Harry Potter: Quidditch World Cup,* as verified by Speedrun.com on 7 Oct 2017.

First player to complete *Disc Jam* (PS4)
Virtual-frisbee phenomenon "Dan-Allen-Gaming" was the first gamer to collect all 12 trophies on High Horse Entertainment's *Disc Jam.* He achieved this feat on 7 Mar 2017 – the game's day of release – mastering its futuristic twist on tennis and frisbee in record time, as verified by PSNProfiles.

Longest-running fantasy sports videogame series
First created for home computers by The Bitmap Brothers in 1988, futuristic sports classic *Speedball* has spawned multiple remakes and updates for 25 years. The most recent release was *Speedball 2 HD,* the 2013 remake of the series' most famous title, *Speedball 2: Brutal Deluxe* (first released in 1990). Other notable entries include Empire Interactive's *Speedball 2100* for PlayStation One in 2000 (when the series went fully 3D for the first time) and Tower Studios' 2011 mobile adaptation, *Speedball 2: Evolution*.

Fastest time to win a match in *Mutant League Football*
Don't say we didn't warn you if you try to take on Twitch broadcaster "TheCasualCleric" (USA) at *Mutant League Football* (1993) for Sega Genesis. Playing as the Maniac All-Stars, he defeated the Sixty Whiners in 3 min 35 sec on 23 Jul 2017, as verified by Speedrun.com. His morally dubious tactic was to bump off the Sixty Whiners' players until they were forced to forfeit the match – something that barely raises an eyebrow in EA's blackly comic twist on American football.

First *Blood Bowl II* world champion
On 29 Jun 2016, Canadian gamer "Guinness" successfully guided his lizardmen team, Razzle Dazzle Rootbear, to the *Blood Bowl II* World Cup trophy. The championship saw more than 3,000 PC players compete over three months, with the eventual final contested between Razzle Dazzle Rootbear and "Mallak"'s (BEL) Eshin Red Raiders.

GAMING GOLD

MEDIC!!!
The sight of robots carting maimed players off the field was a common occurrence in Image Works' *Speedball 2* (1990).

MOTORSPORTS

Ladies and gentlemen, it's time to start your engines! Are you a full-throttle, need-for-speed merchant destined to start on pole position and finish with the chequered flag? If so, you'll want to check out the racing games and the pro drivers that have taken their place on our exclusive podium...

FASTEST THREE LAPS OF BYRON BAY'S DEEP WATER CROSS COUNTRY CIRCUIT IN *FORZA HORIZON 3*

UK speedster "Barthax", aka Andrew Peter Mee, sounds like the kind of person who you would want to ask for a lift if you needed to get somewhere fast. As verified by Twin Galaxies on 6 Sep 2017, "Barthax", who has registered a host of fast times on *Forza Horizon 3*, put his foot down and left his rivals in the dust as he completed three spins around the game's Deep Water Cross Country circuit in 2 min 30.184 sec.

GAMING GOLD

Starter's orders *Indianapolis 500: The Simulation* (EA, 1989) was the **first 3D polygon-based racing videogame**. Its graphics recreated 200-lap, 33-car races.

Most recorded lap times for a *Project CARS 2* track
As of 5 Feb 2018, Austria's Red Bull Ring circuit was the track that fans of Bandai Namco's driving sim had been hitting hardest: 9,129 times had been posted, as verified by www.pcars.13ms.de. The next most popular was Germany's Nürburgring Nordschleife with 9,075 recorded lap times.

Lowest-rated videogame on Steam
There was no place on the podium for *Flatout 3: Chaos & Destruction* (Team6 Game Studios, 2011). As of 2 Mar 2018, a mere 11% of its 1,629 user reviews posted on Steam were positive, giving it the dubious honour of having the lowest rating for a game with at least 500 reviews. "What is the point of this garbage?" asked one frustrated reviewer.

Most followed racing game on Twitter
EA's *Need for Speed* Twitter account had 646,739 followers as of 2 Mar 2018. That easily topped the follower counts for other popular racing games, including Microsoft's *Forza Motorsport* (240,000) and Bandai Namco's *Project CARS* (60,000).

Highest *Forza Motorsport 7* driver level
As of 15 Mar 2018, "HLR PRKid" (USA) had a driver level of 1,838 in Microsoft's 2017 racer. It was the most of any Xbox One gamer, as verified by TrueAchievements.

YOUR NEW FAVOURITE GAME

ONRUSH
Platforms: PS4, Xbox One, PC
Codemasters' new racer promises to throw safety out of the window as it ushers in high-speed thrills. Expect to wreak havoc from behind the wheel of any one of eight vehicle types, in a game that should make *MotorStorm* fans very happy indeed.

FACT!

Thrustmaster's T-GT steering wheel for PS4 and PC – launched in Oct 2017 to coincide with the release of *Gran Turismo Sport* (Sony, 2017) – had a huge RRP of £699 ($799).

Most licensed bikes in a game
As of 28 Feb 2018, Milestone's *Ride 2* (2016) let throttle-jockeys drive 240 real-world bikes – the number of bikes being swelled by eight free DLC packs.

74 POINTS

Brendon Leigh (UK) became the **first F1 eSports Series champion** on 25 Nov 2017, as verified by the event's website. A dramatic last-gasp overtake on the last lap of the third and final race saw him clinch the championship by six points.

LONGEST-RUNNING PLAYSTATION FRANCHISE

Between the Japanese launch of the original *Gran Turismo* on 23 Dec 1997 and the release of *Gran Turismo Sport* on 17 Oct 2017, Sony's seminal racing-sim series (and PlayStation-exclusive franchise) had been providing pedal-to-the-metal thrills for its legions of fans for an amazing 19 years 298 days.

Most of the series' entries have been monster hits, but the **highest-selling *Gran Turismo* game** as of 1 Mar 2018 was *Gran Turismo 3: A-spec* (2001) for PS2, selling 14.98 million copies, as verified by VGChartz. This put it ahead of the PS2's *Gran Turismo 4* (2004) with 11.66 million copies and the PS One original's 10.95 million sales.

Most expensive videogame package
The one existing copy of Codemasters' *GRID 2: BAC Mono Edition* was sold by UK retailer GAME in May 2013. It cost £125,000 ($205,846) and contained a PS3, the game, branded racing wear and a street-legal BAC Mono supercar! The package was promptly snapped up by Canadian DJ "deadmau5".

MARIO KART

With its perfect blend of cartoon graphics, famous characters, glorious power-ups and a healthy dollop of good old-fashioned fun, *Mario Kart* is one of the few games that can work its magic on gamers and non-gamers alike. Strap in as we avoid the banana skins and take the chequered flag.

MOST PLAYABLE CHARACTERS IN A KART-RACING GAME

Mario Kart 8 Deluxe (Nintendo, 2017) power-drifted on to the Switch with a roster of 42 playable characters (excluding variations of the same character). The game includes all the racers from *Mario Kart 8* (2014) for the Wii U, returning favourites Bowser Jr and King Boo, plus new competitors from the *Splatoon* series (Inkling Boy and Inkling Girl).

One very special character must be unlocked before he can be used. Gold Mario (Mario cast in solid gold) requires players to win all 12 Grand Prix races on the toughest 200cc difficulty mode – a task much easier said than done!

12 TROPHIES

France's Florent Lecoanet has won the **most *Super Mario Kart* World Championships trophies**. His victory in the Battle Mode tournament at 2017's World Championships helped lift his trophy tally to eight gold and four silver. Entrants also compete in Time Trial, 150cc Grand Prix and Match Race showdowns.

A ghostly secret
The origins of *Mario Kart*'s speedy shortcuts can be traced back to the Ghost Valley 1 track in *Super Mario Kart* (1992). Plucky players could steal a march by leaping a gap in the track.

FASTEST ALL-CUPS COMPLETION OF *MARIO KART 64*

A fraction of a second separates the top two *Mario Kart 64* speedsters. On 16 Feb 2018, "abney317", aka Beck Abney (USA), finished an all-cups, no-skips run of the 1996 N64 classic in 38 min 37.41 sec. This narrowly eclipsed the time of 38 min 37.60 sec set by "MR" (DEU) on 11 Feb 2018, with just 0.19 sec the difference!

First virtual reality (VR) kart-racing game
Mario Kart Arcade GP VR for the HTC Vive debuted on 14 Jul 2017 at the VR Zone Shinjuku in Tokyo, Japan. Gamers entered a VR Mushroom Kingdom to compete as Mario, Luigi and co.

Fastest completion of the 150cc Mushroom Cup
UK player "DangerMoll" lifted the 150cc Mushroom Cup on the Japanese version of *Super Mario Kart* in 7 min 43 sec on 3 Mar 2018. The racer didn't even think it was a good run!

Most critically acclaimed kart-racing game
As of 29 Mar 2018, *Mario Kart 8 Deluxe* boasted a GameRankings score of 92.39%, aggregated from 52 reviews. The Switch game wrestled the title from Sony's *Crash Team Racing*, a game that had held the record (with a score of 91.78% from 32 reviews) since 1999. One review summed up *Mario Kart 8 Deluxe* as simply "an absolutely fantastic racing game".

Longest-running racing game tournament
The annual *Super Mario Kart* World Championships has been staged on 16 occasions as of its 2017 event, which was held on 15–19 Aug in La Suze-sur-Sarthe, France. Its inaugural event in 2002 had just 16 competitors. By 2017, 54 racers representing 11 nations jostled for the podium spots. The 2018 event is set for 14–18 Aug in Alphen aan den Rijn, Netherlands.

Fastest completion of Rainbow Road in *Mario Kart 8 Deluxe* (200cc)
On 2 Nov 2017, "flc", aka Jeremy Kyle (AUS), completed the gruelling yet colourful Rainbow Road track in a blistering 1 min 33.751 sec.

Best-selling racing game for Nintendo Switch
As of 29 Mar 2018, *Mario Kart 8 Deluxe* had sold 6.95 million copies according to VGChartz. It was the second-best-selling game for

Switch overall, behind Nintendo's *Super Mario Odyssey* (with a total of 8.28 million sales).

Fastest shortcut time for Choco Mountain in *Mario Kart 64*
On 29 Oct 2017, Beck Abney (USA) used mushroom-fuelled turbo-boosts to skip almost the entire Choco Mountain track. He completed the three-lap race in just 16.38 sec. "That's it!" exclaimed the ecstatic gamer.

SOCCER

The joy of winning the title, the despair of relegation, the fear of being fired – all the emotions of soccer can be had in videogames, which is why they and the beautiful game work so well together. They could be said to be the perfect match...

LONGEST GAME OF FOOTBALL MANAGER

The strains and stresses of soccer management in the real world can add years to your appearance, but those who take on the hot seat in the virtual world live a lot longer. As of 22 Nov 2017, Michał Leniec (POL) had played *Football Manager 2016* for 221 in-game years, as verified by the game's developer, Sports Interactive. Michał (pictured) is a real-life Lech Poznań fan.

He had managed his favourite club for the entire game, but also taken on 35 international roles, always simultaneously to his domestic career. While in charge, he won a remarkable 207 national titles. His in-game manager was technically 258 years old! He had played 14,381 matches, winning 10,997 of them and losing just 1,720 – for a win rate of 76%.

MOST EXPENSIVE SOCCER VIDEOGAME

The rumour that there were fewer than 10 copies of the game in existence helped the eBay price of *The Ultimate 11: SNK Football Championship* (SNK Playmore, 1996) reach $10,000 (£6,404). News channel CNN reported the sale on its website on 3 Jan 2011, calling it "a must-have for collectors".

The concept of street soccer as a videogame goes back to the 1980s. Both Epyx's *Street Sports Soccer* and Codemasters' *Street Soccer* were released in 1988 – the **first street soccer videogames.**

$211,651

It was deep into extra time when Guilherme "GuiFera" Fonseca (inset) scored the decisive goal that made him the *Pro Evolution Soccer 2017* World Finals champion. As of 1 Feb 2018, Fonseca had played in only three *PES* tournaments, yet he was still the **highest-earning *Pro Evolution Soccer* player** – as verified by eSportsearnings.com. Of the $211,651.21 (£156,850) he won in events across 2016 and 2017, a huge chunk, $200,000, came in Jun 2017 with that victory over Ettorito Giannuzzi (ITA) at the Emirates Stadium, the north London, UK, home of Arsenal FC. It more than made up for his defeat in 2016's final.

First soccer videogame with female players

When *Michael Owen's WLS 2000* (THQ) was rebranded for the US market, it was known as *Mia Hamm Soccer 64*. Named after the American icon who was twice a Women's World Cup winner, it featured 18 domestic teams, 32 national teams and an all-star team, all female. The game was also notable for having the **first female commentator in a soccer videogame** in the form of ESPN pundit and ex-international forward Wendy Gebauer, who enthusiastically yelled "nice ball" and "she lays it off".

First game to simulate Brexit

Soccer-management game *Football Manager 2017* (Sega/Sports Interactive) features multiple scenarios based on Britain's decision to leave the European Union, most of which affect the transfer dealings of British clubs and the movement of non-British players. The game was released on 4 Nov 2016, which gave developers time to include the possible effects of the Brexit referendum (on 23 Jun 2016).

First real soccer player to headline a game

Released for the Atari 2600 in 1980, *Pelé's Soccer* (Atari) was endorsed by the legendary Brazilian forward and boasted box art featuring the player himself. The game was played from a top-down perspective and was surprisingly convincing for the time, despite having only four players per side. Although he didn't appear in the game, Pelé did star in the Brazilian TV commercial to promote the title.

First soccer videogame "licensed" from a real-life league

Taking its name from the USA's former North American Soccer League, Mattel's *NASL Soccer* (1979) was a two-player game for the Intellivision home console. It introduced a side-view playing perspective, which would be influential for future sims based on soccer.

A game to forget
The **first official World Cup game,** *World Cup Carnival* (1986), rated 0% in one review and was so easy that players could walk the ball into the net!

Most appearances on a videogame cover by a soccer player

As of Sep 2017, the brilliance of Lionel Messi (ARG) had been recognized on 10 soccer game covers of *FIFA* (EA) and *PES* (Konami). Deep breath: *PES 2009*, *PES 2010*, *PES 2011*, *FIFA Street*, *FIFA 13*, *FIFA 14*, *FIFA 15*, *FIFA 16*, *PES 2017* and *PES 2018: Legendary Edition*. See pp.150–51 for the Top 10 *FIFA* cover stars.

FIRST SOCCER VIDEOGAMES

There were three arcade soccer games released in 1973 – Taito's *Soccer* (left), *Super Soccer* (Allied Leisure Industries) and *Soccer* (Ramtek). While owing a big debt to *Pong* (1972) in terms of graphics and paddle controls, these arcade cabinets started the march towards bringing the beautiful game to the world of videogames.

FIFA

Celebrating 25 years of goals, saves, crunching challenges, penalties and dodgy refereeing decisions, the *FIFA* series is a gaming phenomenon. The mercurial Cristiano Ronaldo might feature as *FIFA 18*'s cover star, but it's the gameplay that really hits the back of the net, year in, year out.

HIGHEST-RATED *FIFA 18* PLAYER

Cristiano Ronaldo is accustomed to scoring crucial winners in the real-life version of the beautiful game, and it seems he's just as capable of doing the same in *FIFA 18*. In a devastating turnaround, the Portuguese superstar took the title of **highest-rated player in *FIFA 18*** from Brazilian legend Pelé. How? Well, when *FIFA 18* was first released, the *FIFA 18* Ultimate Team (FUT) card of Pelé – at the height of his powers in the 1970 World Cup – enjoyed an overall rating of 98%, making him the game's highest-rated player (Ronaldo was close behind on 94%). But, on 17 Jan 2018, EA unveiled its FUT Team of the Year (TOTY). The players included in the TOTY each received a new FUT card that boosted their stats to reflect their footballing prowess in the 2017/18 season. Of all the players featured, it was Ronaldo who was the most enhanced – with his overall rating jumping to 99%. The same update saw Ronaldo's La Liga rival Lionel Messi (ARG) draw level with Pelé on 98%.

99
LW

CRISTIANO RONALDO

98 PAC	98 DRI
99 SHO	50 DEF
94 PAS	95 PHY

EXPANDED FRANCHISE

FIFA 17 and 18's fictional footballing hero Alex Hunter (left) is the **most followed fictional videogame footballer on Twitter**. The virtual soccer player had over 58k followers as of 8 Mar 2018.

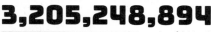

3,205,248,894

As of 9 Mar 2018, Harry "W2S" Lewis (UK) had the **most viewed *FIFA* videogame channel on YouTube**, with 3,262,457,861 views. His was the **most subscribed *FIFA* channel** too, with 12,060,986 subscribers.

GAMING GOLD

Kane, but able? Harry Kane lent his voice to *FIFA 17* (2016) with "uh" mixed "uh" results. Perhaps it's best to let your feet do the talking, Harry?

FACT!

Two players had won the FIFA Interactive World Cup title twice, as of 29 Jan 2018: Bruce Grannec (FRA) in 2009 and 2013, and Alfonso Ramos (ESP) in 2008 and 2012.

203 COUNTRIES

Those who bought EA's *2014 FIFA World Cup Brazil* (2014) had a huge 203 national teams to choose from, making the World Cup tie-in the game with the **most countries in a sports title**. In a move that offered gamers unparalleled potential for patriotic pride, the game featured every team that competed in the World Cup qualifiers across every region. This meant that fans of more nations than ever before (or since) could take their nation through the entire qualification process and claim World Cup glory. In total, a mind-boggling 7,469 players were made available, with each player's likeness faithfully recreated.

XBOX ONE

FIFA 16

EA SPORTS

FIFA 16 LEGENDS

FIRST FEMALE *FIFA* COVER STARS

After an online poll, the most popular female soccer stars from the USA, Canada and Australia were selected to appear on regional covers of *FIFA 16*, alongside Lionel Messi. Canadian fans chose Christine Sinclair, while the Aussies voted for Steph Catley. In the USA, the honour went to 2015 World Cup winner Alex Morgan (above).

Fastest completion of "The Journey" in *FIFA 17*
"The Journey" was a revolutionary new story mode introduced in *FIFA 17* (EA, 2016). It challenged players to become an on-the-pitch sensation in the white-hot crucible of the English Premier League in the form of fictional youngster Alex Hunter (see left). Playing for Arsenal (but on loan to Aston Villa, one of the mode's three Championship clubs), "hcarter57" (UK) finished in 2 hr 46 min 40 sec on 9 Aug 2017, as verified by Speedrun.com. The run involved simulating training sessions and forfeiting league matches – imagine getting away with that in a real match!

Lowest-placed soccer team to have their faces captured for a *FIFA* videogame
Club side Forest Green Rovers, who finished the 2016/17 season in third place in the National League – effectively 95th in the English domestic league system – had their faces captured for *FIFA 18*. The Gloucestershire team, who won promotion to League Two through the play-offs, are not only the lowest-placed club to have their players' likenesses installed in EA's sports series, but also the first team outside any of the top European soccer leagues to be afforded that honour. The move to include them in *FIFA* was in recognition of the club's success in securing a place in the UK's Football League for the first time in 128 years.

Fastest time to complete all *FIFA 18* bronze skill games
On 16 Jan 2018, UK gamer "Pookster007" raced through the bronze-level training drills on *FIFA 18* in 8 min 49 sec, as verified by Speedrun.com. Completing them improves skills in all areas of the pitch, from defending to dribbling to converting scoring opportunities. "Pookster007" eclipsed "NoComment"'s (DEU) time by 2 sec.

SPORTS ROUND-UP

SPORTS

Take soccer, NFL and motorsports out of your sports round-up and what are you left with? Quite a lot, as it turns out. Here, we bring you the best of the rest, from the players who have excelled in gaming's own Winter Olympics to the most notable achievements in hockey, basketball and baseball.

STEEP SPEED-RUNS

In Dec 2017, Ubisoft embraced the 2018 Winter Olympics by releasing *Steep: Road to the Olympics* as a paid-for update to *Steep* (2016) on PS4, Xbox One and PC. The update included downhill skiing and snowboarding as it challenged players to test their skills against the clock.

Statistics provided by the publisher on 15 Feb 2018 revealed who had been quickest on the virtual slopes. As seems fitting for a gamer from a country with such a rich heritage in winter sports, Norway's "SNiiKx" dominated three events. The PC player was **fastest in the Slalom** (50.577 sec), **fastest in the Giant Slalom** (2 min 22.899 sec) and, completing a hat-trick of victories, also the **fastest in the SuperG** (1 min 19.468 sec). **Fastest in the Parallel Giant Slalom** was Xbox One gamer "Bonecrusher2D" (USA), who crossed the finish line in 54.682 sec. PS4 player "cocorider" (BEL) was **fastest in the Downhill,** navigating the course of the blue-riband event in just 1 min 54.899 sec.

MOST APPEARANCES ON THE COVER OF *MLB: THE SHOW*

Since 2012, Sony has produced alternative covers for its baseball title *MLB: The Show* to sell it in different markets. As of 28 Mar 2017, the American-based pitcher Wei-Yin Chen (TPE) had graced the cover of all five releases in Chinese Taipei, starting with *MLB 13: The Show*.

Best-selling action sports videogame series
According to VGChartz, worldwide sales of the *Tony Hawk's...* skateboarding series had reached 54.91 million by 2 Mar 2018, since its launch in 1999, putting it streets ahead of its rivals. To set its sales into perspective, EA's similarly prolific *SSX* snowboarding series had mustered sales of "only" 10.13 million since it debuted in 2000.

Biggest blowout on *NBA 2K17*
It was high-scoring but one-sided as Tristen Geren (USA), playing as 2016's Team USA, recorded an emphatic scoreline of 97–43 against Spanish club Laboral Kutxa Vitoria-Gasteiz in 2K Sports' *NBA 2K17* (2016) basketball title. This was a margin of victory or "blowout" of 54 points. The achievement was accomplished on Xbox One and verified by Twin Galaxies on 12 Dec 2016.

Most critically acclaimed rugby videogame
Across all games with at least 20 critic reviews, the PS2 version of EA's *Rugby* (2001) ran in some match-winning tries to take its place as the most highly praised virtual game of rugger. Based on 25 reviews, the sim boasted an overall GameRankings score of 75.56% as of 2 Mar 2018. That put it marginally ahead of series sequels *Rugby 08* (74.87%) and *Rugby 2005* (74.5%).

Most critically acclaimed PC sports videogame
As of 2 Mar 2018, EA's basketball title *NBA Live 2000* (1999) scored 88% on GameRankings based on 22 reviews. It narrowly outscored *PGA Championship Golf 2000* (87.77%), *NHL 2001* (86.75%), *Tony Hawk's Underground 2* (86.20%) and *Worldwide Soccer Manager 2007* (85.80%).

Longest-running baseball videogame series
The *Family Stadium* Japanese baseball series (aka *Famista*) began in 1986. The most recent was Bandai Namco's *Pro Yakyuu Famista Climax*, released in Apr 2017, meaning that the series had been running for over 30 years.

FACT!

Commencing in 2018, the NBA 2K League is the **first pro eSports league created by an established sporting league.** Hoop-shooting participants will play 2K Sports' *NBA 2K18*.

LONGEST-RUNNING HORSE-RACING VIDEOGAME SERIES
Between the release of the original *Winning Post* (1993) and *Winning Post 8 2018* (2018), Koei Tecmo's thoroughbred series had stayed the course and kept its nose in front of rivals with a total of 33 games over a period of 25 years.

First ice hockey game with playable mascots
When EA's *NHL 18* was released in 2017, it offered the option of a new three-on-three mode that pitched two teams of mascots against each other. They included Fin, mascot of the Vancouver Canucks (left), and Nordy, mascot of the Minnesota Wild, who has the number 18,001 on his squad jersey. This is in reference to the Wild's "Team of 18,000" nickname, which is based on its home arena's capacity.

First basketball videogame with female players
NBA Live 18 (EA Sports, 2017) scored a slam dunk on the virtual court by including players from the Women's National Basketball Association (WNBA). Featured in the title are all 12 teams and their players, including one of the sport's all-time greats, Cappie Pondexter (left), during her association with the Chicago Sky.

GOLD
GAMING

Speakeasy
Jim Hughson's turn as the voice of EA's *NHL* series (from *NHL 97* to *09*) made him **the most prolific commentator in an ice hockey series.**

TOP 10

FIFA COVER APPEARANCES

Since its debut in 1993, EA's **best-selling soccer series** has paraded the world's finest talent on its covers, often picking national icons for special localized editions. As of the release of *FIFA 18* in Sep 2017, these were the most frequently featured *FIFA* cover stars...

≡7	≡7	≡7	≡7	≡5
DAVID ALABA (AUT)	**JAKUB BŁASZCZYKOWSKI** (POL)	**ROBERT LEWANDOWSKI** (POL)	**THIERRY HENRY** (FRA)	**BALÁZS DZSUDZSÁK** (HUN)
3 COVERS	**3 COVERS**	**3 COVERS**	**3 COVERS**	**4 COVERS**
FIFA 14, 15, 16 (all AUT)	*FIFA 11, 12, 13* (all POL)	*FIFA 10, 14, 15* (all POL)	*FIFA 2001* (FRA), *FIFA Soccer 2002* (FRA/UK), *FIFA Soccer 2004*	*FIFA 09, 10, 12, 14* (all HUN)

7

The **most consecutive appearances on a FIFA videogame cover.**
It's a record shared by the UK's Wayne Rooney and Australia's Tim Cahill.

≡5

LANDON DONOVAN
(USA)

4 COVERS

FIFA Soccer 2003, FIFA 07, 11, 12 (all USA)

4

LIONEL MESSI
(ARG)

5 COVERS

FIFA 13, 14, 15, 16, FIFA Street3

≡2

TIM CAHILL
(AUS)

7 COVERS

FIFA 10, 11, 12, 13, 14, 15, 16 (all AUS)

≡2

WAYNE ROONEY
(UK)

7 COVERS

FIFA 06, 07, 08, 09, 10, 11 (various regions), FIFA 12

1

RONALDINHO
(BRA)

9 COVERS

FIFA Soccer 2004, FIFA 06: Road to FIFA World Cup, FIFA 06, 07, 08, 09, 10 (ITA), FIFA Street, FIFA Street 3

FIFA EWORLD CUP

The FIFA eWorld Cup is the **world's largest online game tournament.** Formerly known as the FIFA Interactive World Cup, or FIWC, it had seven million entrants to its 2017 tournament alone. Organized by governing body FIFA and the *FIFA* games publisher EA, it's a prestigious gaming contest that offers huge rewards for the winner. We mingled among the many spectators, coaches and virtual soccer players at the 2017 finals, held in Westminster, London, UK, on 16–18 Aug, and enjoyed a full insight into this fascinating eSport. Here's what we found out...

WSL
FIFA
INTERACTIVE
WORLD CUP
EA SPORTS
PRESENTING PARTNER

The tournament's live knockout stages were held in London's historic Westminster Central Hall and involved agony and ecstasy for the 32 competitors. Some of the finalists earned their places by winning gruelling seasons of *FIFA Ultimate Team* (FUT), played online on consoles.

32

Others had reached its climactic stages through pro-club tournaments featuring eSporters linked to real soccer clubs such as Paris Saint-Germain, Ajax and Wolfsburg. Among the finalists was Ahmed Al-Meghessib, who, amazingly, is a real-life soccer pro from the tiny Arabian state of Qatar!

TOURNAMENT WINNERS

2004	Brazil	2012	Spain
2005	England	2013	France
2006	Netherlands	2014	Denmark
2008	Spain	2015	Saudi Arabia
2009	France	2016	Denmark
2010	USA	2017	England
2011	Portugal	2018	?

46

The number of goals that Spencer "Gorilla" Ealing smashed in during the knockout rounds en route to becoming the 2017 *FIFA* world champion. The Englishman's aggressive and attack-minded style of play made him exciting to watch.

14

The FIFA eWorld Cup (then the FIWC) was launched in 2004. As of the 2018 competition, there will have been 14 tournaments staged (there was no event in 2007). Each year, players compete with the latest iteration of EA's *FIFA* game. Thiago Carrico de Azevedo (BRA) won the inaugural showdown in 2004, defeating Matija Biljeskovic (USA, b. SRB) 2–1 in a nip-and-tuck encounter in Zurich, Switzerland.

$268,000

Prize pool for the 2017 competition (£207,999). Spencer Ealing's top prize of $200,000 (£155,223) instantly made him the **highest-earning *FIFA* player**, with career winnings of $278,054 (£206,230) as of 1 Dec 2017, according to eSportsearnings. Runner-up Kai "Deto" Wollin took home $40,000 (£31,044).

7-3

After three days of elimination matches, the 2017 grand final was a showdown between Xbox One champ Spencer "Gorilla" Ealing (UK) and PS4 winner Kai "Deto" Wollin (DEU). After a thrilling 3–3 draw on PS4, Spencer demolished his opponent 4–0 on Xbox to take the title on a 7–3 aggregate. One of Spencer's decisive goals was scored by Ruud Gullit, who, coincidentally, handed Spencer his trophy. "All of a sudden I am popular again!" laughed the Dutch master. "All the youngsters know me from the game."

WHAT THEY SAID...

"As a pro player, I think that we're going to be on the same level as footballers. I think we'll be selling out stadiums just for people who want to come and watch a *FIFA* match. *FIFA* has the crossover between the regular viewer who watches football; they can jump right into *FIFA* and understand the game."
Aman Seddiqi, FIFA eWorld Cup 2017 grand finalist

"When I first started competitive *FIFA* with *FIFA 15*, I didn't know what I was getting myself into, let alone my parents. But they've understood it once I'd started winning a couple of events. Obviously, there's the money involved as well, but it wasn't as big as it is now. [My parents] support me and understand what I do. I'm only 20 now, so I don't plan to stop anytime soon. I do this as a job – but also as a hobby."
Spencer "Gorilla" Ealing on his career as a pro *FIFA* player

"When I was 10, I never would have thought I'd be a pro *FIFA* player one day. But that would have been my dream. I would work hard every day. The game is changing a lot. The first day you can [practise] crossing, the next day long shots. If you are good at everything – good at crosses, good at defending, good at ball skills – you have a good chance to be a pro player."
FIFA eWorld Cup 2017 runner-up Kai "Deto" Wollin on what advice he would pass on to his 10-year-old self

SIMULATIONS

Ever been to a theme park and thought you could do a better job of building roller-coasters? Or visited a farm and wished you could carve out your own living from the land? Simulation games let you do that and more, then allow you to bask in the glow of your accomplishments…

FASTEST *STARDEW VALLEY* WEDDING (GLITCHLESS)

Who said that fools rush in? Not PC player "Sam_Van_Dam" (USA), who went from New Game to happily-ever-after with one of *Stardew Valley*'s singletons in just 1 hr 6 min 00 sec. It was a glitchless run (which means he did it without any hacks or other help), as verified by Speedrun on 6 Feb 2018.

"Sam_Van_Dam" was able to woo his soon-to-be wife in speedy fashion with gifts, bouquets of flowers and by rapidly upgrading his house to show how reliable a spouse he could be – the old romantic!

LIFE SIMS

If you love to people-watch, then life sims are for you. Whether you're overseeing the whole population of a major city or micro-managing the relationships of virtual people, you'll find hours of entertainment in simply watching your creations go about their daily lives.

MOST EXPANSION PACKS FOR A GAME SERIES

With the release of *The Sims 4*'s *My First Pet Stuff* pack on 13 Mar 2018, EA's ground-breaking life-simulation series had ushered in 71 expansion packs across the entire series. The franchise started with *The Sims* in 2000 and includes *The Sims 2* (2004), 2009's *The Sims 3* and *The Sims 4* (2014). *The Sims: Livin' Large* was the **first *The Sims* expansion**.

It was released on 27 Aug 2000 and required *The Sims* to function.

One of the series' stranger add-ons was 2007's *Bon Voyage* pack for *The Sims 2*. It let you take your Sims on holiday, where they could meet Bigfoot. Those who had *The Sims 3*'s *Seasons* (2012) and *Ambitions* (2010) packs could summon meteors to bombard their virtual suburbanites.

18 MINUTES 32 SECONDS

Fastest time to attract five campers in *Animal Crossing: Pocket Camp*
Camp leader "groteworld" (USA) enticed five happy campers to his campsite in 18 min 32 sec on the Apple iOS version of Nintendo's sim. "Some failed menuing, but almost perfect resource-grabbing pathing," commented the gamer when posting his time on Speedrun on 2 Jan 2018.

19 LIFE SIMS

As the **most prolific life-sim game creator**, Will Wright, the co-founder of games developer Maxis, was the genius behind the best-selling series *Sim City* (1989) and *The Sims* (2000). He also designed *SimEarth: The Living Planet* (1990), *SimAnt* (1991), *SimLife* (1992) and *Spore* (2008). In total, the prolific game designer was involved in the development of 19 life-sim games.

EXPANDED FRANCHISE

The trailer for Double Fine's *Everything* (2017) was so impressive that it won the Jury Prize for animation at the Vienna Independent Shorts film festival. Its victory made it the **first game trailer eligible for an Oscar nomination**.

FACT!

Adam Stevens and Vana Springer's bond over *Stardew Valley* was so deep that he used a crop of in-game tulips to spell out "Marry me?". She said "yes" after discovering his message on 30 Dec 2017.

Highest-rated life-sim game on Steam
The warm feeling of nurturing *Stardew Valley*'s (2016) rural community has spread from the game's Pelican Town and into Steam. As a result, Chucklefish's farming simulator enjoyed a Steam user rating of 95.92% as of 23 Feb 2018.

Fastest time to send a Mii to space in *Tomodachi Life*
On 20 Apr 2018, 3DS player "TheLaggingGamer" (USA) rocketed one of his Miis into space in 5 hr 50 min 41 sec in Nintendo's handheld life sim, as verified by Speedrun. Sending a Mii into space costs $10,000 in-game dollars. "Holy cow this run was insane," said the gamer, who was expecting "to beat this [record] by a fair amount".

Most user-generated creations for a videogame
Matching the massive ambitions that Will Wright had for his creature-creator *Spore* (EA, 2008), its players had designed and uploaded 190,130,484 creatures to Sporepedia (the game's online community) as of 12 Mar 2018. The closest competition – though still trailing far behind – was *LittleBigPlanet* (Sony, 2008), with just over 10 million user-created levels.

Most viewed *Youtubers Life* video on YouTube
It was always likely that U-Play Online's *Youtubers Life* – a tycoon game simulating a YouTuber's life – would attract interest from real-life games broadcasters when it was released in May 2016. As of 12 Mar 2018, a video called: "MOM STEALS MY COMPUTER!! | YouTuber's Life #2" by DanTDM, aka Daniel Middleton (UK), had been watched 7,380,703 times. That is considerably more than the 30,390 in-game views that Middleton managed while playing the title.

Longest-running life-sim series
The *Petz* franchise spans 19 years (and 55 games). It began in 1995 with *Dogz: Your Computer Pet* (Virgin) and had its most recent entry in 2014 with *Petz Countryside* (Ubisoft). Its record might not last much longer, though, with EA's *The Sims* closing in and the *Petz* series seemingly dormant.

VEHICLE SIMS

Name any type of vehicle and the chances are that there's a videogame developer creating a sim of it. Planes, trains and automobiles have been joined by other modes of transport, from warships to galaxy-hopping starships.

Q&A: SCOTT MANLEY

A love of gaming and an astrophysics background have made Scott Manley (USA) an Astronogamer and a *Kerbal Space Program* record-breaker.

What was the biggest challenge in setting your speed record for fastest trip to the Mun and back?
The game had been made harder since my last record [**fastest time into orbit** – 54 sec – since beaten by "DasValdez" (USA)]. I needed a new rocket – a 7,000-part behemoth that pushed the limits of the game physics so hard that it ran at one-third of a frame per second. It would take 2 hr to run the first 5 min of game time. Patience was essential.

Did your background in science and astronomy help your bid?
Optimizing the design required a lot of mathematics. While it might take hours to test a design change, I could use science to eliminate some ideas before building.

What's the best advice for *Kerbal Space Program* newcomers?
Enjoy failure, when things crash or explode. That's the best time to learn something new. If you lose control, it's not because you're a bad player, but because rocket science is hard – fun, but hard. The hardest part to get right is the Mun landing, where you have to stop from a speed of 29,000 km/h [18,020 mph] and gently touch down.

HIGHEST SCORES ON *FTL: FASTER THAN LIGHT* ADVANCED EDITION

On "hard" difficulty, starship captain Joe Jackmovich (USA) racked up 5,847 points on Subset Games' galaxy-rescuing indie spaceship sim, as verified by Twin Galaxies on 23 Jul 2016. Two days later, the same website ratified Jackmovich's record for **highest score on *FTL*'s normal-difficulty mode** (5,275). As of 31 Jan 2018, he had also posted the **highest score on *FTL*'s easy-difficulty option**, with 5,204.

MOST EXPENSIVE DLC FOR A VIDEOGAME (COMBINED)

Released during Nov 2017, the mega-detailed *Train Simulator 2018: Steam Edition* (Dovetail Games) had 420 separate DLC releases available for purchase through the Steam store, as verified on 30 Jan 2018. To snap up every item in the game's wide-ranging DLC would set back the virtual-railway enthusiast £4,684.61 ($6,603.36). And real-life train travellers complain about their own rising fares!

FASTEST RETURN TRIP TO THE MUN IN *KSP*

On 29 Nov 2017, Scott Manley took just 1 hr 1 min 5 sec of in-game time to make a round trip to the Mun in Squad's *Kerbal Space Program* (2015) space-vehicle simulator.

His record was accomplished on the release build of the PC version of the game and verified by the game's developer. To accomplish the journey as quickly as possible, Manley assembled a 7,000-part, 115,200-tonne (253,972,526-lb) rocket, which was key to the blast-off and an

increase in speed. Manley's rocket was comparable to about 42 of the real-world *Saturn V* rockets that fired the first humans to the Moon.

On 10 Aug 2017, "Stratzenblitz75" set the **fastest land speed on *Kerbal Space Program***, an eye-watering 3,469 m/sec (11,381 ft/sec), as verified by the game's developer. "Stratzenblitz75" had to lower *Kerbal*'s graphical settings so that the terrain textures could keep up with him at those great velocities.

FACT!

Published by CRL in 1985 for the Amstrad CPC and ZX Spectrum, *Juggernaut* was gaming's first attempt to realistically simulate driving a truck. *Retro Gamer* called it "very clever" but "frustrating".

Largest warship in *World of Warships*
According to the game's historical consultants, the largest playable warship in Wargaming's historical MMO *World of Warships* (2015) is the German Tier X battleship, the *Großer Kurfürst*, at 300.5 m (985 ft 10 in) long. The craft is based on a class of battleships designed for the German Navy during World War II but which were never built.

Longest-running truck-sim series
Developed by Czech Republic's SCS Software, the PC trucking series *18 Wheels of Steel* had produced eight releases between 31 Aug 2002 and 6 Jan 2011 – a total of 8 years 128 days. The first game was *Hard Truck: 18 Wheels of Steel* and the most recent was *18 Wheels of Steel: Extreme Trucker 2*. The latter tasks players with carting extreme loads across hazardous paths in Montana (USA), Bolivia, Northern Territory (Australia) and Bangladesh.

Rarest trophy in *Professional Farmer 2017*
As of 31 Jan 2018, not a single gamer had won the "Amber Waves of Grain" trophy for owning all available fields on the PS4 version of *Professional Farmer 2017* (VIS, 2016). It is the only one of the game's 18 trophies to have eluded its entire player base, though "I Think I Get It Now", for completing 15 whole growing cycles, had a completion rate of just 1.02%.

Longest-running train-sim series
Debuting in Japanese arcade halls in 1996, Taito's train sims *Densha de Go! (Go by Train!)* had been running along virtual tracks for approximately 21 years by the time a four-screen arcade cabinet was introduced in Nov 2017 (from Square Enix, who relaunched the series in 2010 after acquiring Taito). It had been unveiled during summer 2016 to mark the 20th anniversary of the game.

130,766

As of 31 Jan 2018, the **most liked simulation game on Steam** was *Euro Truck Simulator 2* (SCS Software, 2012). A total of 130,766 players awarded the game a thumbs-up approval. The next simulation game on the list was the farming-themed *Stardew Valley*, which drew 83,266 positive reviews.

Largest real-world tractor in a videogame
Added to *Farming Simulator 17* (2016) by way of the *Big Bud* DLC in May 2017, roving hulk Big Bud 16V-747 is not only gaming's largest agricultural tractor, it's also the **largest tractor** in the real world. Built in Havre, Montana, in 1978, it has a 670-kW (900-hp) engine and weighs 43 tonnes (95,000 lb). Each of its eight tyres is 2.4 m (94 in) in diameter.

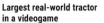

GOLD GAMING

Desert Bus
The deliberately tedious Penn & Teller game (1995) had, as of 2017, helped a charity generate $650K. See pp.94–95.

MANAGEMENT SIMS

These games have come a long way since *SimCity* first challenged us to play mayor in 1989. Since then, we've built prisons, hospitals, dinosaur-filled theme parks and even entire planets – and then watched with a mixture of horror and fascination as our creations have fallen apart at the seams...

LARGEST RIOT IN *PRISON ARCHITECT*

On 16 Dec 2016, US YouTuber "Toast Gaming" had a (very) large-scale emergency on his hands when 10,065 of his inmates went on the rampage in *Prison Architect* (Introversion Software, 2015). What else would you expect to happen when you deny that many prisoners food of any kind whatsoever?

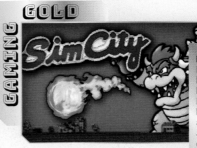

GAMING GOLD

Bowser-zilla! Bowser might usually be content to wreak havoc upon the Mushroom Kingdom, but in 1991 he was an angry visitor to *SimCity* – burning down entire districts in the SNES title.

MOST FOLLOWED SIM GAME ON TWITTER

As of 27 Mar 2018, online web-browser game *Kantai Collection* had 1,381,710 followers on Twitter. Available only in Japan, the title is a complex resource-management sim and strategy game in which players raise fleets of warships that are depicted as female characters (left). It has expanded into a popular manga comic-book series and TV anime.

Fastest any% completion of *Tropico 5*
Coup d'états are usually years in the making, but gamer "Naegleria" (CAN) needed no more than 4 hr 54 min 36 sec to start a revolution on the PC version of Kalypso Media's *Tropico 5* (2014), as verified by Speedrun on 3 Jan 2017.

Most rent earned in one year in *Constructor* **(Xbox One)**
As of 19 Apr 2018, UK gamer "Pool 5hark" had extracted $1,700,561

from his tenants in a single year while playing System 3's 2017 remaster of 1997's *Constructor*. The haul of rent was $941,912 more than the amount taken by the gamer's nearest rival.

Most popular mod for *Cities: Skylines*
A total of 944,806 players had downloaded the "Automatic

Bulldoze" mod in *Cities: Skylines* (Paradox Interactive, 2015) from Steam, as of 27 Mar 2018. Created by "Sadler", the mod simplifies city management by automatically demolishing abandoned and burnt-out buildings.

First movie trailer created in a management sim
In 2016, "JustinBeiberIsPoop" recreated the film trailer for 2007's *Bee Movie* using

RollerCoaster Tycoon 2's editor. Ground tiles were used as pixels to "draw" each frame of the trailer, which were then edited into a stop-motion video.

Longest development time for a park in *RollerCoaster Tycoon 2*
Sebastian Brendgen (DEU) spent 10 years placing 64,516 tiles by hand to create the ultimate (virtual) theme park. When he unveiled it in May 2017, it had 34 roller-coasters.

Highest-rated management sim on Steam
As of 27 Mar 2018, Ludeon Studios' sci-fi colony sim *RimWorld* (2013) had a user rating of 95.33%. "This game is amazing," said one player. "The characters have their own personalities, flaws, strengths, and react to situations like real people."

RIMWORLD

MOST MANAGEMENT SIMS BASED ON A FILM SERIES

With the release of *Jurassic World Evolution* (Frontier Developments, 2018), there have been five management sims inspired by the famous movie franchise that began with *Jurassic Park* in 1993.

The first was *Jurassic Park III: Park Builder* (2001), followed by *Jurassic Park: Operation Genesis* (2003), *Jurassic Park Builder* (2012) and *Jurassic World: The Game* (2015).

Jurassic World Evolution takes its inspiration from the films *Jurassic World* (2015) and *Jurassic World: Fallen Kingdom* (2018). In the game, players build their theme park from scratch, placing their paddocks, choosing which species to house and designing rides. Pay special attention to your park's security, for, as we know from watching the movies, life has a nasty habit of finding a way...

YOUR NEW FAVOURITE GAME

TWO POINT HOSPITAL
Platform: PC
Breaking out in the kind of humour that made *Theme Hospital* (1997) so contagious, Sega's *Two Point Hospital* challenges you to cure patients with ailments you wouldn't find on a regular hospital ward. Premature mummification, anyone?

2,042 YEARS

The computer-controlled guests that visit theme parks in *RollerCoaster Tycoon 2* (Infogrames, 2002) are used to braving over-the-top roller-coasters and other rides. Spare a thought for Beverley P, though, who got a lot more than she bargained for when she entered the gigantic hedge maze of "RogueLeader23" (USA). She emerged 2,042 in-game years later – the **longest time to escape a maze in** *RollerCoaster Tycoon 2*.

FACT!

As of 15 Dec 2017, *Planet Coaster* players had built 10,737,423 km (6,671,925 mi) of roller-coaster track, laid 9,589,423 km (5,958,591 mi) of paths, employed 60,638,930 people and placed 19,503,061 lampposts.

SURVIVING MARS

Surviving Mars' main objective sounds simple, but existing on the Red Planet is anything but easy. Mars' deadly atmosphere makes living in habitat domes a must, but your colonists still aren't safe – meteor strikes, dust storms and freezing cold waves can all turn your communities into ghost towns.

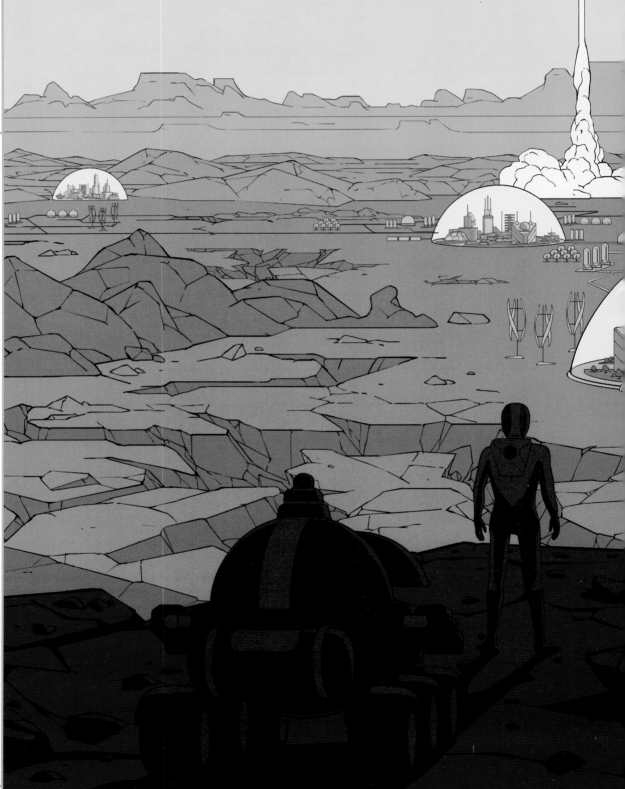

SIMULATIONS

LIFE ON MARS?

Building a colony on a world far different than Earth carries many dangers. Statistics supplied by *Surviving Mars*' publisher Paradox Interactive showed how tough it might be. As of 23 Mar 2018, players had built a total of 1,653,543 domes to keep their colonists safe from the alien planet's atmosphere. But a lack of oxygen is only the start of their problems. Extreme weather and intense cold can destroy even the largest dome, killing hundreds of thousands in the process. The **most common natural disaster in *Surviving Mars*** were meteor storms that had rained down from the skies on 660,770 occasions. The stats also show that certain jobs should come with a health warning. The **most deadly profession in *Surviving Mars*** was that of astrogeologist. On average, 34 space-rock scientists per game had lost their lives in pursuit of their vocation. The overall survival rate for colonists is not great anyway. Of the 88,757,812 colonists who had, so far, braved the Red Planet in the hope of a new life, 37,132,812 (or 42%) had perished. That puts *Surviving Mars*' death rate at an average of 111 colonists per in-game day!

WAY OF THE PACIFIST

Some modern games, such as *Deus Ex*, invite gamers to play peacefully if they want to. The majority of action titles, though, can't be completed without first punching, hacking and blasting through enough bad guys to fill a small country… or can they? Revolutionary gamers are now flipping game design on its head to rebel against this call for aggression. These "pacifist speed-runs" (all verified by Speedrun.com, except for *Fallout 4*, which is on YouTube) are an attempt to finish games as swiftly as possible, while also killing the fewest non-player characters (NPCs) as possible – although dispatching bosses in the name of progress is allowed. Here are some of the best aggression-free examples out there. Peace!

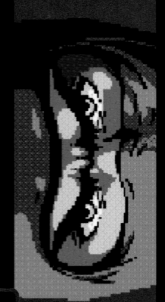

00:14:48
HR   MIN   SEC

"I will get my revenge!"

NINJA GAIDEN (1988)

When they created the classic NES adventure game back in 1988, it's doubtful that Tecmo's development team ever envisaged that Ryu Hayabusa's revenge (above) could have been taken in a non-violent way. But pacifist speed-runner "gusmancini" (USA) had other ideas. On 13 Jan 2016, he took his revenge without killing any enemies (with the exception of unavoidable bosses) and without using health or time-stoppers.

Eager to spread the peace further, the American gamer also tackled the sequels. He recorded the **fastest pacifist completion of *Ninja Gaiden II: The Dark Sword of Chaos*** (NES, 1990) in just 14 min 31 sec on 26 Jan 2016, and the **fastest pacifist completion of *Ninja Gaiden III: The Ancient Ship of Doom*** (NES, 1991), the next chapter in the saga, in a mere 17 min 42 sec on 17 Aug 2014.

POSTAL 2 (2003)

Developed by Running with Scissors, *Postal 2* was hugely controversial when it was first released. The debate was caused by the shooter's satirical black humour and gung-ho gameplay. Scottish PC player "Lonne" finished *Postal 2* on 6 Aug 2017 in the quickest non-violent play-through ever. The achievement was welcomed with an on-screen message of congratulations, saying "Thank you for playing, Jesus!"

`00:32:01` HR MIN SEC

WAY OF THE SAMURAI 3 (2008)

Honouring the Samurai code of chivalry, "Kromer SR" (BRA) set a new high mark in pacifism by completing Spike's feudal RPG without fighting any NPCs. It was a laudable effort on a game with 100 weapons to use. On 2 Oct 2016, he uploaded a video of his feat – called "Way Of The Samurai 3 - Pacifist%" in 12:08,761 (Console WR) – to YouTube. "Faster than Bolt, peaceful like Buddha," he commented.

`00:12:08` HR MIN SEC

SALT AND SANCTUARY (2016)

The ghouls and ghosts of Ska Studios' 2D take on *Dark Souls* were left unharmed by PC speed-runner "Coppie" (SVN), who completed a run-through of the game's eerie environs without damaging a single enemy on 7 Aug 2017. By way of comparison, the fastest any% completion stands at 4 min 30 sec (also by "Coppie"), while the swiftest all-bosses runs tend to last for around 30 min.

`00:05:13` HR MIN SEC

FALLOUT 4 (2015)

Kyle Hinckley (USA), aka "The Weirdist", gave a lot of thought to a pacifist speed-run on the hardest difficulty of Bethesda's RPG, especially as the game director had said completing the game this way was "not necessarily a goal of ours". Incredibly, on 19 Jun 2016, Hinckley finished it without a kill staining his name. His alternative ways of advancing the narrative included hacking robots to attack enemies or exploiting glitches so foes would inadvertently destroy themselves.

`26:35:00` HR MIN SEC

DIABLO II: LORD OF DESTRUCTION (2001)

Canadian gamer "blazer-flamewing" has forged the fastest non-violent path through Blizzard's demon-filled RPG. On 25 Jul 2017, playing as the Paladin, he finished the game without directly attacking any entity. He achieved it by wearing thorn-covered armour and other pieces of equipment that automatically lashed out at any devilish aggressors.

`02:43:11` HR MIN SEC

STRATEGY

Think you can make the right call in a life-or-death situation or plan and execute strategies on a grand scale? Then you have all you need to make it in whichever strategy game you desire. Now all you have to do is outwit all the other budding generals out there looking to do the same...

MOST CRITICALLY ACCLAIMED HANDHELD TURN-BASED STRATEGY GAME

Fire Emblem: Awakening, Nintendo's tactical role-playing *tour de force*, has found a lot of favour with critics. As of 12 Mar 2018, the 11th entry in the *Fire Emblem* saga, released for the Nintendo 3DS in 2012, had an aggregate score of 92.52% from 52 reviews on GameRankings. Critics lauded its finely balanced tactical gameplay that takes the concept of rock, paper, scissors and runs with it – meaning that units are typically strong against one enemy type and weak against another. Its pair-up system, which allows two allies to band together, was also praised.

Its closest rival was the similarly acclaimed *Advance Wars: Dual Strike* (2005) for the DS, which had an average rating of 92.38%.

167

MOBAs

Huge crowds, intense media interest and life-changing prize money – multiplayer online battle arenas (MOBAs) are the pinnacle of professional gaming. Even for those of us who aren't pro gamers, the levels of teamwork and strategy keep us coming back for more...

FIRST GAME TO PAY OUT $100 MILLION

When it comes to eSports, *Dota 2* is king. According to eSportsearnings, it was the first videogame to shell out the scarcely believable figure of $100 million (£78,436,900) in prize money. Valve's MOBA passed the milestone on 12 Jun 2017. The gigantic sum had been shared between 1,952 players in 741 tournaments since 2013.

The annual *Dota 2* championships, known as The International, makes up a huge part of this ever-expanding figure. Just after the $100-million mark was hit, the amount was swelled again by 2017's staging of The International at the Seattle Center's KeyArena in Washington, USA, on 2–12 Aug (main picture). It boasted a prize pool of $24,787,916 (£19,080,300) for the winners and finalists. Team Liquid walked away with the top prize – $10,862,683 (£8,361,450) – the **largest first prize in an eSports tournament.**

HIGHEST-EARNING ESPORTS PLAYER

As of 19 Feb 2018, Kuro "KuroKy" Takhasomi (DEU) had won $3,525,039 (£2,511,310) playing *Dota 2* and *Defense of the Ancients* (2003). Some $2 million (£1.42 million) of that came after his *Dota 2* team, Team Liquid, secured victory at 2017's The International.

Most first-picked *Heroes of the Storm* hero
Based on data tracked by GosuGamers, the spellcaster Jaina Proudmoore had, as of 20 Feb 2018, been picked first by pro gamers 552 times. She just edged out Kael'thas, who was selected 519 times.

FACT!

In a survey by analytics firm Newzoo, covering 10 countries and the top MOBAs (including *Dota 2* and *League of Legends*), it was revealed that 42% of eSports viewers don't play the games they watch.

$18,580,530

As of 20 Feb 2018, Team Liquid still reigned as the **highest-earning eSports team**, scooping an epic $18,580,530 (£13,258,200) from 1,141 eSports events. A large slice was pocketed at The International 2017 *Dota 2* championships in Aug 2017 (just over $10,000,000/£7,135,530), but the team added to their takings from games such as *StarCraft II*, *Quake Champions*, *Heroes of the Storm* and *Hearthstone*. The organization, set up in the Netherlands in 2000, has drawn players from Europe, the Middle East and South America.

3,584 MATCHES

The Haunted Mines map's unique objective of collecting cursed skulls to power up your team's Bone Golem has made it the **most played map in *Heroes of the Storm***. The Haunted Mines in Blizzard's 2015 hero brawler had been visited in 3,584 pro matches, as confirmed on 24 Jan 2018 by GosuGamers. The **least played map in *Heroes of the Storm*** was the Volskaya Foundry, played just eight times as of the same date.

EXPANDED FRANCHISE

Held in Mar 2016, The Shanghai Major was an epic five-day *Dota 2* tournament. The event ended with a special concert based around music for the game, conducted by composer Tim Larkin.

Most revenue by a mobile game
Honour of Kings (Tencent, 2015) is a free2play MOBA for mobiles that's hugely popular in China. Known as *Arena of Valor* in the west, it made $1,881,609,460.19 (£1,322,583,289.57) in digital sales revenue in 2017 alone.

Most eSports world championships won by a country in 24 hours
It's hard enough trying to win one world title, but three? On 4–5 Nov 2017, eSports teams from South Korea won world championships in three different games. First, Samsung Galaxy proved themselves the elite *League of Legends* outfit, beating fellow countrymen SK Telecom T1 in the final. The South Korean national side then successfully defended the *Overwatch* world title against Canada. Finally, South Korean team MVP Black beat Fnatic in *Heroes of the Storm* at the Global Championship finals.

First computer to beat a *Dota 2* world champ in tournament rules
On 10 Aug, at The International's 2017 tournament, the winner of 2015's The International, Syed Sumail "Suma1L" Hassan (PAK), went one-on-one with – and eventually lost to – a bot from AI research outfit OpenAI. The bot showed that it was no fluke the next day when it defeated Danil "Dendi" Ishutin (UKR), the champion of 2011's staging of The International.

Highest-earning *Heroes of the Storm* player
As of 20 Feb 2018, there was little to split fellow South Koreans Lee "Sake" Jung-hyeog and Jeong "KyoCha" Won-ho. According to eSportsearnings, "Sake" had won $306,790.78 (£218,911), but his compatriot was breathing down his neck with $306,468.56 (£218,682). The pair are both members of the hugely successful MVP Black *Heroes of the Storm* eSports team.

LEAGUE OF LEGENDS

How can a game nearly a decade old be as popular now as it has ever been? Simple – *League of Legends'* (*LoL*) perfect mix of strategy and action means that its huge community gets all its gaming kicks, while elite eSports players compete for the big bucks.

MOST DIGITAL REVENUE GENERATED BY A GAME

Depending on the reasons why they are introduced, micro-transactions aren't always a terrible thing. For Riot Games' 2009 free2play *League of Legends* (*LoL*), the sales of outfits, weapon skins and other accessories help satisfy fans' demand for new content – and those same items just so happen to be responsible for the bulk of its revenue. According to SuperData, the hugely popular MOBA generated a total of $2.07 bn (£1.53 bn) in digital sales revenue in 2017 – more than any other game.

Having a massive player base is key to those riches. More than 102 million users played *LoL* every month in 2017, making it the **most played multiplayer online game in 2017**, according to SuperData.

The removal of the Level 30 cap provided another way to view gamer devotion. On 31 Dec 2017, "Nolife Raphael" was the **first player to surpass Level 300 in *LoL*,** as verified by lolnames.gg. He played against AI bots on the three-on-three "Twisted Treeline" map to gain levels rapidly.

MOST FIRST-PICKED *LOL* CHAMPION

Spider queen Elise's all-round qualities have made her a popular first pick for captains. She was the opening choice in 593 competitive *League of Legends* matches as of 14 Feb 2018, according to GosuGamers. That's a first-pick rate of 5%.

FIRST *LOL* PLAYER TO EARN $1 MILLION

League of Legends rewards its superstar players with major tournaments and big money. On 21 May 2017, SK Telecom T1's mid-laner Lee "Faker" Sang-hyeok (KOR) broke through the $1 million (£766,712) barrier in tournament prize money – according to data tracked by eSportsearnings.com. The hot shot, widely regarded as the game's best-ever player,

passed this milestone after his team defeated G2 Esports to win the Mid-Season Invitational event. Inevitably, he was also the **highest-earning *LoL* player.** As of 14 Feb 2018, he'd competed in 39 events and raked in $1,169,713 (£843,111).

With "Faker" on the team, it's little surprise that the three-time world champions SK Telecom 1

have crushed many of the sides that have stood in their way. The crack South Korean outfit stand as the **highest-earning *League of Legends* team.** Esportsearnings reports that, as of 14 Feb 2018, the team had earned $6,598,419 (£4,756,040) in 31 tournaments across the world, over $2.77 m (£2 m) more than the outfit's nearest rival, Samsung.

MOST BANNED CHAMPION IN *LOL* MATCHES

During the pre-match, pro *League of Legends* captains often try to improve their chances of victory by removing the "rune mage" Ryze from their opponent's team. According to GosuGamers, he'd been banned from 2,867 clashes as of 14 Feb 2018. The second most banned hero is LeBlanc, who had been removed on 2,611 occasions.

Largest mechanical wings on a cosplay costume

Leo Simon (UK) said that his costume of *League of Legends* champion Aether Wing Kayle left the public's "minds blown" at gaming events. The outfit took 17 months to create and had wings that stretched 4.26 m (13 ft 11 in), as verified in London, UK, on 27 Jan 2017.

THE NEXT GAMER

Mix *LoL* with reality TV and you have *The Next Gamer*. At stake was $10,000 AUD (£6,152; $7,983) and a pro eSports team spot. Jarod "Get Back71" Tucker won series one.

Largest walkabout puppet based on a videogame
At 3.42 m (11 ft 3 in), Thresh is head and shoulders above the rest. This puppet version of the *League of Legends* Champion was created by US FX studio Buddy Builds in Jul 2016 and commissioned by Riot Games.

1 HOUR 34 MINUTES 37 SECONDS

Two epic records were set in Seoul, South Korea, in one game on 20 Jan 2018. Jin Air Green Wings (JAG) and SK Telecom T1 battled to the **longest professional *League of Legends* game**. The clincher game in a 2–1 victory for JAG lasted 1 hr 34 min 37 sec. In helping JAG to this win, Park "Teddy" Jin-seong racked up the **most minions killed in a *League of Legends* pro game** – 1,465. "I was way too focused to pay attention," he told Invenglobal.com.

GAMING GOLD

Doing damage
Making the most of a "crazy insane" bug, *LoL* YouTuber "Brofresco" did 20,597.4 points of damage in one hit in Mar 2016.

Most wins of the *League of Legends* World Championship
Between its inaugural tournament in 2011 and the culmination of its 2017 event on 4 Nov, the world title had been won by South Korea's SK Telecom T1 three times: in 2013, 2015 and 2016. Star players "Faker", aka Lee Sang-hyeok, and "Bengi", aka Bae Seong-ung (both KOR), were the only two players to feature in the team on all three occasions. There was to be no

fourth global title in 2017. SK Telecom T1 reached the final of the tournament, which was held for the first time in China, but were beaten 3–0 by the Samsung Galaxy team, who took the title for a second time.

Most followed MOBA game on Twitter
A total of 4,287,909 followers made *League of Legends'* Twitter channel more popular than any other MOBA on the social-media platform, as of

14 Feb 2018. It was ahead of *SMITE* (1,081,355), *Dota 2* (782,487) and *Heroes of the Storm* (496,714).

Highest win rate for a Champion in *League of Legends*
Based on pro matches tracked by GosuGamers, "the star forger" Aurelion Sol had been on the winning team in 69% of contests in which he had been selected, as of 14 Feb 2018 – though he'd been chosen on only 47 occasions.

First female pro *LoL* player
On 12 Aug 2015, Maria Creveling, aka "Remilia" (USA), effectively became the first female player to turn professional when her team Renegades qualified for the lucrative *League of Legends* Championship Series (LCS). Maria, who played in a support position in the game, had previously secured her reputation by obtaining the highest rank of Challenger in the game's online multiplayer.

STRATEGY ROUND-UP

"If you know the enemy and know yourself, you need not fear the result of a hundred battles." So said Sun Tzu in his treatise *The Art of War*. His advice still rings true to strategy-game stalwarts 25 centuries later. Strangely, he didn't add "be sure you know your keyboard shortcuts..."

MOST ACCLAIMED *WARHAMMER* GAME

Cave trolls looking to turn the Empire's finest knights into tin cans? Orcs and goblins gleefully roaring "WAAAGH!" as they charge into battle once more? It can mean only one thing – yet another gamer is playing a title based on Games Workshop's fantasy tabletop game *Warhammer*.

Of all the games inspired by *Warhammer* (strategy or otherwise), Creative Assembly's real-time epic *Total War: Warhammer II* (Sega, 2017) has impressed the critics the most. As of 6 Feb 2018, its average review score was higher than any other entry based on the *Warhammer* fictional universe, with an aggregate score of 87.26% according to GameRankings. It seized the top spot from THQ's sci-fi strategy *Warhammer 40,000: Dawn of War – Dark Crusade*, which was released in 2006.

MOST ACCLAIMED SWITCH STRATEGY VIDEOGAME

Mario + Rabbids Kingdom Battle (2017) saw Ubisoft's Rabbids invade Nintendo's Mushroom Kingdom, posing new problems for Mario and co. The fusion proved popular with gamers and the press alike. As of 5 Feb 2018, the turn-based crossover title had a GameRankings score of 84.81% from 55 reviews.

MOST MONEY EARNED IN STRATEGY TOURNAMENTS

As of 5 Feb 2018, Lee "Jaedong" Jae-dong (KOR) had been rewarded for his prowess on *StarCraft* and *StarCraft II* to the tune of $627,936.35 (£444,696), putting the pro gamer just ahead of fellow countryman Young Ho-lee.

Most flawless missions in *XCOM 2*
As of 5 Feb 2018, strategy maestro "Th3 On1y Shming" had orchestrated 1,062 "flawless" missions in Firaxis' turn-based alien-battler *XCOM 2* (2016) on Xbox One, as verified by TrueAchievements. For a mission to be recorded as flawless, players must guide their XCOM team to victory without its members sustaining any damage.

AGE OF EMPIRES IV
Platform: PC
The original *Age of Empires* set the bar high for real-time strategy with its 1997 release, and *Age of Empires IV* will look to do exactly the same. Expect to once more take control of enormous armies as some of history's legendary generals.

FACT!

On 21 Oct 2016, to align with the release of *Civilization VI*, pro eSports organization Team Liquid announced the founding of the **first** *Civilization* **eSports team**.

Most prolific real-time strategy videogame series
As of 1 Mar 2018, *Command & Conquer*, the real-time strategy (RTS) game created by Westwood (now owned by EA), had 56 separate releases, including expansions and ports to other systems. The series spans 17 years, starting with the original for PC in 1995. The most recent entry was 2012's *Command & Conquer: The Ultimate Collection*. The nearest RTS series is Sega's *Total War* franchise, with 46 separate releases.

Highest-rated strategy game on Steam
As of 6 Feb 2018, the real-time strategy-come-survival title *Factorio* (Wube Software) boasted a user-approval rating of 96.54% on the PC distribution platform. A total of 32,364 players liked the part-crowdfunded title, while only 438 had given it the thumbs down. It was also the **highest-rated indie game on Steam** and the second most highly rated overall, behind *Portal 2*.

Most *Halo Wars 2* multiplayer matches won
Nimble-fingered "Gh0stR3aPeR" (DEU) has won the most *Halo Wars 2* multiplayer matches, notching up an impressive 3,344 victories. This puts the Xbox One player 161 victories ahead of his nearest rival, "Viper Skills", who has won 3,183 matches. His feat was verified by TrueAchievements.com on 6 Feb 2018.

Most watched eSports match for a mobile videogame
The ClashCon 2015 Clan War final between Sweden 1 Star and Glory China I on 24 Oct 2015 had been watched 4,122,157 times on YouTube as of 6 Feb 2018. The *Clash of Clans* match ended in a tie, but China's Glory China I took the trophy based on the percentage of damage inflicted. The showdown, hosted in Helsinki, Finland, was the **first dedicated convention for a mobile game** and saw 1,200 *Clash of Clans* fans from 39 countries gather at the Messukeskus Expo and Convention Centre.

11,810,159

MOST SUBSCRIBERS FOR A GAME CHANNEL ON YOUTUBE
The loyal and committed fan base of mobile strategy game *Clash of Clans* has shown such devotion to following the latest news and watching the showdowns between the best players that, as of 5 Feb 2018, Supercell's official YouTube channel boasted a formidable 11,810,159 subscribers. This placed *Clash of Clans* well ahead of other gaming channels, including *League of Legends* (8,728,782), *PlayStation* (6,273,934), *Call of Duty* (5,231,111) and *Rockstar Games* (3,855,563).

MOST PICKED
DOTA 2 HEROES

What do the *Dota 2* pros look for when poring over the options for their eSports team in the all-conquering MOBA? Our data – as verified by GosuGamers on 12 Mar 2018 – proves that it's brains, not brawn, that is the most highly prized quality in *Dota 2*'s heroes.

10
SAND KING
PICKED 5,571 TIMES
Main attribute
Strength

9
PUCK
PICKED 5,721 TIMES
Main attribute
Intelligence

8
DISRUPTOR
PICKED 5,769 TIMES
Main attribute
Intelligence

7
CLOCKWERK
PICKED 5,813 TIMES
Main attribute
Strength

6
QUEEN OF PAIN
PICKED 5,902 TIMES
Main attribute
Intelligence

As of 20 Feb 2018, Batrider, with 12,035 bans, is the **most banned Dota 2 character**. His speed and vision make him just too deadly to take on in tournaments.

5
INVOKER
PICKED 6,194 TIMES

Main attribute
Intelligence

4
DARK SEER
PICKED 6,664 TIMES

Main attribute
Intelligence

3
VENGEFUL SPIRIT
PICKED 6,911 TIMES

Main attribute
Agility

2
BATRIDER
PICKED 7,121 TIMES

Main attribute
Intelligence

1
RUBICK
PICKED 9,155 TIMES

Main attribute
Intelligence

PLAY YOUR CARDS RIGHT

Once thought of as something of a novelty, online collectable card videogames have now hit the jackpot, with winning hands that have seen their popularity rocket. Here, we look at some of the major titles that have raised the stakes and discover what they bring to the gaming table.

HEARTHSTONE
(Blizzard Entertainment, 2014)
Few come bigger. With 70 million registered players as of 1 May 2017, Blizzard's take on the genre is a sensation, thanks in part to it being playable on PC, smartphone and tablet. Its roots in the *Warcraft* universe guarantee an audience, but its success also springs from its easy-to-learn, tough-to-master gameplay. Strategies can be mind-spinningly complex, involving chess-like levels of planning and execution.

POKÉMON TRADING CARD GAME
(Nintendo/Wizards of the Coast, 1996)
Originally available in physical form only, the *Pokémon* card game expanded to include an online version. Just like the *Pokémon* games, the key is to make use of the right type in every battle. Watch out if your opponent has a Rare Candy card – this powerful card lets its owner evolve any basic Pokémon!

HEX: SHARDS OF FATE
(Cryptozoic Entertainment, 2016)
Funded via a successful Kickstarter campaign that raised $2.27 m (£1.37 m) in 2013, *Hex* differs from other collectable card games in that it's also a massively multiplayer online (MMO) game. Essentially, *Hex* combines card collecting and deck building with the communal aspects of an MMO. If you want to make friends as you work out strategies, then this is for you.

HAND OF FATE 2
(Defiant Development, 2017)
Released in late 2017, *Hand of Fate 2* isn't an online collectable card game, but is instead an adventure game that changes based on the cards in your hand. As you progress, more and more cards are added to your deck. Only once you've gained every card will you be able to collect every magical item and hidden weapon necessary to win.

GWENT: THE WITCHER CARD GAME
(CD Projekt Red, 2018)
Available in beta form since 2016, the card-game offshoot from *The Witcher III: Wild Hunt* has made a big splash on the pro scene. Live Twitch streams feature players from as far and wide as China, Germany and the USA battling for enormous sums. The Gwent World Masters series, announced in Aug 2017, offered a total prize pool of $850,000 (£659,545).

ARTIFACT
(Valve, TBC)
The speculation is that this spin-off from Valve's all-conquering *Dota 2* MOBA may not be widely available until 2019. But, when it does land, there's every chance that it will challenge *Hearthstone* in terms of its player numbers.
Artifact works a little differently from most online card games in that players manage three heroes (to represent *Dota 2*'s lanes) at once. Each hero's result has a knock-on effect on the others.

THE ELDER SCROLLS: LEGENDS
(Bethesda Softworks, 2017)
As with *Hearthstone*, *The Elder Scrolls: Legends* is based in the same universe as its parent franchise: in this case, *The Elder Scrolls*. *Legends* divides its playing arena into various lanes, which assign different abilities to your cards and determine which lane you can and can't attack. There's lots to learn, but the tactical options available make it a satisfying experience.

Fairy Ring

Morokei, the Deathless
Summon: If you started the game with no duplicate cards in your deck, you gain 5 health and restore a rune.

BRAWLERS

Going *mano a mano* to overcome your rival is what brawlers are all about, and few other genres provide such a stern test of skill. Striking with a devastating combo at the perfect moment is the key to victory – just be sure you've got a back-up plan if your opponent counters...

LIVE, NOW!

INJUSTICE 2

MAXIMILIAN vs SONICFOX

2017 TOP MOMENTS

"FIGHTING GAMES GIVE YOU SO MUCH CREATIVITY. THEY'RE ABOUT AWESOME CHARACTERS DOING EVEN MORE AWESOME STUFF!

MAXIMILIAN DOOD

MOST SUBSCRIBERS FOR A YOUTUBE CHANNEL DEDICATED TO FIGHTING GAMES

US YouTuber Maximilian Dood (aka Maximilian Christiansen) has been posting videos since 7 Jun 2007 indulging his passion for fighting games. As of 4 Apr 2018, he'd built up a subscriber base of 806,844 fellow enthusiasts.

Seen below (second left) with the YoVideogames crew, Max explained why fighting games are so popular: "There's nothing quite like landing something you've been practising for hours and hours in an actual match, to eventually have that thing become second nature."

Of all fighting games, his favourite is Capcom's 1999 classic *Street Fighter III: 3rd Strike*. "It's a pinnacle of classic sprite-based animation," he said.

SUPER SMASH BROS. BOSS RAGE

HOW TO EXTEND COMBOS

REACTION

FIGHTING

Fighting games are so well balanced and finessed these days that battles are often as much about strategy as brute strength – like chess but with bigger muscles! For elite eSports pros, major money is on offer. But, no matter who you are, unleashing huge combos is still the coolest way to show off.

LONGEST ONE-HANDED COMBO IN *DRAGON BALL FIGHTERZ*

Dishing out body-bruising, 100-plus hit combos is complex enough with two fully functioning hands in Bandai Namco's *Dragon Ball FighterZ* (2018). Imagine the difficulty of trying to do exactly that with one hand tied behind your back – or, in the case of fighting-game maestro "desk", one hand broken.

As demonstrated in an unbelievable clip sent directly to us on 4 Mar 2018, "desk" employed the formidable team of Super Saiyan Goku, Teen Gohan and Yamcha to dole out a blistering array of 441 hits to a hapless Cell. His technique was to pull Cell's team-mate (Android 16) into the fray to double-up the hits-landed count, then end with a Super move. Just imagine what he'll manage once his hand's healed!

Rarest *Nidhogg 2* trophy
The elusive "Hogglike" trophy had yet to be awarded to any PS4 player as of 23 Feb 2018, as verified by PSNProfiles. To unlock the trophy, players must complete the single-player mode without dying – a notoriously difficult task in a game where life is cheap and death is but a sword-swipe away. PC players had fared slightly better, with 0.1% of players managing to grab the "Hogglike" achievement on Steam.

MOST POPULAR CHARACTER IN *STREET FIGHTER V*

Poster boy Ryu is the fighter that pro *Street Fighter V* players turn to the most. As of 23 Feb 2018, he'd been used by 726 players, with a Usage Score of 1,581 according to Eventhubs (the score based on where the character fits in each pro's top three picks). Fiery female Karin was in second place with a score of 1,056, and Special Forces soldier Charlie Nash was third with 1,022.

EXPANDED FRANCHISE

From May 2017, DC Comics bridged the gap between the games *Injustice: Gods Among Us* and *Injustice 2* with a comic-book series. Superman is behind bars, Batman doesn't know who to trust and the future of the planet hangs by a thread.

BEST-SELLING FIGHTING GAME (PS4 & XBOX ONE)

"Get over here!" According to VGChartz, *Mortal Kombat X* (Warner Bros., 2015) had sold 3.21 million copies on the PS4 as of 23 Feb 2018. The same source confirmed the game's dominance on Xbox One, too, with 1.55 million copies shifted as of the same date.

Highest first prize for a fighting game tournament
The world's best *Street Fighter V* players went toe-to-toe in the finals of the 2017 Capcom Cup, held on 8–10 Dec in Anaheim, California, USA. A prize pool of at least $370,000 (£275,269) was split among the top eight combatants. "MenaRD", aka Saul Leonardo Mena Segundo (DOM), faced off against "Tokido", aka Hajime Taniguchi (JPN). "MenaRD" eventually emerged victorious and claimed the $250,000 (£185,993) top prize. The winner's sum was $20,000 (£14,879) more than the previous year's cash purse.

Most competitive players of a fighting videogame
According to Eventhubs, *Ultra Street Fighter IV* had 14,200 competitive players as of 23 Feb 2018. Behind it were *Ultimate Marvel vs. Capcom 3* (with 7,776 players), *Super Smash Bros. for Wii U* (with 5,857) and *Street Fighter X Tekken* (with 5,008).

First fighting game with weapons
A new era was ushered in with the Oct 1979 arcade release of Tim Skelly's *Warrior* (Vectorbeam). The two duelling, vector-drawn knights in the one-on-one brawler wielded swords. Contrary to the norm for later fighting games, it used a top-down perspective. Original arcade cabinets for *Warrior* are extremely rare, with only 10 registered at the Vintage Arcade Preservation Society (VAPS) as of Feb 2018.

Longest online winning streak on
Marvel vs. Capcom: Infinite **(Xbox One)**
Mikhail Krauser (CAN) kicked, punched and super-cancelled his way through 151 victorious online battles of Capcom's fighter as of 26 Feb 2018, according to TrueAchievements. The same source verified the feats of "BigDaddyUltima" (USA) and "Forla 77", who, with win streaks of 144 and 140 respectively, had been snapping at Krauser's heels.

Longest wait for a game re-release
In Nov 2017, to mark 30 years of *Street Fighter*, Capcom re-released the SNES version of *Street Fighter II* on an NTSC cartridge. The new cartridge, priced at $100 (£74), was limited to a 5,500 run (with 1,000 in a "Glow-in-the-dark Blanka green"). Its release came 14 years after the SNES console ceased production.

GAMING GOLD

YOU DANCE VERY WELL.

Dancing keen
Zangief is joined by a surprise fan at the end of *Street Fighter II* (1991) as former Soviet political leader Mikhail Gorbachev busts some moves.

26 YEARS

On 20 Mar 2017, YouTuber "desk" posted a video showing the discovery of new combos some 26 years after *Street Fighter II*'s arcade release in Feb 1991. The new combos target the masked fighter Vega (called Balrog in Japan). It exploits a glitch that allows Vega to be hit while grounded after a sweep attack. It is the **longest time to find a *Street Fighter II* combo**.

BEAT-'EM-UPS

Most of us would reach for our phone to call the police if our loved ones were kidnapped by notorious crime lords or alien invaders. Not so the stars of videogame beat-'em-ups, who much prefer to suit up and head on out to punch their way to vengeance.

FIRST CEL-SHADED BEAT-'EM-UP VIDEOGAME

When *Viewtiful Joe* came to GameCube on 26 Jun 2003, jaws were well and truly dropped. Capcom's highly stylized beat-'em-up was the first game in the genre to make its graphics appear hand-drawn and animated to the quality you'd expect of a cartoon. Capcom took full advantage of this dynamic visual style to complement the game's story, which sees a film buff – the titular Joe – plunged into a movie and transformed into a superhero. The game was also notable for letting players chain together combos by freezing and fast-forwarding time. "Henshin a-go-go, baby!" as Joe would say.

Fastest completion of *Brawlhalla*
Danish gamer "ThStardust" completed Blue Mammoth's 2015 free-to-play fighting game in just 3 min 32 sec on 15 Jan 2017, as verified by Speedrun. "ThStardust" had a message of consolation for previous record holder "ImLogic" (USA), posting: "Sorry logic, but im gonna need to take that 1st place back" when he uploaded his new benchmark time to Speedrun's leaderboard.

The pain game
Until Taito's *Renegade* (1986), beat-'em-up bad guys could always be knocked out in one hit. *Renegade*'s enemies could actually absorb multiple blows!

70 INJURIES

Arcade game *Sonic Blast Man* (Taito, 1990) challenged players to don boxing gloves and hit a pressure-pad controller to knock down enemies. It was recalled in 1995 after 70 cases of game-related injuries emerged – the **most real-life injuries for players of a beat-'em-up game**. Taito had to pay $50,000 (£32,226) for not filing incident reports. Ouch!

First videogame adaptation of a movie based on a game
Double Dragon was a one-on-one fighter based on the 1994 movie adaptation of SNK's side-scrolling beat-'em-up series. It was released in Japan as a NeoGeo arcade game on 3 Mar 1995. This predated Capcom's *Street Fighter: The Movie* videogame adaptation by three months. Alas, the *Double Dragon* game – alternatively known as *Double Dragon '95* – wasn't a critical success, being roundly panned for its sub-par graphics.

Longest time in the same videogame role
Japanese actress Masako Nozawa has been voicing Son Goku (as well as other characters) in the *Dragon Ball* game series for 24 years 312 days, between the releases of *Dragon Ball Z: Super Butōden* on 20 Mar 1993 and *Dragon Ball FighterZ* on 26 Jan 2018. Her games include one-on-one brawlers and side-scrolling beat-'em-ups.

Longest-running side-scrolling beat-'em-up franchise
Following the release of *Double Dragon IV* (Arc System Works) on 30 Jan 2017, Technōs' seminal side-scrolling fighter series had been running for approximately 30 years. The original game, *Double Dragon,* was first released in arcades in 1987 and has become the **most ported fighting videogame**, appearing on 24 platforms ranging from the Atari 2600 to the PS4.

Fastest completion of *Mother Russia Bleeds*
Playing on the "easy" difficulty on 4 Apr 2017 and choosing the Boris character, France's "Pringi" completed Devolver Digital's super-grisly 2016 side-scrolling fighter in 54 min 38 sec, as verified by Speedrun. "I begin to think that sub-50 [min] is possible," he said.

HIGHEST-RATED FIGHTING GAME ON STEAM

As of 12 Mar 2018, Silver Dollar Games' kung fu brawler *One Finger Death Punch* (2013) had a 95.71% user-approval rating on Steam. A total of 13,172 martial arts devotees awarded it a positive review, with just 203 users giving it the thumbs down.

FACT!
In 2009, a beat-'em-up based on DC Comics' Justice League was cancelled. Developed by Double Helix, the game would have let players take on goons as Superman, Batman, Wonder Woman and others.

HACK-AND-SLASH

Sharpen your sword, grind your axe and strap on your favourite suit of armour – it's time to take to the battlefield to slice-and-dice yet another horde of unsuspecting bad guys. Here, we cut a swathe through the games that let sharp metal, not fists, do the talking.

MOST PROLIFIC HACK-AND-SLASH SERIES

Not counting the series' first entry (on account of it being a one-on-one brawler), there had been 33 *Dynasty Warriors* hack-and-slash games as of 14 Mar 2018 – eight main series games, 13 standalone expansions and 12 spin-offs.

It's also the **best-selling multi-platform hack-and-slash series**, selling 20.49 million copies from the PS One to the PS4 eras as of 14 Mar 2018, according to VGChartz.

Hello world!
There's a twist at the end of the arcade version of *Golden Axe* (Sega, 1989). Just when you thought they were defeated, the bad guys climb out of an in-game arcade cabinet to run amok in the real world!

First audio-only hack-and-slash game
A Blind Legend (Dowino, 2015) has hack-and-slash combat yet it contains no graphics. It's played through headphones using binaural 3D sound with audio effects and voices. Movement is made via a smartphone touchscreen.

Longest development time for a hack-and-slash game
The development of *Ryse: Son of Rome* (Crytek) began in 2006, yet it wasn't until 22 Nov 2013 that it was released – seven years later. Though eventually emerging as an Xbox One launch title, it was originally intended to be a Kinect-enabled Xbox 360 game. A decision was taken to rework it for the Xbox One, but, despite the wait, it met with a muted reception.

Most character death animations in a game
Bayonetta (PlatinumGames, 2009) recorded the most death animations in hack-and-slash history. This was arguably because the game was so famously difficult to master. There are no fewer than 48 contextual demises for the game's heroine, the grandest being "Armageddon", in which Earth itself explodes. The record just beats the 47 unique demises that befall Leon S Kennedy in Capcom's survival horror *Resident Evil 4* (2005).

Longest marathon on a hack-and-slash RPG
Peer Bresser and Jimmie Smets (both DEU) spent 24 hr 25 min on *Diablo III* (Blizzard, 2012) at Pro7 Games in Cologne, Germany, on 8–9 Nov 2017.

BAYONETTA 3
Platform: Switch
The return of the gloriously deadly Umbra Witch caught many off guard when PlatinumGames revealed a trailer for *Bayonetta 3* on a Nintendo Direct. Expect the jibes to flow as rapidly as the hacks and slashes when it comes to Switch.

FACT!

God of War's bald-headed protagonist Kratos was originally designed with long, flowing hair and, for story reasons that never made the final cut, an infant child strapped to his back!

MOST HONOURABLE KILLS IN *FOR HONOR*

In Ubisoft's 2017 combat game that sees knights, samurai and vikings clash swords, a kill is classed as "honourable" if a player dispatches an opponent in a one-on-one duel. Unsurprisingly, kills achieved by back-stabbing an already wounded player, teaming up on an enemy or nudging an opponent off a ledge to their demise do not count as honourable kills.

As of 14 Feb 2018, the player to most closely respect this code of honour was Xbox One gamer "ShinIzanagi" (UK), who had taken the lives of 36,654 players in honourable single combat, according to TrueAchievements. "ShinIzanagi" might well be responsible for your death when you take to the online arenas, but at least he'll pay you the respect of looking you in the eyes...

Largest land-based game boss
He isn't as big as Gongen Wyzen, who grows beyond the size of planets in *Asura's Wrath* (2012), but the Titan Cronos in *God of War III* (Sony, 2010) is the largest game boss on land. Estimates for his dimensions vary from 5,500 ft (1,676 m) to one claim that he could be as tall as 29,000 ft (8,839 m) – almost the equal of Mount Everest!

Fastest completion of *DmC: Devil May Cry*
Sword-slashing, pistol-toting "RedPapaSmurf" (USA) set the fastest completion of Capcom gunslinger *DmC* – 1 hr 19 min 56 sec, according to Speedrun.com. The gamer blazed a trail on 26 Feb 2017 through the New Game+ mode on "Human" difficulty. "I'm comin for that 1:18," said the gamer.

COMBAT SPORTS

It's time to grab yourself a ringside seat as we get ready to rumble! No matter which game you're playing you'll want to keep your guard up, stay off the ropes and roll with the punches if you want to avoid throwing in the towel.

A CALL TO *ARMS*

Nintendo's latest brawler *ARMS* (2017) lets gamers throw punches from entirely new angles. Using the Switch's motion controls, players use their fighter's extendable, bendable arms to catch their opponents off guard, no matter where they are in the ring.

Fighting as the boxer Spring Man (main picture), Mexico's "maraboto95" pummelled his way to the **fastest "Normal" completion of *ARMS***, finishing a single-player Grand Prix in 16 min 33 sec, as verified by Speedrun on 1 Feb 2018.

The same gamer also holds the record for the **fastest "Hard" completion of ARMS**, concluding another single-player GP – but this time with the hardest (Level 4) difficulty enabled – in 18 min 9 sec on 17 Feb 2018.

First arm-wrestling game
After the success of the boxing game *Punch-Out!!* (1983), Nintendo was swift to adapt the "dodge and counter-attack" formula to create *Arm Wrestling*. The 1985 coin-op was the last game that Nintendo independently developed specifically for the arcade market.

TWO LEGENDS LIVE ON

Muhammad Ali (right) called himself "The Greatest" and plenty agree, including games publishers. As of 29 Mar 2018, the three-time world heavyweight champion had graced the covers of eight games – the **most appearances on a game cover by a boxer** – starting with *Champions Forever Boxing* (NEC, 1991).

Martial arts legend Bruce Lee (left) has the **most game appearances by a martial artist**. The fighter and star of the silver screen had featured in 13 games as of 1 Mar 2018.

Best-selling fighting game for Nintendo Switch

As of 29 Mar 2018, *ARMS*, Nintendo's anarchic take on boxing, had punched well above its weight. The game had notched up impressive sales of 1.62 million units, according to VGChartz.

Its success has led to *ARMS* being taken seriously on the eSports scene. The brawler was a fixture at 2018's EVO Japan fighting game extravaganza (held on 26–28 Jan). In total, 327 entrants competed in the *ARMS* event, with Japan's "Pega" eventually emerging victorious.

First 3D boxing game

4D Sports Boxing (Distinctive Software) for the Apple Macintosh was a watershed game for the 3D combat-sport genre. Released in Jun 1991, EA's early boxing sim used motion-capture to make the animation of its 3D polygonal graphics as smooth as possible.

Longest-running boxing game franchise

The *Punch-Out!!* series has gone the full 12 rounds and beyond. Starting with 1983's *Punch-Out!!*, it had seen eight unique entries across 26 years, including the 1985 spin-off *Arm Wrestling* (see below left). The most recent entry was the standalone WiiWare title *Doc Louis's Punch-Out!!* (Nintendo, 2009).

First videogame to feature real-life boxing footage

Rather than create animated characters, *Prize Fighter* (Sega, 1993) used full-motion video of four stuntmen – Jimmy Nickerson, Manny Perry, Billy Lucas and Ben Bray – to create its roster of in-game fighters. Players could then take on the filmed fighters from a first-person perspective. It took the game's developers, Digital Pictures, five weeks to train the "fighters" so that they were ready when the cameras started rolling.

88.18%

Most critically acclaimed combat sports game

The long-reigning champion of this particular category is EA Sports' 2005 golden oldie *Fight Night Round 2* for the original Xbox. Its GameRankings score of 88.18% is based on 44 reviews. It's closely followed by *Fight Night Round 4* (EA, 2009) on the PS3 with 88%.

4 SECONDS

FASTEST SINGLE-PLAYER KNOCKOUT IN *UFC 3*

"VaultDude21" (CAN) is obviously a believer in the mantra that fighters aren't paid for overtime. Seeing no reason to hang around, the Xbox One gamer notched a 4.56-sec knockout in EA Sports' 2018 fighter *UFC 3* on 11 Feb. The rapid time was set just nine days after the game's launch.

To give his martial arts game *Karateka* (1984) a fluid feel, developer Jordan Mechner created the **first motion-capture animation in a game**. He filmed his karate instructor and traced over the footage.

FASTEST KO OF MIKE TYSON IN *PUNCH-OUT!!*

A blur of fists from the ring-savvy "Summoningsalt" (USA) was enough to topple *Punch-Out!!*'s final obstacle, "Iron" Mike Tyson, in 2 min 5.82 sec. The time was verified by Speedrun on 1 Mar 2017 and was exactly 1 sec faster than the second-placed boxer, "zallard1" (USA).

WWE

With its larger-than-life characters and death-defying stunts, WWE is perhaps the perfect sport to be given the videogame treatment. It's time to dig out your best leotard, perfect your signature takedown and get ready to make your entrance into the squared circle...

LARGEST ROSTER IN A WWE WRESTLING GAME

If you combine those wrestlers included on the disc for *WWE 2K18* (2017) with those then added as part of its various DLC packs, the latest game in 2K's long-running wrestling series features a total of 184 unique playable characters.

We've decorated the background of this spread with just a small sample of the game's decades-spanning line-up, but the full roster includes such legendary wrestlers as Ric Flair, The Rock, The Undertaker, Ultimate Warrior, Andre the Giant and "Macho Man" Randy Savage.

Current stars are well represented, from *WWE 2K18*'s cover star Seth Rollins (right) and AJ Styles to Roman Reigns and gamer/YouTuber Xavier Woods (aka Austin Creed). There are also 32 playable female wrestlers, including Ruby Riott, Sasha Banks, Alicia Fox and Trish Stratus.

GAMING GOLD

Say it with roses Elizabeth Ann Hulette (aka Miss Elizabeth) was the **first WWF/WWE Diva to appear in a videogame** – she appeared in the end credits of 1989's *WWF Superstars* arcade game.

51 APPEARANCES

As of 14 Mar 2018, The Undertaker had been playable in 51 out of the 66 licensed WWF/WWE games made – making him the **most prolific wrestler in videogames**. Players were first able to take control of the "Demon of Death Valley" in *WWF Super WrestleMania* (Sculptured Software, 1992) for the Super NES and Sega Genesis. His most recent outing was in 2K's *WWE 2K18*. In 2008's *SmackDown vs Raw 2009*, he could even use a mystic urn – usually held by his former manager Paul Bearer – to turn opponents into zombies.

FIRST 3D WWF/WWE TITLE

Until the late 1990s, WWF games were confined to 2D bouts. In 1998, Iguana West's *WWF War Zone* introduced fully 3D wrestler models and ring environments. It was also the first WWF/WWE title to show wrestlers entering the virtual ring.

FIRST WRESTLING-THEMED VEHICULAR COMBAT GAME

Car combat and wrestling stars clashed in THQ's demolition derby-style game *WWE Crush Hour* (2003) for PS2 and GameCube. WWE stars were taken out of the ring and put behind the wheels of heavily armed and outlandishly customized vehicles as they fought their way to a final showdown with the evil Vince McMahon.

23 MINUTES 21 SECONDS

"Chris32156" recorded the **fastest 100% completion of *WWE 2K17*'s Hall of Fame Showcase** on 3 Aug 2017, as verified by Speedrun. The American PS4 player demolished all seven of the mode's classic bouts, which include 1988's match between Sting (below) and Ric Flair, SmackDown 2000's clash between Jacqueline and Ivory, and 1999's "Armageddon" between Big Show and Big Boss Man.

Most watched *WWE 2K18* match
As of 14 Mar 2018, a total of 2,937,189 YouTube viewers had watched WWE superstars Seth Rollins and Austin Creed play their digital selves in a 20-man Royal Rumble in 2K's *WWE 2K18*. The video – "WWE 2K18: SETH ROLLINS & AUSTIN CREED enter the ROYAL RUMBLE! – UpUpDownDown Plays" – was uploaded a few days after the game's release.

First mature-rated wrestling game
Acclaim's *ECW Hardcore Revolution* (2000) holds the dubious honour of being the first game judged as suitable for adults only by USA's Entertainment Software Rating Board (ESRB). Unfortunately, all the "extreme wrestling action" and "strong language" that was included still couldn't save the game from landing with a dull thud when it was released and then soon forgotten.

Most prolific developer of combat sports games
As of 14 Mar 2018, Japanese developer Yuke's had created a total of 43 combat sports games – from 1995's *Shin Nippon Pro Wrestling: Toukon Retsuden* to 2017's *WWE 2K18*. Titles from Yuke's also include 2004's all-female *Rumble Roses* (and its 2006 sequel) and 2011's tie-in to the robo-boxing movie *Real Steel*, which starred Hugh Jackman.

First videogame to feature real-life wrestling footage
The select screen for *WWF Rage in the Cage* (Sculptured Software, 1993) for the Sega CD featured full-motion-video (FMV) clips of all 20 playable wrestlers as well as the signature moves of icons such as Bret Hart, Shawn Michaels and The Undertaker. Upon winning the game's tournament mode, the player's chosen wrestler also celebrated in an FMV clip.

Most watched wrestling machinima
Dream-team matches abound in "WWE'12: Marvel vs DC Comics". A YouTube posting on 18 Jan 2012 from "FantasyCaws" used the "Create a Wrestler" mode from *WWE '12* (Yuke's, 2011) to pit the likenesses of Spider-Man, Thor, Iron Man and Captain America against Superman, Batman and The Flash in a virtual WWE ring. It had racked up 63,221,781 views on YouTube as of 14 Mar 2018.

TOP 10

WRESTLING COVERS

Wrestlers have been brawling to find out who the king of the ring is for decades – but perhaps the true test of their claims is to see who has body-slammed themselves on to the most game covers. As of 1 Mar 2018, these were the most-seen wrestlers on videogame boxes...

1
THE UNDERTAKER
(USA)
19 COVERS

Known for her signature move, the explosive Luna Bomb, Canadian-born Luna Vachon was the **first female cover star of a wrestling game** (*WWF Raw*, 1994).

=2
TRIPLE H
(USA)
17 COVERS

=2
DWAYNE "THE ROCK" JOHNSON
(USA)
17 COVERS

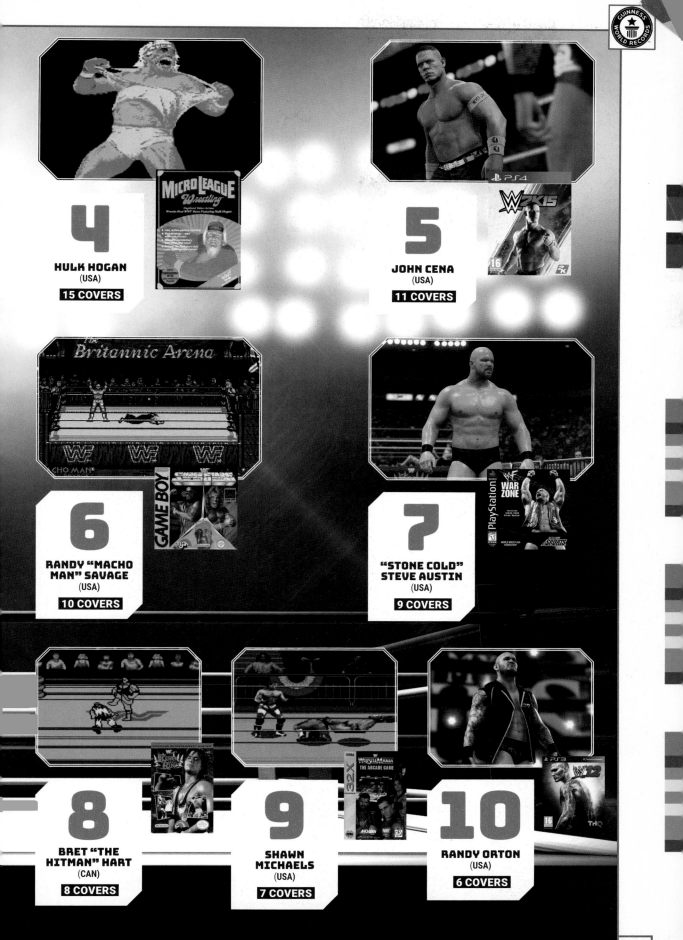

4
HULK HOGAN
(USA)
15 COVERS

5
JOHN CENA
(USA)
11 COVERS

6
RANDY "MACHO MAN" SAVAGE
(USA)
10 COVERS

7
"STONE COLD" STEVE AUSTIN
(USA)
9 COVERS

8
BRET "THE HITMAN" HART
(CAN)
8 COVERS

9
SHAWN MICHAELS
(USA)
7 COVERS

10
RANDY ORTON
(USA)
6 COVERS

FEATURE

PLAYER

1P
DOGURA

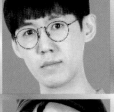

itCash

Highest-ranked *Guilty Gear Xrd* **player (ever)**
NAME: Ryo Nozaki
ALIAS: Dogura
NATIONALITY: JPN
CHARACTER: Raven
LIFETIME SCORE: 226,193
CAREER EARNINGS: $26,560 (£19,078)
TOURNAMENTS WON: 31

Highest-ranked *Street Fighter V* **player (ever)**
NAME: Hajime Taniguchi
ALIAS: Tokido
NATIONALITY: JPN
CHARACTER: Akuma
LIFETIME SCORE: 224,867
CAREER EARNINGS: $207,921 (£149,355)
TOURNAMENTS WON: 47

Highest-ranked *Tekken 7* **player (ever)**
NAME: Hyun-jin Kim
ALIAS: JDCR
NATIONALITY: KOR
CHARACTER: Dragunov
LIFETIME SCORE: 287,701
CAREER EARNINGS: $53,531 (£38,452)
TOURNAMENTS WON: 27

PRO FIGHTERS

Street Fighter V might let you do battle with one of Ryu, Ken, Akuma and co., while *Injustice 2* presents you with an entire cast of superheroes and dastardly villains to pick from. But our Player Select presents an altogether more dangerous prospect. Here, you'll discover the best fighting-game pros the world has to offer, as well as the character with which they dominate their chosen game. Just make sure you "Choose your fighter" carefully...

SELECT

2P
SONICFOX

Highest-ranked *Super Smash Bros. for Wii U* player (ever)
NAME: Gonzalo Barrios
ALIAS: ZeRo
NATIONALITY: CHL
CHARACTER: Diddy Kong
LIFETIME SCORE: 2,792
CAREER EARNINGS: $181,291 (£130,226)
TOURNAMENTS WON: 10

Highest-ranked *Marvel vs. Capcom: Infinite* player (ever)
NAME: Christopher Gonzalez
ALIAS: NYChrisG
NATIONALITY: USA
CHARACTER: Morrigan
LIFETIME SCORE: 61,825
CAREER EARNINGS: $40,452 (£29,057)
TOURNAMENTS WON: 8

Highest-ranked *Injustice 2* player (ever)
NAME: Dominique McLean
ALIAS: SonicFox
NATIONALITY: USA
CHARACTER: Deadshot
LIFETIME SCORE: 213,664
CAREER EARNINGS: $449,342 (£322,744)
TOURNAMENTS WON: 14

SPEED-RUNS

In this special speed-running chapter, competition is fierce and there's no time to rest on your laurels. Every demonstration of raw pace you'll see on this and the following 11 pages was verified by Speedrun on 2 Apr 2018. Now get ready… get steady… and GO!

MOST SPEED-RUN GAME EVER

Super Mario 64 has been around since 1996, but its speed-run community shows little sign of slowing down. If anything, it's speeding up. Nintendo's masterpiece had enticed 6,727 speed-runners to post their best times on Speedrun, as of 2 Apr 2018.

The hotly contested times include runs to complete the game with 120, 70, 16, 1 and 0 stars. The last three accomplishments require players to exploit glitches in *Mario 64*'s ageing code that enable Mario to face off against Bowser long before he should be able to. The absolute minimum number of stars needed to beat the game without using glitches is 70, while the 120-star victory involves pocketing every star there is to collect.

TOP 10: GAMES WITH MOST SUBMITTED SPEED-RUNS

Despite his advanced gaming age, Mario still has a fleetness of foot that means he rules the podium places on the all-time list of speed-run games. As, indeed, does Nintendo. The Japanese publisher has created eight of the 10 most speed-run games, with only *Portal* (Valve, 2007) and *Undertale* (Toby Fox, 2015) able to make a dent in its dominance.

GAME	PUBLISHER	RELEASE	#
Super Mario 64	Nintendo	1996	6,727
Super Mario Odyssey	Nintendo	2017	6,546
Super Mario Sunshine	Nintendo	2002	4,726
The Legend of Zelda: Ocarina of Time	Nintendo	1998	4,273
Super Mario World	Nintendo	1990	3,866
Super Metroid	Nintendo	1994	3,279
The Legend of Zelda: A Link to the Past	Nintendo	1991	3,225
Super Mario Bros.	Nintendo	1985	2,741
Undertale	Toby Fox	2015	2,704
Portal	Valve	2007	2,441

SPEED-RUNS

ARMS (2017)
Nintendo's latest brawler is bringing gamers together. When previous record holder "plp" (USA) gave way to "Mileve" (CAN) – by less than half a second – he proposed a pairing, saying: "Mileve, we should play sometime." We haven't yet heard who won the head to head…

Axiom Verge (2015)
The side-scrolling "Metroidvania" has proven a hit with speed-runners. Fastest player "Zecks" (FIN) said he was delayed by the boss Uruku (right) but survived, admitting "gotta count my blessings".

Batman: Arkham Asylum (2009)
The USA's "Nivlak" overcame the rioting inmates of Gotham's asylum for the criminally insane faster than anyone else – taking on Scarecrow, Bane, Joker and more. We're not sure if even Batman himself could have done it any better!

GAME	RUN TYPE	PLACE	PLAYER	TIME	SYSTEM
Ape Escape	Any%	1	eednob (USA)	00:44:48	PS2
		2	SSBMstuff (USA)	00:45:04	PS2
		3	El_Dorado (JPN)	00:45:26	PS2
ARMS	1P Grand Prix; Any ARMS; Easy	1	Mileve (CAN)	00:10:05.7	Switch
		2	plp (USA)	00:10:06	Switch
		3	RampantEpsilon (USA)	00:10:35.6	Switch
Axiom Verge	Any%; Normal	1	Zecks (FIN)	00:34:57.4	PC
		2	Ryn2075 (USA)	00:35:24.5	PC
		3	BlueyLewis	00:36:48.1	PC
Bastion	Any% No MMS; New Game	1	HaosEdge (AUT)	00:13:29	PC
		2	valentinoIAN (USA)	00:13:32	PC
		3	SomeDude1316 (USA)	00:13:35	PC
Batman: Arkham Asylum	Any%; Easy	1	Nivlak (USA)	01:19:08	PC
		2	Psychotik (CAN)	01:19:36	PC
		3	cojosao (USA)	01:19:51	PC
The Binding of Isaac: Afterbirth	1 Character	1	karolmo (ESP)	00:05:35	PC
		2	BrainTM (USA)	00:05:43	PC
		3	Dea1h (RUS)	00:05:52	PC
Blaster Master	Any% (JP)	1	IluvMario (USA)	00:25:55	NES
		2	Dugongue (USA)	00:26:36	NES
		3	ShiningDragoon (USA)	00:26:43	NES
Bubble Bobble (NES)	Any% (1 Player)	1	Zimond (SWE)	00:31:43	NES
		2	AND4H (USA)	00:34:18	NES
		3	RottDawg (CAN)	00:40:32	NES

GAME	RUN TYPE	PLACE	PLAYER	TIME	SYSTEM
Bully: Scholarship Edition	Any%	1	SWEGTA (SWE)	02:37:34	PC
		2	joystiquebr (BRA)	02:37:57	PC
		3	GuyWhoLied (USA)	02:40:29	PC
Castlevania (NES)	Any%	1	Janthe (FRA)	00:11:31.8	NES
		2	FuriousPaul (USA)	00:11:32.7	NES
		3	kmac (USA)	00:11:32.9	NES
Cave Story	Best Ending	1	magmapeach	00:56:32	PC
		2	PPU (JPN)	00:57:11	PC
		3	Shadax	00:57:23	PC
Celeste	Any%	1	TGH (USA)	00:32:24	PC
		2	yp (CAN)	00:32:53.5	PC
		3	Millay (FRA)	00:33:56.6	PC
Dishonored: Death of the Outsider	Any%	1	bjurnie (NLD)	00:09:15	PC
		2	seeker_ (FRA)	00:09:21	PC
		3	Metro72 (USA)	00:10:42	PC
Fire Emblem Warriors	New Game; Single	1	DKRF (USA)	01:49:26	Switch
		2	GodSlayerLaharl (UK)	01:50:14	Switch
		3	AvionDS (CAN)	02:00:02	Switch
Firewatch	Any%	1	Kevbot43 (USA)	01:05:04	PC
		2	snoborder88 (USA)	01:05:12	PC
		3	ZaturnuX (SWE)	01:06:23	PC
Five Nights at Freddy's	Any%; PC	1	Richard1764 (FRA)	00:01:08.4	PC
		2	flower (RUS)	00:01:09	PC
		3	ZeldaCrasher (USA)	00:01:10.2	PC
For Honor	NG+ Any%	1	Bandana (USA)	01:16:58	PC
		2	Mr.KillshotTV (BLR)	01:26:10	PC
		3	Cropax (DNK)	01:29:00	PC

Celeste (2018) Split-second reflexes are required to set the fastest possible times in Matt Makes Games' platformer. Remembering the levels' layouts will also save you vital seconds, as "TGH" (USA) demonstrated in his run.

Firewatch (2016) Day 77 of Campo Santo's first-person narrative adventure proved a stumbling block for our top speed-runner. American "Kevbot43" lost vital seconds in the wilderness, but it didn't stop him from eclipsing his fellow fire-lookouts.

SPEED-RUNS

Hellblade: Senua's Sacrifice (2017)
Ninja Theory's psychological adventure won all kinds of awards for its slow-burning story (see pp.12–13), but don't think that's stopped a slew of speed-runners from blazing a trail through it.

Injustice 2 (2017)
"JerQ_Q" (FIN) wasn't quite as fast as a speeding bullet when he took on the DC Universe in *Injustice 2*'s Story mode, but he might be one day... "Next time we go for sub 1 hour!" he announced after his record run.

GAME	RUN TYPE	PLACE	PLAYER	TIME	SYSTEM
Furi	Speedrun Mode; Legacy	1	Dircashede (AUS)	00:29:23	PC
		2	angelym (FRA)	00:29:43	PC
		3	Platypus_Funk (FRA)	00:31:20	PS4
Half-Life	WON; Scriptless	1	Maxam (SWE)	00:29:03.6	PC
		2	ProtoAus (AUS)	00:29:39.5	PC
		3	d0t (SWE)	00:29:42.7	PC
Half-Life 2	New Engine	1	raintnt (RUS)	01:11:37.03	PC
		2	chili_n_such (USA)	01:13:32.61	PC
		3	deathwingua (UKR)	01:14:11.19	PC
Heavy Rain	Any%	1	dragonbane0 (DEU)	03:23:32	PS3
		2	Kevbot43 (USA)	03:29:27	PS3
		3	loafofbread (USA)	03:41:03	PS3
Hellblade: Senua's Sacrifice	Any%	1	s8n (DEU)	01:42:50	PC
		2	Pestis616 (DEU)	01:58:39	PC
		3	qvaku (POL)	02:04:50	PC
Hotline Miami 2: Wrong Number	NG+ Any%	1	Uzikoti (FRA)	00:32:49	PC
		2	Ashmore (FRA)	00:33:42	PC
		3	Jackintoshh (IRL)	00:33:50	PC
Injustice 2	Story Mode	1	JerQ_Q (FIN)	01:00:09	PS4
		2	peck324 (USA)	01:02:07	PS4
		3	PoisonTrace (USA)	01:13:30	PS4
Jet Set Radio	Any%; PC	1	Faila (ARG)	00:36:11	PC
		2	kitcarsonn (USA)	00:36:21	PC
		3	maxylobes (USA)	00:37:44	PC

GAME	RUN TYPE	PLACE	PLAYER	TIME	SYSTEM
Kirby: Planet Robobot	Any%	1	shirokirby (JPN)	01:41:54	New 3DS
		2	yosshiV3 (JPN)	01:42:59	New 3DS
		3	Kobral (DEU)	01:48:52	New 3DS
L.A. Noire	Any%; Normal; w/o DLC	1	SeductiveSpatula (NOR)	03:42:57	PC
		2	Ectortutu (RUS)	03:47:22	PC
		3	Duders (USA)	03:54:44	PC
Legacy of Kain: Soul Reaver	Any%	1	Veictas (ITA)	00:24:57	PC
		2	Twincross (UK)	00:27:50	PC
		3	DaeMord (UK)	00:28:47	PC
The Lion King (SNES)	Any%; Difficult	1	Akiteru (CAN)	00:13:54	SNES
		2	TheMexicanRunner (MEX/POL)	00:14:19	SNES
		3	AlfredoSalza (CHL)	00:14:47	SNES
Luigi's Mansion: Dark Moon	Any%	1	Banananana (USA)	03:00:05	3DS
		2	RiiDOLSK (USA)	03:01:51	3DS
		3	StarlightKick (USA)	03:17:43	3DS
Mafia II	Any%	1	kdstz (NLD)	03:08:54	PC
		2	Kabalie (FIN)	03:12:01	PC
		3	Vojtas131 (CZE)	03:12:20	PC
Mafia III	Any%	1	Kabalie (FIN)	05:47:28	PC
		2	Mattmatt10111 (ATA)	07:24:02	PC
		3	Kinfath92 (ITA)	07:24:07	PC
Mario + Rabbids Kingdom Battle	Any%; No DLC; Easy	1	StKildaFan (AUS)	05:25:36	Switch
		2	BnH247 (USA)	05:42:09	Switch
		3	N/A		

***Luigi's Mansion: Dark Moon* (2013)**
Boo! Luigi's adventure through the haunted Evershade Valley has sucked in speed-runners like ghosts up a Poltergust 5000 vacuum cleaner. The USA's "Banananana" has the fastest time, coming within just 5 sec of cracking the 3-hr barrier.

TOP 10: GAMES WITH MOST SUBMITTED SPEED-RUNS IN 2017

We opened our speed-running chapter with a look at the games that have the most submitted speed-runs ever, but what about more recent titles? We asked Speedrun to send us their statistics on which games had seen the most speed-runs during 2017 – and, yet again, it was a certain Super Mario who was way out in front…

***Super Mario Odyssey* (2017)**
Showing you just can't keep a good plumber down, *Super Mario Odyssey* was the 2017 release with the most submitted runs. All the more impressive was that *Odyssey* wasn't released until 27 Oct!

GAME	PUBLISHER	RELEASE	#
Super Mario Odyssey	Nintendo	2017	3,424
Super Mario 64	Nintendo	1996	2,738
Super Mario World	Nintendo	1990	1,681
Super Metroid	Nintendo	1994	1,653
Resident Evil VII: Biohazard	Capcom	2017	1,583
Super Mario Bros.	Nintendo	1985	1,448
Mario Kart 8 Deluxe	Nintendo	2017	1,407
Undertale	Toby Fox	2015	1,172
White Tiles 4: Piano Master	Brighthouse	2014	1,142
Refunct	Dominique Grieshofer	2015	1,120

SPEEDRUN.COM

GAME	RUN TYPE	PLACE	PLAYER	TIME	SYSTEM
Mass Effect 2	Any%; with DLC	1	tentaclepie (SWE)	01:29:02	PC
		2	vacuity615 (FRA)	01:42:57	PC
		3	Rainbow_Lizard (UK)	01:43:35	PC
Mega Man X4	Zero 100%	1	ArielRx (ECU)	00:42:06	PC
		2	Qttsix (TPE)	00:42:22	PC
		3	LuizMiguel (BRA)	00:42:26	PS One
Mirror's Edge Catalyst	Any%	1	MazkuD (FIN)	01:16:44	PC
		2	matchboxmatt (USA)	01:17:07	PC
		3	alexhxc15 (USA)	01:19:02	PC
Monster Hunter: World	Any%; 1 Player	1	Shepard (USA)	07:51:58.6	PS4 Pro
		2	P4ntz (CAN)	16:48:16.6	PS4
		3	N/A		
Moss	Any%	1	towai (USA)	00:48:42	PS4 (PS VR)
		2	MileyMouse (BEL)	00:49:45	PS4 (PS VR)
		3	UpdogDrew (USA)	01:03:06	PS4 (PS VR)
Naruto Shippuden: Ultimate Ninja Storm 4	Any%; New Game	1	TrueStorySeamus (UK)	01:26:01	PC
		2	Unicorn_Mots (POL)	01:38:56	PC
		3	joystiquebr (BRA)	01:49:17	PC
Nefarious	Any%; Bad Ending	1	oreoplaysthings (USA)	00:52:25	PC
		2	Watson690 (UK)	00:53:24	PC
		3	bardninja (USA)	00:59:43	PC
NieR: Automata	[A]; Normal; NG; Any Weapon; Glitched	1	Kanaris (AUS)	01:24:54.3	PC
		2	Kasserne (DNK)	01:26:11.7	PC
		3	-MarbleSoda- (USA)	01:28:58.8	PC
Ninja Gaiden Black	Normal; Any%	1	JTB123 (UK)	01:52:37	Xbox 360
		2	unwary (CAN)	01:56:04	Xbox 360
		3	KrisTheHylian (SWE)	02:04:49	Xbox 360

Ninja Gaiden Black (2005)
Turn to pp.164–65 to read how the *Ninja Gaiden* series has inspired a spate of pacifist speed-runs. For gamers who prefer their ninjas to be rather more ruthless, the UK's "JTB123" has been busy showing them how it's done.

Moss (2018)
Tearing through Polyarc's VR adventure means solving its puzzles as quickly as possible, while making sure you direct Quill down the fastest route. Top player "towai" (USA) reckoned a time under 48 min was "probably possible".

Pikmin 3 (2013)
French gamer "IceCube" has proven himself to be the ultimate Pikmin wrangler. He whipped the helpful creatures into shape to have them assist Captain Olimar in completing his third adventure in double-quick time.

GAME	RUN TYPE	PLACE	PLAYER	TIME	SYSTEM
Ori and the Blind Forest: Definitive Edition	All Skills; No OOB/TA	1	UncleRonny (ISR)	00:28:43	PC
		2	Willson (SWE)	00:28:49.6	PC
		3	Elojimmini (UK)	00:28:49.9	PC
Overwatch	Tutorial; PC	1	Midnight (NLD)	00:03:50.9	PC
		2	Burchase (USA)	00:03:52.0	PC
		3	nijQ (DEU)	00:03:52.5	PC
Persona 5	Hard, True Ending	1	Neviutz (DEU)	17:05:12	PS4
		2	Darkkefka (USA)	18:43:04	PS4
		3	Liv (UK)	19:06:04	PS4
Pikmin 3	Any%	1	IceCube (FRA)	00:50:07	Wii U
		2	JHawk4 (USA)	00:51:27	Wii U
		3	BielR3 (ESP)	00:51:29	Wii U
Pyre	Undefeated; Reduced	1	Ihrving (USA)	02:33:56	PC
		2	Savusukka (FIN)	02:35:34	PC
		3	LivingLooneyBin (AUS)	02:36:50	PC
Ratchet & Clank	NG+	1	doesthisusername (DNK)	00:27:51	PS4
		2	nickfredy (USA)	00:27:52	PS4
		3	Scaff (AUS)	00:28:08	PS4
Rayman	Any% PS1; USA	1	Thextera (BEL)	01:12:43	PS2
		2	Glackum (USA)	01:13:06	PS2
		3	Arttles (PRT)	01:13:31	PS One
Rayman 2: The Great Escape	Any%	1	Darnok_PL (POL)	01:52:39	PC
		2	Glackum (USA)	01:55:28	PC
		3	lagpu1 (ESP)	01:57:08	PC

Pyre (2017)
America's "Ihrving" helped Pyre's exiles return from banishment almost before they knew it. The gamer emerged undefeated, meaning the speedster won every match in the Rites – a sport that's best described as "magical basketball".

SPEED-RUNS

GAME	RUN TYPE	PLACE	PLAYER	TIME	SYSTEM
Resident Evil 4	New Game; PC; Professional	1	Yuushi (JPN)	01:29:17	PC
		2	Morse66 (FRA)	01:29:42	PC
		3	MikeWave (USA)	01:30:00	PC
RiME	Any%	1	UnMind (FRA)	01:22:27	PC
		2	Ark_ (USA)	01:23:38	PC
		3	Tech (USA)	01:24:30	Xbox One
Salt and Sanctuary	Any% no OOB	1	Coppie (SVN)	00:09:36	PC
		2	seanpr (USA)	00:10:33	PC
		3	ermagherddon (AUS)	00:11:09	PC
Shadow Warrior 2	NG Any%; Easy	1	Unicorn_Mots (POL)	00:45:24	PC
		2	Raaikken (FIN)	00:46:44	PC
		3	Punchy (UK)	00:47:30	PC
Shantae: ½ Genie Hero	Shantae Mode; Any%; Glitchless	1	Tky619 (UK)	01:04:08	PS4
		2	CakeSauc3 (USA)	01:04:20	PC
		3	JTNoriMaki (USA)	01:07:22	PC
Shovel Knight	Any%; Shovel Knight	1	Smaugy (SWE)	00:42:28	PC
		2	applesauc (USA)	00:43:05	PC
		3	Primorix (USA)	00:43:27	PC
Silent Hill	NG (Easy)	1	Punchy (UK)	00:31:43	PS TV
		2	Aaron (UK)	00:31:44	PS3
		3	Plywood (USA)	00:32:13	PS2
Snipperclips: Cut It Out, Together!	Any%; Solo; Base Game	1	Nutt (AUS)	00:09:07	Switch
		2	N/A		
		3	N/A		

Resident Evil 4 (2005)
Japan's "Yuushi" urged fellow speed-runners to "never give up" after a year-long quest to top *Resident Evil 4*'s leaderboard came to a successful conclusion.

Shovel Knight (2014)
Sweden's "Smaugy" showed himself to be a master of Yacht Club Games' shovel-swinging, treasure-gathering platformer. The player raced through *Shovel Knight* in just 42 min 28 sec.

Star Wars Battlefront II (2017)
Even in a galaxy far, far away, speed-runners can still be at the mercy of misfiring technology – just ask Australian gamer "Iako3000". The player did claim the top spot in *Battlefront II*, but said that an even faster run was ruined by a corrupt video file.

GAME	RUN TYPE	PLACE	PLAYER	TIME	SYSTEM
Solitaire	Draw One	1	DDos-Dan (AUS)	00:00:08	PC
		2	Strucht DeRügel	00:00:10	PC
		3	Georg Sandner	00:00:11	PC
SOMA	Any%	1	Teravortryx (CAN)	00:59:50	PC
		2	Sychotixx (USA)	01:00:31	PC
		3	amzblk (EST)	01:02:02	PC
South Park: The Fractured but Whole	Any%	1	Firepaw (AUT)	03:48:24	PC
		2	ZanderGoth (USA)	04:19:43	PC
		3	BnH247 (USA)	06:04:35	PC
Splatoon	Any%	1	movefish (USA)	00:51:19	Wii U
		2	TonesBalones (USA)	00:51:56	Wii U
		3	BEAT (JPN)	00:52:31.1	Wii U
Splatoon 2	Any%	1	hashedrice (JPN)	01:32:31	Switch
		2	movefish (USA)	01:32:44	Switch
		3	TonesBalones (USA)	01:35:02	Switch
Spyro: Year of the Dragon	Any%	1	jeremythompson (USA)	00:24:08	PS TV
		2	Zeuspot (DNK)	00:25:55	PS TV
		3	grantchil (USA)	00:26:11	PS TV
Star Fox 64	Any%; Console	1	Hayate (JPN)	00:22:24	N64
		2	Stivitybobo (USA)	00:22:27	N64
		3	LylatR (CAN)	00:22:29	N64
Star Wars Battlefront II	Any% w/ Bonuses	1	Iako3000 (AUS)	00:47:51	PC
		2	ctc (USA)	00:48:43	PC
		3	rakv (SWE)	00:48:54	PC
Star Wars: Knights of the Old Republic	Any%	1	glasnonck (USA)	01:14:59	PC
		2	Sheepmetal (DNK)	01:21:04	PC
		3	indykenobi (USA)	01:24:10	PC

Splatoon 2 (2017)
It doesn't matter how fast you are, no one escapes without being covered from head to toe in paint in Nintendo's huge (and hugely messy) hit.

SPEED-RUNS

***Thumper* (2017)**
The gameplay in this psychedelic and unsettling rhythm shooter already unfolds at breakneck speed. US gamer "RaulTheGhoul" upped its pace to the maximum, cruising through its stages in exactly 3 hr.

***Uncharted 4: A Thief's End* (2016)**
One of the most impressive aspects of the speed-running community is the respect players have for each other. After setting the fastest time in *Uncharted 4*, Mexico's "OmarZarco" praised Japan's "AO", whose record he'd just taken. "Excellent job of finding [the] various shortcuts," he said.

***Super Mario Run* (2016)**
Some people are never satisfied! Though sitting top of the pile in Nintendo's Mario game for mobile phones, the UK's "Really_Tall" posted the comment "it was still fairly bad" when uploading his time to Speedrun.

GAME	RUN TYPE	PLACE	PLAYER	TIME	SYSTEM
SteamWorld Dig	Any%	1	anxest (FRA)	00:22:18	PC
		2	Berumondo (BEL)	00:22:38	PC
		3	renozealot	00:22:57	PC
Super Mario Run	Main Levels; Any%	1	Really_Tall (UK)	00:18:37	Android
		2	jarod (USA)	00:19:00	iOS
		3	MrCafecito (MEX)	00:19:04	iOS
The Talos Principle	Any%; Messenger; Unrestricted	1	Kraeft (SWE)	00:04:08	PC
		2	syros	00:04:11	PC
		3	Extodasher (CAN)	00:04:15	PC
Thumper	Play All Levels (Any%)	1	RaulTheGhoul (USA)	03:00:00	PC
		2	BrofessorScales (CAN)	03:11:11	PS4
		3	N/A		
Titan Souls	Any% (Beat the Game); Normal	1	Scrublord (USA)	00:11:37.7	PC
		2	Zic3 (USA)	00:11:47.9	PS4
		3	3l3ktr0 (FRA)	00:11:54.3	PC
Titanfall 2	Any%; Any%	1	Bryonato (USA)	01:22:44	PC
		2	Joshwa04 (UK)	01:25:27	PC
		3	Overzero (USA)	01:25:38	PC
Trine	NG+ Any%	1	Evertrn (SWE)	00:29:52	PC
		2	MaximumLeech (USA)	00:30:25	PC
		3	Janmumrik (SWE)	00:33:47	PC

GAME	RUN TYPE	PLACE	PLAYER	TIME	SYSTEM
Uncharted 4: A Thief's End	Any%	1	OmarZarco (MEX)	03:39:12	PS4
		2	AO (JPN)	03:42:42	PS4
		3	lighteninggod (NGA)	03:45:03	PS4
Uncharted: The Lost Legacy	Any%	1	Erims (FRA)	01:13:05	PS4
		2	Mattmatt10111 (ATA)	01:15:14	PS4
		3	osskari (ISL)	01:17:16	PS4
Undertale	Neutral	1	SnowieY (CAN)	00:56:10	PC
		2	TGH (USA)	00:56:32	Linux
		3	Magolor9000 (CAN)	00:56:43	PC
Vanquish	Any% Casual; DLC	1	Neptas (CAN)	01:25:16	PC
		2	nordanix (SWE)	01:29:35	PC
		3	DaisyFan (CAN)	01:30:17	PC
Wolfenstein II: The New Colossus	Any%	1	DraQu (FIN)	01:05:59	PC
		2	forgiven_ (USA)	01:09:08	PC
		3	CreeperHntr (USA)	01:09:58	PC
Xenoblade Chronicles 2	Any%; Normal; No DLC	1	Tort (USA)	05:31:01	Switch
		2	Gren (USA)	05:41:45	Switch
		3	docmob (FRA)	05:51:50	Switch
Yoshi's Woolly World	Any% (Classic Mode); Normal	1	be_be_be_ (JPN)	02:24:51	Wii U
		2	Vallu (FIN)	02:25:39	Wii U
		3	Jolteon92 (UK)	02:32:09	Wii U

Xenoblade Chronicles 2 (2017)
A speed-run record that takes over 5 hr of solid gameplay – such as that by "Tort" (USA) on *Xenoblade Chronicles 2* – is some achievement. But if you think that's a long time, spare a thought for *Persona 5* enthusiasts. A good run for them still takes over 17 hr!

Super Metroid (1994)
Planet Zebes doesn't just make for one of gaming's most iconic locations – it's also a fantastic place to speed-run. The best players have Samus leaping across platforms with pixel-perfect precision and know exactly where to find the game's secret shortcuts.

TOP 10: SNES CLASSIC MINI GAMES WITH MOST SUBMITTED SPEED-RUNS

Little did Nintendo's bosses know that the release of the Super NES Classic Mini would provide yet another platform for speed-runners to challenge themselves. As of 2 Apr 2018, Nintendo's classic sci-fi adventure *Super Metroid* was the game that speed-runners had applied themselves to the most, with more than a hundred times being submitted.

GAME	PUBLISHER	RELEASE	#
Super Metroid	Nintendo	1994	114
Super Mario World	Nintendo	1990	64
The Legend of Zelda: A Link to the Past	Nintendo	1991	42
Star Fox 2	Nintendo	2017	29
EarthBound	Nintendo	1994	27
Super Mario World 2: Yoshi's Island	Nintendo	1995	10
F-Zero	Nintendo	1990	6
Contra III: The Alien Wars	Konami	1992	5
Super Ghouls 'n Ghosts	Capcom	1991	4

CONTRIBUTORS

STEVE BOXER

Steve has been writing about games since the early 1990s, now primarily for *The Guardian*, *The New European*, *Metro* and *TechRadar*. He's old enough to have owned an Atari VCS with its launch line-up of games, and learned any social skills he may possess in the arcades.

Which games did you play most this year?
So far, the glory that is *Monster Hunter: World*. Plus *Ni no Kuni II: Revenant Kingdom* (above), *Far Cry 5* and *Sea of Thieves*.

What was the year's most exciting event?
Seeing Nintendo's Switch turn out to be a console of utter genius, thereby expunging the memory of the lame Wii U.

MATT BRADFORD

Matt is a Canadian writer, editor and voice actor whose fondest gaming memories include playing *Tron: Deadly Discs* with his dad and *Super Mario Odyssey* with his son. He can also be heard on the podcasts *Video Game Outsiders* and *Zombie Cast*.

Which games did you play most this year?
Assassin's Creed Origins, *Prey* (above), *Horizon Zero Dawn*, *Chime Sharp*.

What was the year's most exciting event?
Personally? Voicing the lead role [of Ryan] in Moonray Studios' videogame *Debris*. As a gamer? Jumping back on the Nintendo train with the Switch.

ROB CAVE

Rob is a writer and editor on videogames, popular science and pop culture. He's worked on every *Gamer's Edition* and has broken or worn out more console controllers than he feels comfortable acknowledging.

Which games did you play most this year?
Fortnite (above), which will hopefully help keep me distracted as I continue to eagerly await the arrival of *The Last of Us Part II*.

What was the year's most exciting event?
The most exciting gaming event of the year has got to be the Nintendo Labo, which brings cardboard engineering and a new layer of imaginative joy to the already pretty impressive Nintendo Switch.

DAVID CROOKES

David has been writing about computers and videogames since 1993. He has contributed to the *Gamer's Edition* since 2009 and he regularly writes for *Retro Gamer*, *gamesTM* and *The Independent*.

Which games did you play most this year?
I've become rather addicted to *Fortnite Battle Royale*, but I've also been playing the resurrected *Shadow of the Colossus*, *Night in the Woods* (above), *Far Cry 5* and *Sea of Thieves*. I enjoyed reacquainting myself with some classic games on the C64 Mini.

What was the year's most exciting event?
For me, seeing the Nintendo Switch go from strength to strength.

PAUL DAVIES

Paul is a games design consultant to developers and publishers. His books for Titan include *The Art of Horizon Zero Dawn* and *Tales from the Sea of Thieves*. Paul lives in London with his wife and son.

Which games did you play most this year?
When I wasn't playing *Overwatch* excessively, I dived deep into *Horizon Zero Dawn* and attempted to get good at *SMITE* and *League of Legends*. I also took a shine to *Quake Champions* (above), but my brain was too slow.

What was the year's most exciting event?
The Overwatch League and the arrival of *Destiny 2*. Nintendo Labo caught me by surprise. It's already on my little one's near-psychic videogame radar.

MATT EDWARDS

Matt has written for *Eurogamer*, *gamesTM*, *Edge* and *Retro Gamer*. He now works as a community and eSports manager for Capcom and co-hosts CapcomFighters, a weekly *Street Fighter* Twitch stream.

Which games did you play most this year?
Street Fighter V: Arcade Edition, *Monster Hunter: World*, *God of War* and *Divinity: Original Sin II* (above).

What was the year's most exciting event?
I'm a big fan of competitive fighting games. I often have the Capcom Pro Tour or Gfinity Elite Series streaming to my tablet while I play through another game on my PS4 or PC.

STACE HARMAN

Stace is a writer, author (*Independent by Design: Art & Stories of Indie Game Creation*), game consultant and virtual itinerant. He's one half of indiebydesign.net and one quarter of the Harman household.

Which games did you play most this year?
Hearthstone continues to claim its share of cash and time. On Switch, *Darkest Dungeon* (above) and *Super Mario Odyssey* vied for top spot.

What was the year's most exciting event?
Watching my son get to grips with his first videogame in the form of Nintendo Labo was exciting for both of us. Watching my wife indulge her love of *PixelJunk Monsters* via its unexpected sequel was endearing.

JOHN ROBERTSON

A journalist, author and photographer focused on covering videogames and their cultural impact, John is always on the lookout for new stories featuring games and how they affect people. He's been in the games industry for over a decade, working on games as well as covering them.

Which games did you play most this year?
Fortnite, *Football Manager 2018*, *Yakuza 6* (above) and *Shadow of the Colossus*.

What was the year's most exciting event?
The incredible impact of *Fortnite Battle Royale* across all demographics.

INDEX

Bold entries in the index indicate a main entry on a topic; **BOLD CAPITALS** indicate an entire chapter.

INDEX

PICTURE CREDITS

Cover Paul Michael Hughes/GWR, Warner Bros., Microsoft, EA, Bandai Namco, Activision, Epic Games, LucasArts, Nintendo, Capcom; **1** Capcom, Blizzard, Nintendo, Epic Games; **6** Paul Michael Hughes/GWR, Kevin Scott Ramos/GWR, Paul Michael Hughes/GWR, Paul Michael Hughes/GWR, Paul Michael Hughes/GWR; **7** Paul Michael Hughes/GWR, Paul Michael Hughes/GWR, James Ellerker/GWR, Paul Michael Hughes/GWR; **8** 123RF; **10** Shutterstock; **18** Paul Michael Hughes/GWR; **21** Jennifer Willoughby; **25** Ryan Schude/GWR, Marius Herrmann; **27** Steingrimur Arnason; **28** Nintendo; **29** Square Enix; **30** Alamy; **34** YouTube; **38** Paul Michael Hughes/GWR; **48** Hosokawa Shingo; **50** Shutterstock; **52** Lucius Kwok; **53** Paul Michael Hughes/GWR; **54** James Ellerker/GWR; **56** CCP hf. **60** Electronic Arts; **64** Nintendo, Getty; **66** Shutterstock; **68** Boardgame Geek; **70** Kevin Scott Ramos/GWR; **78** Shutterstock; **81** Kevin Scott Ramos/GWR; **82** Diana Dakin; **84** Stock Unlimited, Alamy, Getty; **85** Shutterstock, Alamy, Reuters; **86** Paul Michael Hughes/GWR; **88** MIT, Myron Krueger, National Archives, Oculus VR LLC, Google, HTC Corporation, THE VOID; **89** Shutterstock, Kickstarter, Microsoft, Sony, HTC Corporation; **92** Alamy; **93** Twitch, Akash; **94** Alamy; **96** Paul Michael Hughes/GWR; **98** James Ellerker/GWR;

99 Getty; **100** Paul Michael Hughes/GWR; **102** Paul Michael Hughes/GWR; **104** Paul Michael Hughes/GWR; **106** Shutterstock; **108** Shutterstock; **109** Warner Bros.; **113** Alamy, Kevin Scott Ramos/GWR; **116** Capcom; **117** Capcom; **118** D M Duijverman, Vanessa Gavalya, Alamy, Getty; **119** Gnsin, Tiia Monto, Joerg Metzner, Getty, Shutterstock; **120** Ben MacMahon/GWR; **122** Capcom; **123** Philip & Andrew Oliver; **124** Dreamstime, New York Daily News; **128** Nintendo, Philip & Andrew Oliver; **129** Nintendo; **130** Nintendo, Shutterstock; **131** Shutterstock, Nintendo; **132** Alamy; **133** Ranald Mackechnie/GWR, iStock; **136** EA Sports; **140** Moby Games, Getty; **142** Getty; **144** Marcin Rajczak; **145** Moby Games; **149** Getty; **152** Getty; **153** Ben Hoskins, Ben Hoskins, Shutterstock; **154** Chucklefish LTD; **155** Chucklefish LTD; **156** Electronic Arts, Alamy; **164** Shutterstock; **166** Nintendo; **168** Shutterstock; **170** Riot Games, Paul Michael Hughes/GWR; **172** Red Bull; **174** Valve Corporation, Shutterstock; **175** Valve Corporation, Shutterstock; **176** Alamy; **177** Alamy, iStock; **183** Arcade Flyer; **186** Shutterstock, Arcade Flyer Archive; **190** Shutterstock; **192** Twitter, Shutterstock; **193** Kevin Scott Ramos/GWR, Red Bull, Red Bull; **214** Paul M Morgan, Getty

ACKNOWLEDGEMENTS

Guinness World Records would like to thank the following for their help in compiling *Gamer's Edition 2019*:

2K Games (Gemma Woolnough); Activision Blizzard (Jonathan Fargher, Emily Woolliscroft, Maxim Samoylenko, Steven Khoo, Kevin Scarpati, Dustin Blackwell); Atlus (Robyn Mukai Koshi, Jacob Nahin, Michael Quijano); Bandai Namco (Lee Kirton, Ruby Rumjen, Edwin Chuah, Ryan Sinclair); Bethesda (Mark Robins); Capcom (Laura Skelly, Matthew Edwards, Tim Turi, Tristan Corbett); CCP Games (Paul Elsy, George Kelion, Klaus Wichmand); CD Projekt Red (Robert Malinowski); Sami Cetin; Maximilian Christiansen; Chucklefish (Molly Carroll, Eric Barone, Tom Katkus); Cloud Imperium Games (David Swofford, Chris Roberts); Raymond "Stallion83" Cox; D'Avekki Studios (Tim Cowles); Walter Day; Daybreak Game Company (Raquel Marcelo); Nathaniël "Nathie" de Jong; Dead Good Media (Stu Taylor); Decibel PR (Sam Brace); Defiant; Desk; Digital Leisure (Paul Gold); Double Fine Productions (James Spafford); Edelman (Jules Delay); Electronic Arts (Catherine Vandier, Kyle Riley, Bryony Benoy, Tristan Rosenfeldt); ESL (Anna Rozwandowicz, Chrystina Martel, Christopher Flato); eSportsearnings.com; Freejam Games (Martin Snelling, Andy Griffiths); Frontier Developments (Daniela Pietrosanu); Gameloft (Jack Wilcock); GameRankings; Joseph "Stampy Cat" Garrett; Tristen Geren; Global Game Jam (Seven Siegel, Gorm Lai, Jo Summers); GosuGamers (Victor Martyn, Ed Harmer); Grayling (Sam Gavin); Jace Hall; Headup Games (Gregor Ebert); Marius Herrmann; Hope & Glory PR (Sheeraz Gulsher, Pieter Graham); Housemarque (Lauri Immonen); id Software (Tim Willits); Indigo Pearl (Caroline Miller, Alex Holt-Kulapalan); Raheem "Mega Ran" Jarbo; Jelly Media (Mark Bamber); Johnny Atom Productions (Simon Callaghan); Isaiah TriForce Johnson; Callum "SeaPeeKay" Knight; Koch Media (Daniel Emery); Konami/Voltage PR (Steve Merrett); Laminar Research (Marty Arant); Lick PR (Kat Osman, Lucy Starvis); Limited Run Games (Josh Fairhurst, Douglas Bogart); Kurt J Mac; Madmorda; Scott Manley; Dominique "SonicFox" McLean; MCV (Seth Barton, Marie Dealessandri); Microsoft (Kumar Manix, Rob Semsey); Mojang; Nintendo (Emma Bunce, Kalpesh Tailor, Oliver Coe); Numantian Games (Miguel Corral); Outrageous PR (Danielle Woodyatt); Overbuff.com; Douglass Perry; Stefano Petrullo; Premier PR (Will Beckett, Lauren Dillon, Yunus Ibrahim, Tom Copeland); PSNProfiles (Matt Reed); Psyonix (Stephanie Thoensen, Joshua Watson); PUBG Corporation (Shane Rho); Lorenzo Ramondetti; Red Consultancy (Graham Westrop, Natasha Zialor, Beth Mitchell); Sonja "omgitsfirefoxx" Reid; Riot Games (Becca Roberts, Jessica Frucht); Roblox (Brian Jaquet); Rockstar Games (Craig Gilmore, Hamish Brown); Rocksteady Studios (Gaz Deaves); Roll7 (Simon Bennett); Jeremy Sanchez; Sega (Peter Oliver); Shoryuken.com; Sony Computer Entertainment (Jo Bartlett, Hugo Bustillos); Speedrun.com (Peter Chase); Sports Interactive (Ciaran Brennan, Neil Brock, Miles Jacobson); Spotify (Martin Vacher); Square Enix (Yunus Ibrahim); SRK FGC Stats (@SRKRanking); StudioMDHR (Ryan Moldenhauer, Chad Moldenhauer); SuperData (Sam Barberie, Albert Ngo); SwipeRight PR (Kirsty Endfield); thatgamecompany (Jennie Kong); Think Jam (Ellie Graham, Chris White); Ross "TommyT999" Thompson; Dr Thomas Tilley; TrueAchievements (Rich Stone); Tai-Ting Tseng; TT Games; Twin Galaxies; Twitch (Chase); Ubisoft (Stefan McGarry, David Burroughs, Olivia Garner, Tom Goldberger); VGChartz; Warhorse Studios (Tobias Stolz-Zwilling); Warner Bros. (Mark Ward, Hannah Jacob); Dan "Silentc0re" White; YouTube Gaming (George Panayotopoulos); Zebra Partners (Beth Llewelyn).

COUNTRY CODES

Code	Country	Code	Country	Code	Country
ABW	Aruba	GNB	Guinea-Bissau	PHL	Philippines
AFG	Afghanistan	GNQ	Equatorial Guinea	PLW	Palau
AGO	Angola			PNG	Papua New Guinea
AIA	Anguilla	GRC	Greece		
ALB	Albania	GRD	Grenada	POL	Poland
AND	Andorra	GRL	Greenland	PRI	Puerto Rico
ANT	Netherlands Antilles	GTM	Guatemala	PRK	Korea, DPRO
		GUF	French Guiana	PRT	Portugal
ARG	Argentina	GUM	Guam	PRY	Paraguay
ARM	Armenia	GUY	Guyana	PYF	French Polynesia
ASM	American Samoa	HKG	Hong Kong		
		HMD	Heard and McDonald Islands	QAT	Qatar
ATA	Antarctica			REU	Réunion
ATF	French Southern Territories	HND	Honduras	ROM	Romania
		HRV	Croatia (Hrvatska)	RUS	Russian Federation
ATG	Antigua and Barbuda			RWA	Rwanda
AUS	Australia	HTI	Haiti	SAU	Saudi Arabia
AUT	Austria	HUN	Hungary	SDN	Sudan
AZE	Azerbaijan	IDN	Indonesia	SEN	Senegal
BDI	Burundi	IND	India	SGP	Singapore
BEL	Belgium	IOT	British Indian Ocean Territory	SGS	South Georgia and South SS
BEN	Benin			SHN	Saint Helena
BFA	Burkina Faso	IRL	Ireland	SJM	Svalbard and Jan Mayen Islands
BGD	Bangladesh	IRN	Iran		
BGR	Bulgaria	IRQ	Iraq		
BHR	Bahrain	ISL	Iceland		
BHS	The Bahamas	ISR	Israel	SLB	Solomon Islands
BIH	Bosnia and Herzegovina	ITA	Italy	SLE	Sierra Leone
		JAM	Jamaica	SLV	El Salvador
BLR	Belarus	JOR	Jordan	SMR	San Marino
BLZ	Belize	JPN	Japan	SOM	Somalia
BMU	Bermuda	KAZ	Kazakhstan	SPM	Saint Pierre and Miquelon
BOL	Bolivia	KEN	Kenya		
BRA	Brazil	KGZ	Kyrgyzstan	SRB	Serbia
BRB	Barbados	KHM	Cambodia	SSD	South Sudan
BRN	Brunei Darussalam	KIR	Kiribati	STP	São Tomé and Príncipe
		KNA	Saint Kitts and Nevis		
BTN	Bhutan			SUR	Suriname
BVT	Bouvet Island	KOR	Korea, Republic of	SVK	Slovakia
BWA	Botswana			SVN	Slovenia
CAF	Central African Republic	KWT	Kuwait	SWE	Sweden
		LAO	Laos	SWZ	Swaziland
CAN	Canada	LBN	Lebanon	SYC	Seychelles
CCK	Cocos (Keeling) Islands	LBR	Liberia	SYR	Syrian Arab Republic
		LBY	Libya		
CHE	Switzerland	LCA	Saint Lucia	TCA	Turks and Caicos Islands
CHL	Chile	LIE	Liechtenstein		
CHN	China	LKA	Sri Lanka	TCD	Chad
CIV	Côte d'Ivoire	LSO	Lesotho	TGO	Togo
CMR	Cameroon	LTU	Lithuania	THA	Thailand
COD	Congo, DR of the	LUX	Luxembourg	TJK	Tajikistan
COG	Congo	LVA	Latvia	TKL	Tokelau
COK	Cook Islands	MAC	Macau	TKM	Turkmenistan
COL	Colombia	MAR	Morocco	TMP	East Timor
COM	Comoros	MCO	Monaco	TON	Tonga
CPV	Cape Verde	MDA	Moldova	TPE	Chinese Taipei
CRI	Costa Rica	MDG	Madagascar	TTO	Trinidad and Tobago
CUB	Cuba	MDV	Maldives		
CXR	Christmas Island	MEX	Mexico	TUN	Tunisia
CYM	Cayman Islands	MHL	Marshall Islands	TUR	Turkey
CYP	Cyprus			TUV	Tuvalu
CZE	Czech Republic	MKD	Macedonia	TZA	Tanzania
DEU	Germany	MLI	Mali	UAE	United Arab Emirates
DJI	Djibouti	MLT	Malta		
DMA	Dominica	MMR	Myanmar (Burma)	UGA	Uganda
DNK	Denmark			UK	United Kingdom
DOM	Dominican Republic	MNE	Montenegro	UKR	Ukraine
		MNG	Mongolia	UMI	US Minor Islands
DZA	Algeria	MNP	Northern Mariana Islands		
ECU	Ecuador			URY	Uruguay
EGY	Egypt	MOZ	Mozambique	USA	United States of America
ERI	Eritrea	MRT	Mauritania		
ESH	Western Sahara	MSR	Montserrat	UZB	Uzbekistan
ESP	Spain	MTQ	Martinique	VAT	Holy See (Vatican City)
EST	Estonia	MUS	Mauritius		
ETH	Ethiopia	MWI	Malawi	VCT	Saint Vincent and the Grenadines
FIN	Finland	MYS	Malaysia		
FJI	Fiji	MYT	Mayotte		
FLK	Falkland Islands (Malvinas)	NAM	Namibia	VEN	Venezuela
		NCL	New Caledonia	VGB	Virgin Islands (British)
FRA	France	NER	Niger		
FRG	West Germany	NFK	Norfolk Island	VIR	Virgin Islands (US)
FRO	Faroe Islands	NGA	Nigeria		
FSM	Micronesia, Federated States of	NIC	Nicaragua	VNM	Vietnam
		NIU	Niue	VUT	Vanuatu
		NLD	Netherlands	WLF	Wallis and Futuna Islands
FXX	France, Metropolitan	NOR	Norway		
		NPL	Nepal	WSM	Samoa
GAB	Gabon	NRU	Nauru	YEM	Yemen
GEO	Georgia	NZ	New Zealand	ZAF	South Africa
GHA	Ghana	OMN	Oman	ZMB	Zambia
GIB	Gibraltar	PAK	Pakistan	ZWE	Zimbabwe
GIN	Guinea	PAN	Panama		
GLP	Guadeloupe	PCN	Pitcairn Islands		
GMB	Gambia	PER	Peru		

STOP PRESS!

Gaming records don't stop being broken just because our printing presses have started to whirr into motion. Here is just a small taste of the record-setting achievements that either came too late for the rest of the book or that we simply couldn't cram in anywhere else!

First playable female in the *Far Cry* series
When it released on 27 Mar 2018, *Far Cry 5* became the first game in Ubisoft's long-running first-person shooter with a playable female character (left). At the beginning of the game, players can choose between being male or female, as well as alter facial features, skin tone, eye colour and other aspects of the character you play as during the game.

Largest gathering of people dressed as Lara Croft
Bad guys, beware! The largest gathering of people dressed as *Tomb Raider* heroine Lara Croft consisted of 316 participants. It was achieved by Warner Bros. Pictures (China) in Beijing on 8 March 2018, to mark the cinematic debut of the latest *Tomb Raider* movie.

First completion of the *Dark Souls* trilogy without being hit
On 8 Mar 2018, Twitcher "The_Happy_Hobb" (UK) completed all three of Bandai Namco's notoriously tough *Dark Souls* games without any of the series' fiendish foes laying a sword, tooth or claw on him. Having come close in multiple attempts over the previous year, the gamer was understandably excited. "Gaming history! *Dark Souls* history! No hits... It's easy!" he said.

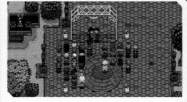

Fastest *Stardew Valley* wedding (glitchless)
Quick-fire Casanova "TheHaboo" (USA) wed his *Stardew Valley* love even faster than fellow American "Sam_Van_Dam" (pp.154–55). On 27 Mar 2018, the PC gamer wooed his intended in just 58 min 58 sec. The time was put down to a high number of rainy days, which meant he didn't waste time on watering crops.

Most concurrent viewers for a Twitch stream by an individual
Twitch streamer "Ninja", aka Richard Tyler Blevins (USA), broke his own record (pp.92–93) on 21 Apr 2018. An incredible 667,000 people streamed the "Ninja Vegas 18" event held in Las Vegas, USA. "Ninja" played nine games of *Fortnite Battle Royale* (Epic, 2017), awarding $2,500 (£1,779) to match-winners or anyone who killed him during a game.

Fastest half marathon dressed as a videogame character (male)
Sporting Super Mario's iconic red-and-blue overalls and an almost-as-bushy moustache, Peter Wood (UK) ran the Great North Run half marathon – in Newcastle, UK, on 10 Sep 2017 – in 1 hr 31 min 59 sec. Happily, the 21.09-km (13.1-mi) course was free of koopa troopas and goombas on the day!

Deadliest machine in *Horizon Zero Dawn*

As of 7 Mar 2018, the Sawtooth was *Horizon Zero Dawn*'s (Sony, 2017) deadliest creation. The beast, which resembles a huge mechanized saber-toothed cat, had crushed, mangled and otherwise exterminated 20.9 million unlucky players since *Horizon*'s release on 28 Feb 2017, as verified by Sony.

First *Monster Hunter: World* monster added as DLC

On 22 Mar 2018, the Deviljho was added to Capcom's 2018 hit *Monster Hunter: World* as free downloadable content (DLC). The formidable beast has the unique ability to swat away hunters by swinging around smaller monsters. "No one is safe from the deadly jaws of the Deviljho – not even other monsters," said Capcom's official blog.

Earliest space-race victory in *Civilization IV*

In *Civilization IV* (2K Games, 2005), a space-race victory is achieved by building a spaceship and sending it to Alpha Centauri, the closest star system to our Solar System. On 22 Mar 2018, "WastinTime" achieved it during the in-game year of 90 CE. Having started the game in 4,000 BCE, he first launched his spacecraft in 210 BCE. That's 2,170 years before, in the real world, Yuri Gagarin made the **first manned spaceflight** in 1961! The *Civilization* veteran's craft then took 299 years to reach its destination.

FARTHEST HUMAN-CANNONBALL FLIGHT

To celebrate the release of its open-world pirate-filled adventure game *Sea of Thieves* (2018), Microsoft arranged for "The Bullet", aka David Smith Jr (USA), to attempt to beat his human-cannonball record of 59.05 m (193 ft 8 in). On 13 Mar 2018, at the Raymond James Stadium in Tampa, Florida, USA, the stuntman was blasted 59.43 m (195 ft) from a *Sea of Thieves*-themed pirate ship. The new attempt was 0.38 m (1 ft 2 in) farther than his previous best attempt.

Highest-altitude videogame stream

On 13 Oct 2017, Microsoft streamed gameplay of *Super Lucky's Tale* (2017) from a height of 365.7 m (1,200 ft) above the ground! The game was streamed on Xbox's Mixer channel from a hot-air balloon as it sailed high above Albuquerque, New Mexico, USA.

Most concurrent players involved in a single multiplayer battle

A total of 6,142 players took part in *EVE Online*'s "Siege of 9-4R" on 23 Jan 2018, as players looked to either destroy or defend the system's Keepstar space station. At EVE Fanfest on 14 Apr 2018, CCP Games celebrated the achievement on stage. "Our community is at the very core of what we do, and this award is theirs," said Svenni Guard, CCP Games' Senior Community Development Lead (near left), during the event.

MARIO QUIZ ANSWERS (PP.126–27)

From left to right:

Super Mario Bros.
Super Mario 64
Paper Mario: Sticker Star
Mario Golf World Tour
Super Mario Sunshine
Mario Party 6
Mario vs Donkey Kong
Mario Slam Basketball
Mario Super Sluggers
Mario Tennis
Mario vs Donkey Kong: Mini-Land Mayhem!
Mario & Sonic at the London 2012 Olympic Games
Super Mario World
Super Mario Galaxy
Mario Kart 7
Super Mario Maker
Dr Mario: Miracle Cure
Super Mario 3D Land
Mario + Rabbids Kingdom Battle
Mario Party: The Top 100

UNLOCK A WORLD
OF NEW RECORDS

GUINNESS WORLD RECORDS 2019

GUINNESS WORLD RECORDS 2019

OUT NOW!